Mr **Shankly's** Photograph

Praise for *Mr Shankly's Photograph*:

'So who would be the greatest football managers if you were to perm, say, any three from the past 50 years? Shankly, Busby and Clough – or Paisley, Ferguson and Wenger? Kelly's superb semi-fictional work on Liverpool in their 1960s heyday goes a long way to providing the answer . . . This is *Fever Pitch* for the new decade – but better.' The *Sunday Times*

'A wonderful book about adolescence, work and love.' *Sportspages*

'Unashamedly romantic but ringing with authenticity. *Mr Shankly's Photograph* will be enjoyable reading for anyone who loves football, music or the sixties – or all three.' *Manchester Evening News*

'Beats any fictional football book I have ever read . . . a captivating read . . . if you are sick of coming home from a hard day's work to be faced with docu-soaps and dodgy dramas then this book is the perfect antidote.' Nathan Davies, soccergrounds.com

Mr **Shankly's** Photograph

A Journey From the Kop to the Cavern

Stephen F Kelly

ROBSON BOOKS

This paperback edition first published in Great Britain in 2004 by
Robson Books, The Chrysalis Building, Bramley Road, London W10 6SP

An imprint of Chrysalis Books Group plc

Copyright © 2002, 2004 Stephen F Kelly

The right of Stephen F Kelly to be identified as the author of this work has been
asserted by him in accordance with the Copyright, Designs and Patents Act 1988.

The author has made every reasonable effort to contact all copyright holders.
Any errors that may have occurred are inadvertent and anyone who for any
reason has not been contacted is invited to write to the publishers so that a
full acknowledgement may be made in subsequent editions of this work.

British Library Cataloguing in Publication Data
A catalogue record for this title is available from the British Library.

ISBN 1 86105 646 X

Typeset by SX Composing DTP, Rayleigh, Essex
Printed by Creative Print & Design (Wales), Ebbw Vale

Contents

To Thomas Kelly
1914–1983

Preface

This book began life as a work of non-fiction, designed to plot the life of Liverpool Football Club and the city of Liverpool over the forty years between 1960 and 2000. But somehow along the way it took on a different dimension and became a snapshot of life in Liverpool during the heady years of the 1960s.

It is essentially the story of one boy's love for Bill Shankly and the city of Liverpool. Apart from obvious realities, such as Shankly himself, the Beatles and my parents, it is a journey into fiction. It should therefore be stressed that any resemblance between anyone living and any of the characters in this book is purely coincidental.

Thanks must be given to a number of people who have encouraged this work. In particular, I shall be ever grateful to Andrew Serraillier who repeatedly read updates of the manuscript and, more than anyone, urged me to follow my instincts, and turn what was a non-fiction work into fiction.

My gratitude must also go to a number of other people who read the original manuscript as it was being written. David Fraser was generous and objective in his criticism, while Roisin Tambour suggested some constructive and crucial changes. Sadly, David

Fraser died just days before the hardback edition of this book was published. He will be missed by his many friends.

I must also place on record my appreciation to Jeremy Robson at Robson Publishing, who received a manuscript somewhat different from the one he was anticipating but who, nevertheless, was prepared to stand by and publish what I had produced. It was a courageous decision and I hope that his intuition will be repaid. My thanks also to Jane Donovan, my editor at Robson, to Richard Emerson and Laura Ward, as well as to Richard Mason for the cover design. My agent John Pawsey should also be mentioned for his cheering support throughout this project. Others who have helped include Anthony Rowe Jones, Marjorie Rowe Jones, the staff of Liverpool Central Library, Chris Prior and various others who answered my internet queries about Liverpool.

I should also like to thank my wife Judith Jones for so many useful suggestions and ideas on the structure, as well as for her enduring support over the years. Also to Nicholas Kelly and Emma Kelly who have put up with my grumpiness while this and other books were being written. One day, I promise that I'll stop being grouchy. Thanks finally to my mother for so many special memories and for all her devotion and encouragement over the years – and, of course, to my late father, who stimulated in me a love of football and politics.

Stephen F Kelly

one

Ferry Cross the Mersey

Thomas Caesar Kelly tugged his swanky Ilford camera from his jacket pocket, unravelled it from its leather casing and painstakingly began to line up the shot. Holding the camera at waist level, he wavered one way, then the other, carefully positioning himself so that the sun was at the back of him and the shadow of the house was out of shot.

'Where do you want 'im t' stand, Tommy? Shall I be lifting 'im over t' fence?' asked Uncle Horace, his rich Yorkshire accent as deep and sensuous as his tanned looks. I glanced nervously at my father, then at my grandfather.

'No, he's alright there. Just stand him in front of Mr Shankly on this side of the fence. Away from the roses, though.'

I peered over my shoulder at the figure looming over me. His skin was pale, his imposing forehead bare and furrowed. There was a small scar to one side of his head, maybe the result of some footballing accident, I thought.

'What about me, am I alright here?' asked Mr Shankly.

'A bit more to your left. Yes, that's it.' Mr Shankly placed his hands on my shoulders. I could feel their weight and warmth burning into me. Yet heavy as they were I had never felt so secure, as though I had no reason to fear. These four men, my father, my grandfather, my uncle and his next-door neighbour, all swaddling me in their decency and care. I suddenly felt so grown up.

'Terrible business in Munich,' broached my father, continuing to experience some difficulty in focusing his camera. The disaster still loomed heavy in people's minds.

'Oh, aye,' tutted Mr Shankly. 'Dreadful. Dreadful. Such wonderful players. So sad. But I hear Matt Busby's coming home soon. That'll be good. I spoke to Jean, his wife, last week. They're really pleased with his progress. They've had him up and walking about the hospital. He's a great friend, you know, known him for many years.' A watery sun peeked briefly through a cloud.

'There y'are, sun's come out for you Tommy,' joked Uncle Horace. Dad, gripping his precious camera, moved to the side a fraction, as the house's shadow lengthened and darkened.

'Come on Tommy. Mr Shankly hasn't got all day,' grumbled Grandfather. Dad was in danger of becoming an embarrassment.

'Ah, nae problem, don't worry, take yer time,' said Mr Shankly.

'Now, ready? Smile.' A moment's silence. I forced a grin and the camera clicked. 'That's it, lovely,' said Dad raising his eyes in the direction of the Huddersfield manager. 'Thank you very much, Mr Shankly. Say thank you, Stephen.' I nodded half-hearted gratitude.

Uncle Horace beamed and Mr Shankly removed his hands from my shoulder. I was alone again and once more as nervous as any other ten-year-old. No protective arms, no comforting smiles, no longer the focus of attention with the famous man next door. But a moment had been frozen that would live with me forever.

I like to think that my life had got off to a portentous start, even before that photograph with Mr Shankly. On the sultry night of my first birthday, in June 1947, Liverpool Football Club had clinched their fifth league championship. It was unusually late in the season but the Siberian winter of 1946 had forced umpteen postponements. Slag heaps had frozen, rail points had iced over, the trains had ground to a halt and the snow had piled high on football pitches around the country. Football was out of the question and so the season dragged on well into the summer as the backlog of fixtures was finally resolved.

That June evening, Liverpool entertained Everton in the

Liverpool Senior Cup final at Anfield. But the really crucial game was taking place a hundred miles away at Stoke, where City and Sheffield United had kicked off fifteen minutes earlier. A win for Stoke and they would be champions. Anything less and Liverpool would be crowned kings. With a quarter of an hour still remaining at Anfield, they announced the result of the Stoke–Sheffield game over the tannoy. Stoke had been beaten: Liverpool were champions. A packed Anfield erupted – well, the Red part. As for the other lot, they were handing over the trophy they had won in 1939 and had held throughout the War years. Kicking off with the league title and handing it over to your deadliest rivals must have been mortifying, to say the least. Fans raced on to the pitch to shake hands with their heroes, yet somehow or other the players had to continue until the final whistle before they could eventually give vent to their delight.

Home for me was a two-up, two-down terrace in Birkenhead with a coal fire in every room, along with an inside and outside toilet and a back yard the size of a sheep dip. And that was where I lived with my parents. No brothers, no sisters. Admittedly the house was new, having been rebuilt in 1947 after one of Herr Hitler's famous incendiary bombs had flattened its predecessor. Doubtless the pilot was aiming to hit the docks, which were just half a mile down the road, but as a result of some inaccurate navigation most of the street went up, or down rather, along with the popular cinema at the top of the road. Anyhow, that was where I lived with my parents. My father, Thomas Caesar Kelly, was in his early thirties when I was born and worked as a fitter for the Gas Board, while my ever-youthful mother generally looked after me and the house.

At school they had taught me that Caesar was a Roman name. 'No it's Manx, an old Manx name,' my aunt explained one day. Well, you could have fooled me. 'Your father was named after his father, he was Caesar as well. His name was Stephen Caesar and you were named Stephen after him,' they told me. At least I could be thankful not to have inherited both his names.

Apart from having to live with the name Caesar, there were no traumas in our household, no divisions, no violence, no drunkenness. It was comfortable and secure, even though money was tight. I grew up an only child, wallowing in the attention my doting parents focused on me. Not that I ever missed having a brother or sister as there were plenty of other lads in the street, and all of similar ages. We were the post-war baby boom. But although we all played football in the park almost daily, the other lads lacked my commitment to the game. They didn't collect football programmes, didn't go to matches, didn't know one player from another, and never read *Charlie Buchan's Football Monthly*. But all that was about to change.

Aged nine, I was in the back entry that separated us from the next row of terraced houses, kicking a threadbare tennis ball against the back-yard door. It was a breathless May afternoon. A flick here, a flick there. It wasn't difficult, just practice and concentration. On the shin, bounce, against the door, onto the knee, bounce, onto my instep, bounce. Just keep concentrating, don't let the ball race away from you. Keep it under control. Not always easy when it was landing on cobbles. On the shin, bounce, against the door, onto the knee, bounce, against the door, bounce, onto the instep, bounce. Concentrate, concentrate, concentrate. But from the corner of an eye I was conscious of being discreetly spied upon.

Standing in the open doorway of another house ten yards down the entry was a lad roughly the same age as me. He was wearing a Davy Crockett hat, its tail hanging loosely over his shoulder. He was staring at me, watching my every move to the extent that I was now being made self-conscious by his presence. It was putting me off. I tried to ignore him, flicking the ball up a little higher before bouncing it off my knee and on to the wall. But I was only showing off and not surprisingly the ball spun off my hip, dropped to the ground and raced down the cobbles towards the other boy. He stepped out of the doorway, grabbed the ball and stood there holding it. I glared at him. But in response he began to throw the ball against his yard wall in an increasingly threatening manner, hurling it harder and harder yet each time catching it with the comparative ease of a slip fielder, bending one way, then stretching the other. He was slightly taller than me and more wiry; he seemed comfortable with a ball. I was beginning to think that I had seen the last of it but just as I turned to go back into my house he shouted. ''Ere,' and threw the ball towards me. Thankfully, I caught it smartly.

'Thanks,' I said. 'You're new here aren't you?' He was staring at me again and didn't answer immediately. He took his hat off to reveal a mop of blazing ginger hair, freckles and a bleached face.

'Yeah.'

'What's your name?'

'Er, Peter,' he replied in a shrill, hesitant voice, his eyes painfully avoiding my look.

'I like your hat.'

'Yeah, me mum made it for me.'

'Have you seen the film?'

'Yeah.'

'Do you live there?' I asked nodding towards his house.

'Yeah.' There was a pause. 'Is that your house?' he asked.

I nodded. 'How long have you been here?'

'Just a couple of weeks. And you?'

'We've been here for years. I've always lived here,' I answered.

'Is dat your mum in your house talking to my mum?'

'Yeah.'

'Where did you use to live?' I asked.

'Down that way,' he said, pointing in the general direction of the bottom of the entry. 'Down by the docks. That's where me dad works.'

'Which school do you go to?' I wondered.

'Our Lady's. Where do you go?'

'Bidston Avenue. Will you start going to my school now?'

'No, that's a Protestant school. I go to a Catholic school.'

'Is your mum and dad a Catholic?'

'Yeah, of course they are. Are you a Proddie then?'

I looked at him blankly and confessed that we didn't even go to church. He looked horrified and quickly crossed himself.

'Warra you doin'? What's that for?' I asked.

'I'm crossing myself,' he said. 'You're a heathen.' I still didn't understand.

'Do you like football?' I asked.

'Oh yeah,' he answered. 'Me dad used to be a footballer. He signed for Tottenham just before the war.'

'Wow,' I replied. 'Dat's pretty good.'

'Yeah. He was a good player. He was spotted by a Tottenham scout and signed for them and went off to London on the train. But when he got to the station he took one look and caught the next train home. He didn't like it. He was only young and he says London is no place for a young man. He could have been playing for Tottenham now. Shame really.'

'Warra bout you. Do you want to be a footballer?' I asked.

'Yeah, sure. I wanna play for Manchester United when I get bigger. I don't wanna play for anyone else.'

'My dad knows a famous footballer.'

'Who?'

'I dunno, can't remember his name. I don't think he's that famous now. But der's a lad in our school says he knows Rocky Marciano.'

'Marciano? How can he? He lives in America.'

'Yeah, well, so does this lad. He's American.'

'An American in your school. Go 'way.'

'Honest.'

'What's he doing in your school?'

'Dunno but he comes from Colorado. And he reckons Marciano'll hammer Cockell.'

'No he won't. My dad says Don Cockell's gorra good chance, even though Marciano's a dirty fighter.' There was pause. He wiped his nose on his sleeve. 'Do you collect football programmes?' I nodded. 'Have you got any swaps?' I nodded again, and with that we both darted into our respective houses before emerging with large bundles under our arms.

'By the way, what's *your* name?' he asked, as we sat down on the back-yard step to flick through each other's collection.

'Do you fancy a game of headers in the entry after tea?' I suggested. I now had a comrade in arms.

Liverpool in the mid-1950s. A bustling city. People spilling out everywhere. Row upon neat row of terraced streets, wharves, factories, kids kicking balls around in the streets, trains, trams, smoke and, of course, the unmistakable smell of the sea. And everywhere evidence still of Mr Hitler's misdoings. To think that this was once a city of windmills and piazzas, of elegant Grecian-columned buildings, of docks crammed with four-masted schooners, of whalers and of paddle steamers, happily tripping across the Mersey.

As east–west trade flourished once more, the river, which had always been the *raison d'être* of the city's existence, was again choked with ships. Liners, cargo vessels, oil tankers, tugs, even the occasional visiting destroyer, would queue up in the Mersey awaiting a free berth on the next tide. The two-funnelled *Empress of England*, the *Saxonia*, the *Carinthia*, the *Reina del Mar* and the ill-fated *Empress of Canada*, which finished its days as a burnt-out wreck in Gladstone Dock, every one of them a liner boasting elegance and first-class service. All could regularly be spotted from a packed ferry boat as it ploughed its majestic course across the Mersey towards Birkenhead, weaving in and out of the anchored traffic. And smoke drifting lazily from every funnel. You needed to be a watchful pilot in those days, not like today when you can look up and down the river and never spot a ship. The river was the city's main artery, pumping life and energy into its population. And forming the backdrop, its three imposing buildings: the Royal Liver Building, topped with its mythical Liver Bird, the elegant offices of the Cunard Steamship Company and the white-domed offices of the Mersey Docks and Harbour Board, our version of St Paul's Cathedral. Images that broke hearts and raised the spirits of sailors and passengers, departing or arriving from afar.

Liverpool was the gateway to the West. On the quayside hundreds waved their farewells, as they tossed a final goodbye to the old land and were swept away to exciting adventures in America, Canada, South Africa, Australia or wherever. There were few, if any, of the streamers being hurled over the side of ships that you see in the movies. It was from these very docks that Melville, Hawthorne and Conrad sailed, their heads stuffed with images of Liverpool and the Old World that would one day be recreated in the New. Hawthorne enthused, calling it 'the greatest commercial city in the world'. His friend, Melville, talked of the city's 'shifting sands, everything changing, always changing'.

Admittedly, by the 1950s it was never as busy as it had been in the early years of the century when liners were steaming away at the rate of one a day for New York or Boston, packed mostly with Irish emigrants. Or the days when you could spot the distinct red funnel of a Cunarder through the back streets that bordered the docks. Yet even in the fifties there were still plenty of liners and the land-sharks that Melville so resented, as well as bucketloads of tears on the quayside. We'd shed some ourselves, waving Auntie

Alice off to Australia, taking the bus from our house where she'd stayed overnight, and a mountain of luggage down to the pierhead, me squatting in the downstairs front seat buried beneath leather suitcases that were tagged for Sydney. We put her on the boat and kissed her goodbye in her posh cabin before the ship slipped its moorings and made off into the mists of the Mersey. We never saw her again. It was the way of a thousand such departures for travellers and sailors alike.

The sea seeped into men's souls and stole them away from their families. To go to sea was an adventure and a respectable occupation for many a Scouser. A merchant sailor, pick of the girls and all that. They sailed aboard an armada of shipping lines – Elder Dempster, Canadian Pacific, Bibby, Blue Funnel, Harrison, Holt, Brocklebanks – to far-off places. The elite of Cunard White Star were known as 'Cunard Yanks'.

'Where've you been, Jim?'

'Just back from a run to New York. Off to Valparaiso next week on the *Arcadia*.'

And, of course, all the girls loved a sailor, especially when they had a pocketful of pound notes and just wanted to spend, spend, spend. The sailors brought records home, too, the kind you couldn't buy in Liverpool, or anywhere else in Britain for that matter – rhythm and blues, jazz, the blues. The merchant sailors of Liverpool boasted some unique collections.

At the turn of the nineteenth century it was claimed that on any single day there could be as many as ten thousand seamen from all corners of the globe passing through the city. It wasn't a bad life. Lots of pals, free lodgings, adventures, see the world. You had to be young. You worked hard and cursed the skipper but then there wasn't much else to do and there was certainly nothing to spend your money on. Each night, watching a plump sun drop like a delicious peach over the horizon. But they always came back, returning with tales of gin joints, of card games, of fights, of riches, of girls, of savage skippers, of New York fashions, of long-forgotten relatives and of sun-kissed beaches. When you got back home you were a millionaire and could boast to all those stay-at-homes. Sometimes they hopped ship, usually in Boston or New York, deserting for months on end until the money ran out and then inevitably hopped on another boat bound for Liverpool. They may have travelled, even widened their horizons, but Liverpool was never more than a stone's throw from their souls.

The docks were the hub around which the city revolved. Workers shuffled like ants off the overhead railway each morning as the wooden train rattled its way above the docks that hugged a seven-mile stretch of the Mersey. Folks called it the 'dockers' umbrella', because it was elevated – in much the same way that the New York subway is even to this day. It provided a convenient shelter for the dockers as they marched shoulder-to-shoulder to their workplaces, where they might, or might not, get the tap on the shoulder for a day's work. Sometimes it depended on your religion, your football team, which Parish you lived in, which Lodge you belonged to. It was politely called 'casualisation'. 'Corruption' might have been a better word. The entire city's economy was built on casual labour and the gang system. It defined levels of poverty and aspirations. Equally, work depended on such variables as the weather, the tide, the wind and trade. You never knew from one day to the next what you might earn. Liverpool was into freelancing long before it became the pattern of the e-commerce culture.

The names of the docks rekindled memories of Victorian pride: Victoria, Albert, Queens, Prince's, Canning, Stanley, Coburg, Huskisson, Gladstone, Brunswick, Herculaneum. Attenshun! Each of them a memorial to enterprising capitalism. In the nineteenth century Liverpool boasted more wealthy families and millionaires than any city in the land, apart from London. Fortunes had been amassed from shipping, banking, insurance, slavery and cotton. And scattered around these docks were all the other lucrative ancillary trades that go hand-in-hand with them – rope-makers, chandlers, flag-makers, carters, ship-repairers, sail-makers, hauliers, painters, tarpaulin-makers and so on. If you didn't earn your living *on* the sea, then the likelihood was that you earned it *from* the sea. At one time the docks employed sixty thousand directly, with an equal number employed indirectly. By the 1950s the number was already down to twenty thousand.

Over the water in Birkenhead the story was much the same, though never on such a grand scale. Liverpool had the stylish architecture of the Pier Head and its imposing docks hidden behind many an elegant Victorian edifice. In Birkenhead it was much cruder, each jetty open to view; no grand walls hiding luxurious liners. Instead each wharf was chock-full of dreary-looking cargo ships of one sort or another. Sometimes double-parked, they disposed their cargo of choking red iron ore onto the quayside. It wasn't a pretty picture. And always there were the cryptic, wizened faces of Asian sailors, glaring from portholes or wandering aimlessly about dockland, a little too scared to venture much further than the iron roadbridge that marked the border between the docks and so-called civilisation.

On the Birkenhead docks they even had their own union. Not for them the mighty Transport and General Workers' Union, who ruled the roost over the water, but instead the little-known National Association of Stevedores and Dockers, or the Blue Union, as it was commonly known. The Birkenhead dockers hated Deakin, Brown and the rest of the T&G leadership who had done so little to end the corrupt gang system of dockland. They even spent six weeks on strike in the mid-fifties as a bitter inter-union dispute saw Mersey docker pitted against Mersey docker, brotherly solidarity tossed aside.

When an old, rusting Russian crate dropped anchor one morning word spread like wildfire and by tea-time Peter and I were down at the quayside hailing these strange fellows from the East with their rough white faces hewn out of icebergs. Such an event might even have merited a paragraph in the *Liverpool Echo*.

'*Russian captain toasts the city of Liverpool with vodka*'.

'*When Russian captain Yvgeny Raskin and his crew sailed into Birkenhead this morning aboard the* SS Bulganin *they became the first Soviet sailors to cast anchor in the Mersey docks since the Russian Revolution of 1917 . . .*'

Not that we would have fully understood the political implications, but those foreign faces. Wow! I wonder what they made of us in our prosperous capitalist slums. We shouted to them but they didn't understand. Instead they hurled tinny red lapel badges to us grasping kids as they waved from the forecastle of their rusty ship. It was better than nothing and it was proof that we had seen the visitors from outer space. Next morning I wore my prize to school: the hammer and sickle with a feisty V I Lenin adorning my lapel.

Prior to the 1840s Birkenhead had been little more than an

attractive hamlet on a hill that offered a delightful panorama across the Mersey. In the mid-1820s, William Laird, a Scotsman and pioneering builder of iron ships, had set up a small iron works and shipyard in the Wallasey pool. It didn't amount to much until his son, John Laird, took over the business. John not only turned it into one of the finest shipyards in the world, but also became the town's first Member of Parliament. That development coincided with the expansion of the docks, turning Birkenhead into something of a boom town.

Apart from the energetic John Laird, the town's existence was almost entirely due to the generosity, or perhaps it should be called the exploitation, of a handful of Liverpool shipping merchants. When they ran out of dock space on the north side of the river, these entrepreneurs set about raising more money and did the only sensible thing possible: they began to construct docks on the south side of the river. This was 1847. Within the space of a few years the population of Birkenhead had mushroomed from a mere 110 in 1810 to more than 84,000 in 1881. By 1921 it was had risen even higher, to 147,000. So phenomenal was the growth that one Scottish newspaper was rashly predicting that at this rate Birkenhead would be the biggest city in the kingdom by 1970. The same paper called Birkenhead 'one of the greatest wonders of the age and indeed one in which the character of our age is most strongly expressed'. It never happened, although part of that description could have applied just as well to Birkenhead in the 1980s. Trade peaked by the turn of the century, and the population rose by a mere hundred or so between 1921 and 1931. Then came the 1930s; unemployment set in, devastating the whole of Merseyside, and with this the population began a steady decline. Birkenhead would never be quite the same again.

In character the town was much like Liverpool: sprawling docklands, though less romantic, but with the same regimented streets of terraced houses, gasometers, bomb sites and red-bricked Victorian schools. Liverpool had its Liver Building and walled Victorian docks; Birkenhead had little to boast about. It was the poor relative. People in Liverpool had sentiment, history and wealth on their side. We just had deprivation. Even the smell of the sea was never so fresh on our side of the Mersey.

Football for us was Tranmere Rovers, the wretched of the third division north who never got to inhabit the upper reaches of the Football League. But at least it was close, even walkable, and with a hole in the fence known to only a handful of us boys. Liverpool and Everton were the rich uncles on the other side of the water, who you only visited maybe once a year at Christmas or Easter. In the fifties it was not uncommon to support both teams: Everton's ground, Goodison Park, one week and Anfield the next, especially as Liverpool, still managed by Phil Taylor, were languishing in the lower league and could hardly be described as rivals. Even so, there was none of the vitriol that haunts today's game. You cheered for your team but you didn't despise the opposition. If you wanted to see the superstars, the glory sides, then you had to go to Everton. And, like most kids, I did. Watching Liverpool against the likes of Leyton Orient, Doncaster Rovers or Grimsby Town didn't hold much romance for a ten-year-old. I wanted to see the Spurs, the Busby Babes, Stanley Matthews, Wolves and the Arsenal. Well, come on – give us a break. I was only ten!

One Friday evening, scanning the sports' pages of the *Liverpool Echo*, I spotted that Everton were to play Manchester United in a league fixture the following Wednesday afternoon. The mind boggled. United were top of the table, league champions the previous season and already looking set to win another league title while still going well in the FA Cup. Not that I was a United supporter, far from it, but you did have to admire their record and it was a chance to see a few England internationals, something that Everton certainly did not boast.

But how to persuade my parents. In these pre-floodlight days, mid-week games kicked off anywhere between 2 p.m. and 3 p.m. I might have been on half-term holiday from school but my father certainly wasn't, so I needed someone to take me. The solution came in the shape of my new friend, Peter, and more importantly, his fifteen-year-old brother, John. Like me, Peter had never been to a first division game and, as a United supporter, was desperate to go. His brother was also a United fan and, what's more, was willing to take us both. First problem solved, though not until my mother had held a summit meeting with Peter's mum over numerous cups of tea. Next problem: where to get the money. That was the one condition my mother laid down: I had to pay.

Now finding enough money to pay the fare and entrance fee was no small task, even though both transport and the entrance fee to any football match were far from prohibitive.

'I could get some money from me gran,' I suggested to Peter, as we strolled home from our daily kick-about in the park. 'I could go on my bike and see her this afternoon.' It was not uncommon for Peter to come with me, then hang around outside while I went in, said a few words of kindness and collected my earnings. Then we would run off and spend it.

'Well, it's a start,' he replied. 'How much'll she give you?'

'Sixpence, maybe,' I said, trying to juggle the ball on my toes as we made for home.

'That won't get us far. We need to come up with something better,' said John. In the absence of anything better, we decided to have a word with Peter's mum.

'Well, you could try taking some empties back to Jimmy's shop,' she suggested. 'He'll give you tuppence a bottle.'

'But where do we get the empties from?'

'Well, I've got a few in the shed and you could go ask Peter's grandad next door. I know he's got some under the stairs. Try some of the neighbours as well, they'll probably have some hanging around. They'll be glad to get rid of them. Hasn't your mum got some, Stephen?'

For want of a better idea we decided to give it a try, but only after we'd tapped Granny for sixpence. This was capitalism working-class style and, much to our surprise, it worked! By the end of the day we had accumulated enough money to pay our fares, entrance fees and a programme. Sadly, our success at making money didn't last long.

Wrapped in warm winter coats, scarves and gloves on a chilly spring day we duly took a bus to Woodside where we caught the ferry over to Liverpool. Then it was another bus from the Pierhead, and up Scotland Road towards Goodison Park. The atmosphere in the bus was heavy with smoke, noisy talk, pushing and the rank smell of beer. At Goodison Park, John ushered us through the turnstile and into the Boys' Pen, bought us a programme and perched us on a bar.

It was a breathtaking sight. We were in a high corner of Goodison, overlooking the Gwladys Street goal end and the

Bullens Road paddock. I knew that Everton had one of the biggest grounds in the country but had never expected it to be on this scale. The one thing that really stuck in my mind was the blue criss-cross trade mark that ran the length of Archibald Leitch's stands.

Of the game I remember little except that we gawped in youthful admiration at the mighty Duncan Edwards and his England compatriots, Tommy Taylor and Roger Byrne. But what I do remember was the crowd. More than 72,000 were reported to have been packed into Goodison Park that afternoon, a record gate for a mid-week game. They had come to pay genuine homage to the finest team of the era, and I'm not talking about the Royal Blues. Everton's days of eminence had long past. They weren't even an average side. It was a dispiritingly far cry from the pre-war years when Everton ruled supreme. But at least I had seen my first major football match – and the great United side.

A year later the Busby Babes were dead. In the sludge and snow of Munich, the United BEA Elizabethan aircraft had crashed on take-off. The plane had briefly stopped over at Munich to refuel on its journey from Belgrade to Manchester after United had booked themselves a place in the European Cup semi-finals. It was the third time the pilot had attempted a take-off from Munich that afternoon, twice having been forced to abort and return to the terminal. In the immediate aftermath, in all, twenty-one lay dead. Two others, including Duncan Edwards, would later add to that appalling toll. There were eight United players among the list of victims, which also included club officials and journalists as well as a handful of fans and cabin crew.

I heard the news on the radio that grey February afternoon. I immediately ran over to Peter's. He'd just heard as well and was in tears. His brother had retreated to his bedroom, distraught. His father sat motionless and silent over his dinner.

'We're going to go to church later to say a mass for them,' Peter told me, as he sat staring blankly into the fire. 'They don't expect Duncan Edwards to live.' I wasn't sure what he meant by mass and last rites but I sensed it was something he felt had to be done. Along with Tommy Taylor and Roger Byrne, who had been killed, the young Duncan Edwards was his favourite player. There was little else that could be said. I wandered back to my own house.

For once I recognised the significance of the moment. It was my first personal encounter with death. It may not have been family, or even my own team, but I could relate to it, and in particular I could feel Peter's grief.

two

Hello, Mr Shankly

If anything, our journey begins, not in Liverpool, but some eighty miles to the east. Money might have been tight in our household but the one thing Dad always insisted on was regular holidays. Mostly they would be to the south coast during the summer but there would also be Easter breaks to see my grandparents in Yorkshire. Beyond gloomy Manchester, deep into the furrowed Pennines, and down the Colne Valley where millstone grit meets the soft limestone of the West Riding. Where carefully rolled cricket pitches and Wesleyan chapels jockey for space alongside tall-chimneyed woollen mills. This was textile country, the land of non-conformism. As the Oldham Road drops through the valley, it skirts a dozen similar woollen communities before it falls gently through the dampness and mist into Huddersfield, a rather private Yorkshire town, but full of tradition and surprise. Yes, you've guessed the link. Well, maybe not quite.

In my life there was another link. My mother hailed from Huddersfield, born there just a few days after the General Strike came to its inconclusive end in May 1926. Arthur Scargill's Yorkshire miners might have been renowned for their militancy in the 1980s but in the 1920s the nine-day strike had barely been noticed in many parts of Yorkshire. They might have been militant in the cotton mills of Lancashire, and maybe even around the coalfields of Barnsley, but not where there was wool, and certainly not in Huddersfield. The mills of the Colne Valley kept running. For 'wool' read 'wealth', read 'prudence'. No picket lines here; only the trams and trains came to a halt. And even then, after a few days the noise of the trams could be heard once more. They simply got on with life in Huddersfield, ten thousand of them turning up outside the Town Hall on the eve of the great strike to cheer Town's championship football team. No food shortages, no violence; Huddersfield might just as well have been on another planet. There wasn't a coal mine within ten miles of Huddersfield and in those days ten miles might just as well have been the other side of the country. And the local paper certainly didn't side with the miners, calling them 'destructive'.

Huddersfield was a woollen town, its mills the purveyors of the finest worsteds in the world. They made and cut the cloth here for a thousand suits. They dressed Hollywood film stars, New York businessmen, maharajas from Rahjastan and exiled princes who lived by the sea in Monte Carlo. Huddersfield and its folk had grown rich on worsted. And fittingly in the twenties they had boasted the foremost football team in the land, winner of three consecutive league titles, runners-up on a further three occasions and Wembley finalists five times. Only Arsenal could match their superiority and that was after they had poached Town's imperious manager Herbert Chapman from Leeds Road to Highbury. They also had the finest trolley buses in the land, cheerfully red, and so quiet that all you could hear was a friendly buzz like that of a bee on a gentle summer's day.

And yet for all its natural conservatism, Huddersfield was non-conformist with a grand Liberal tradition stretching back over the years. It could tolerate all colours of opinion. That enigmatic socialist Victor Grayson had been a neighbouring MP before he mysteriously disappeared, never to be seen again, though some say he was spotted years later in Australia with a pretty girl on his arm. And many a well-known socialist, from Keir Hardie to Harold Wilson, had harangued the public in the Mechanics' Institute. Immediately after the Second World War, Curly Mallalieu was to become the town's first Labour MP, a man who fittingly loved football as much as politics. Huddersfield was New Labour decades before Tony Blair was converted. Their ideology was founded in employment. There were jobs and everyone wanted to preserve them. The thirties and the Depression had passed Huddersfield by without even a casual glance over the shoulder. They didn't forget that.

But by the 1950s Huddersfield was living on its past. Wool had been challenged by a range of new and considerably cheaper fabrics coming out of America. Nylon and rayon were the new kings. The townsfolk still had their trolley buses but the football team was not what it used to be. Town had begun the fifties in the first division, were then relegated, but returned the following season only to be relegated once more before the decade ended.

My mother had grown up in this rather private, slightly suspicious town, working in the mills before war broke out and interrupted everybody's lives. She had a boyfriend in the RAF who she jitterbugged with every Saturday evening at the Cambridge Road baths dance until one week he failed to return from a flying mission. He was presumed dead. But apart from that, and one bomb dropped by a Luftwaffe plane off course from Sheffield, and which anyhow failed to explode, Huddersfield could be said to have had a 'quiet war'. By 1945 my mother had moved to Merseyside, meeting a man in a convalescent home in Southport. She had had her appendix taken out; he had had his kidney removed. They agreed to meet in Manchester, conveniently halfway between Huddersfield and Liverpool, but forgot that there were three stations. They both duly arrived at different stations, got annoyed, and went off into town to have a cup of tea and – astonishingly – finished up in the same tea-rooms.

That was the end of my mother's life in Huddersfield. But it wasn't altogether the end of her association with the town. Most of her relations still lived there and, as a family, we paid regular visits, usually at Easter or, in summers when there was no money for a more adventurous holiday, staying with my grandparents in their Yorkshire stone house near the park. It sounds grand but, in fact, the garden was overgrown with rhubarb and the toilet was down the ginnel. Getting caught short in the night was not something you would want to do too often.

It was on one such visit to Huddersfield that our odyssey really begins. Picture the scene. My guess is that this was Easter or even Whit 1958. We are strolling through a suburb of Huddersfield, not that they really had suburbs in the 1950s, but what *we* might describe as suburban today. Semi-detached houses in roads – not streets mind you – lined with blossom trees and the occasional car. It's a Sunday morning, sparkling sunshine, a fresh warmth in the air. Grandad, Father and I have taken a pre-Sunday-lunch stroll across the top o' the bank to see Uncle Horace and Auntie Gertie, leaving Grandma and my mother back at home dutifully preparing dinner.

Uncle Horace was Grandad's brother; an Edwardian gentleman – always was and always would be. He was possibly the wealthiest man I knew as a child and had been something grand in the Huddersfield Co-operative Society. Perhaps this does not sound so impressive today, but in those days the Co-op was a formidable institution. Years later I came across a book in which he was thanked for his remarkable services to the movement during the War. He didn't serve behind the counter or anything like that. Oh no, Uncle Horace was something big in management. As far as I was concerned Uncle Horace *was* the Huddersfield Co-op. I liked to be able to boast about it.

He was a smartly dressed man with a fine head of swept-back silver hair, soft warm skin, almond eyes, and a sharply clipped moustache. Tall and straight-backed, he always, but always, wore a three-piece woollen suit, tie, suede spats and brogues. Even on a Sunday morning, he would not forsake his spats, not even in the sunshine. I liked Uncle Horace; to a ten-year-old he was a figure of fascination. So debonair, and such a rich, soft Yorkshire accent. He had standards, a firm handshake, status and a case full of books, as well as a chess set. Anyone who had a chess set had to be important. Seated by his fireplace, I could glance at the shelves: Longfellow, Carlysle, Tennyson, *Culpeper's British Herbal* and, of course, copious leather-bound volumes of Dickens. They even had a telephone. But, without getting too carried away here, my fondness for Uncle Horace was probably more to do with the simple fact that he always squeezed half a crown into my palm as I shook hands to leave. Half a crown, so much money. A child could be forgiven for liking him. But I was never certain that his own brother liked him that much. Huddersfield folk can be perversely suspicious, even of their own kind. Grandfather would grunt at the mention of his name. The word back home was that Grandad always had to do the visiting and that Horace rarely crossed t' bank to repay a call. Books, chess set, half a crown; I liked all these things and yet the most interesting thing about Uncle Horace was undoubtedly his next-door neighbour.

Horace's wife, Auntie Gertie (always Gertie, never Gertrude) would, as usual, be pottering about the garden, maybe pruning her prize roses, occasionally nipping indoors to check the Sunday roast. She was a kind-natured lady, slightly majestic, with an internal smile and, like her husband, invariably dressed ready to receive visitors. She had immaculately coiffured grey hair, but despite her imposing appearance, to me she was always jolly. They were both well into their sixties and retired. On this particular Sunday we had wandered into the garden to say goodbye to Gertie.

Over the fence, a middle-aged man was tugging at some weeds. He seemed unduly preoccupied. He was dressed in brown trousers, a woollen, sleeveless cardigan and a shirt buttoned up at the collar but without a tie. He looked fairly innocuous.

Uncle Horace pointed him out to my father, whispering something. Father, in turn, nudged me. 'That's Mr Shankly,' said Uncle Horace, looking at me. I knew a little about Mr Shankly, though not much more than the simple fact that he was the manager of Huddersfield Town Football Club and the next-door neighbour of Uncle Horace.

The previous day I'd been to Leeds Road with Dad and Grandad to see Town, something of a ritual whenever we came to Huddersfield. We'd stood on the old open end by the gasometer. Twenty minutes to go and Town were 2–0 down. Then, the man standing next to me shouted 'Mackeson!' Mackeson was a stout, and there was an advert at the time about Mackeson working wonders. We all laughed when the man shouted it. Then Town were promptly awarded a penalty and pulled a goal back. The man shouted it again, and once more Town scored. He then shouted it a third time and, would you believe, Town scored yet again and wound up 3–2 winners. It had been a good afternoon. As we poured out of the ground, everyone was slapping this chap on the back, and still laughing, as if he had been the divine inspiration behind Town's dramatic reversal of fortune. Well, it was a good yarn and made us all laugh as we caught the trolley bus home.

Mr Shankly had been at Huddersfield for three years, initially as coach and now as manager after Andy Beattie had been sacked. I had a vague memory of a cigarette card at home showing a portrait of him in Preston – or was it Scotland? – colours. Beyond that there was no reason why I should know any more about him.

Mr Shankly looked up. 'Hello Horace. Are you well? I'm just doing a bit of weeding. Nice day, isn't it?'

'Aye, it's a grand day.'

'Your garden's looking nice,' he said, pulling himself up uneasily and letting out a groan. 'I was out playing footbae with the youngsters down the road this morning,' he said, rubbing his leg. 'That little Jimmy Ray kicked me in the calf. He's all of twelve, he is, dirty little player.'

Horace laughed. 'Got some of the family over from Liverpool,' he said, pointing to my father and myself. 'And this is the brother, Frank.' Grandfather and my father nodded politely.

'Did well to pull back those goals yesterday,' said my father. I wanted to tell Mr Shankly all about the man who had stood by us, but didn't dare.

'Aye, they did alright, showed a lot of fight. Should never have got themselves in that position in the first place, though.'

The grown-ups all nodded sympathetically, except for me, who was too busy tugging at my father's sleeve.

I'd remembered that Dad had tucked his camera into his pocket. 'Dad, could you take my picture with Mr Shankly?' I asked furtively.

'Oh, best not fuss him now,' said Dad.

'Go on Dad, please.' Uncle Horace was looking at us.

'He wants to know if we can take his photograph with Mr Shankly,' said Dad. We all looked across the fence.

'Aye, of course he can. Have you got a camera?' asked Mr Shankly. And so the photograph was taken that would have such an uncanny influence on my life. But, for the moment, like any football-mad kid, I still wasn't fully satisfied.

'Do you think you could ask him to get me the autographs of the Town players as well,' I asked Uncle Horace. They all laughed at my audacity. The autograph I really wanted was that of Denis Law.

He was a seventeen-year-old lad, already catching the eye. He'd been injured the day before, crashing to the ground, as he swept arrogantly into the penalty area. They stretchered him off towards the dugout, but as they walked behind the goal Law held an arm aloft for them to stop. He pulled himself up and watched as Town slotted the resulting penalty into the back of the net. A committed Town player was Denis. They expected him to be a great player one day.

'Bill, the lad here wants to know if you can get him some autographs as well,' asked Uncle Horace, smiling benevolently at his next-door neighbour.

'Certainly, I'll do what I can,' he replied, half smiling at me. 'Can't promise it immediately, but as soon as I get time.'

A young girl, probably my age, poked her head out of the kitchen door and shouted something. And with that, Mr Shankly hobbled into his house, still rubbing his leg and waving us farewell. He never reappeared. No doubt he was worried about his injured player, I thought. Ten minutes later we were gone, me gratefully clutching the half crown that Horace had carefully taken from his purse, and Grandad eager to get back for his roast beef and Yorkshire pudding. Well, Grandma's Yorkshire pudding was rather special. And that was the nearest I got to meeting the famous Mr Shankly . . . well, for the time being.

Months later a letter arrived from Uncle Horace. Enclosed was a sheet of autographs. Bill Shankly, Eddie Boot, Bill McGarry, Raymond Wilson, Kevin McHale, they were all there, and yes, Denis Law. It was a prize possession. Its arrival triggered my memory. I'd forgotten all about the photograph. I jogged Dad's memory in turn and he dutifully took the film around the corner to the chemist's for developing. A week or so later he picked up the prints and, along with photographs of Grandma and Grandad outside the Brontës' vicarage at Haworth, was this neat picture with crinkled edges of me and Mr Shankly, standing by Uncle Horace's garden fence. 'Oh I do wish you'd smile on photographs,' said Mum. 'But it's a good likeness. We must put it in the photo album.'

Two years on. A chilly December evening in 1959 and my father has returned home from work in the encroaching darkness, giving his usual whistle as he opens the back-yard door. Not whistling to me but to our budgie, who always recognised his footsteps coming up the entry and the opening catch on the yard door. The bird whistled back, his tiny head bouncing excitedly as he did so. It happened every evening.

'Well,' said Father, walking through the kitchen and straight into the back room, 'have you heard the news?' Of course I hadn't. What news was he talking about? My mother looked at him curiously.

'Bill Shankly is to be the new manager of Liverpool,' he said, pulling a newspaper out of his coat pocket to show me. Now that was a rarity. Dad never bought a newspaper. 'He's leaving Huddersfield and starting with Liverpool at the beginning of next year,' he added.

Sports news in those day came, of course, via the back pages, not through television or radio. Hence, I'd not heard, but there it was in bold typeface on the back page of the *Liverpool Daily Post*.

Bill Shankly Liverpool's New Manager
To Take Over at Anfield In A Month

And alongside was a photograph of the man I had seen over Uncle Horace's garden fence. The caption read. 'The face of a man with a mission. Bill Shankly, newly-appointed Liverpool manager has a solitary aim – to put Liverpool back in the first division. If he succeeds he's the friend for life of all Liverpudlians.' I liked that; it sounded good to me. After all, he had been true to his word and all the autographs of the Town players, including Denis Law as well as Bill Shankly, had duly arrived on a neatly folded piece of white paper, care of Uncle Horace. And now he was coming to Liverpool. What's more, I'd had my photograph taken with him.

'We're going to live by the seaside,' he had told his daughters as a means of tempting them to Merseyside. Hmmm, well, I'm not so sure about that. Apart from Southport and New Brighton, there wasn't too much seaside close to Liverpool. And what sand there was was covered in a slimy oil. But a little white lie at least ensured that his daughters were keen to move. Dad seemed pleased as well. I was never quite sure how Grandad, Uncle Horace and the rest of the Town supporters reacted to the news, but for us on Merseyside the tale was about to begin.

All of which neatly takes us to another family footballing link. My father had known William Ralph Dean all his life. Their families had grown up together, living in the same street and attending the same school while my father's sister had us believe that she had once been a sweetheart of Dean's. I'm not sure that I believed her but it was a harmless yarn. It was not surprising then that Dad should be a lifelong fan of Dean. As a lad he had cheered him from the terraces at Tranmere as the seventeen-year-old scored 27 goals in 27 league games, and then later at Goodison where he continued his goalscoring feats. My father had watched from the Gwladys Street end the day Dean struck his record-breaking sixtieth goal of the season. Years later, when Dean ran a pub in Chester, I would be lifted up to peer inside at the man behind the bar, the greatest goalscorer of them all. When Dean returned to Birkenhead he would become an occasional visitor to our house and a frequent drinking companion of my father at the club where they were both members.

On one such occasion, Dean called as I was preparing for bed. It was early into the New Year, not long after Shankly's appointment. I had probably met him before but this was my first genuine memory of talking to him. He was ushered into the living room where I was kneeling, in pyjamas and dressing gown, in front of the fire. A short, squat figure, nothing like the giant I had imagined who must have once leapt fearlessly above towering defenders. I was introduced, shook his hand and sat in awe, waiting for the memories to trip off his tongue. Of course they didn't. The pair of them talked about decorating.

They say that you are just one handshake away from fame. And in shaking Dean's hand I had touched fame. Think of all the hands he had shaken – Stan Matthews, Tommy Lawton, Charlie Buchan, Billy Wright, Alex James, Pongo Waring, Babe Ruth, Jack Dempsey, King George! I was one handshake away from the King.

At the time Bill – he was always Bill, never Dixie to his friends – was working as what is euphemistically known these days as a security guard but what in those days was better known as a cocky-watchman. It was a bottom-of-the-pile job, lousy hours, lonely nights, not much pay, and in winter piercingly cold with only a brazier to keep you warm. And this man had not only scored 60 goals in one season for Everton but had also represented his country 16 times. That evening Mr Dean didn't stay long. Pasted in sweat and looking older than his fifty-odd years, he wearily pulled himself up from his armchair. 'I'd better go now, Tommy, get to work,' he said. It was now or never, I had to ask him something, anything, to do with football. I had to hear this man, this legend, talk about the game. I plucked up the courage and spilled it out. 'What do you think Everton's chances are this season, Mr Dean?'

'Oh, interested in football, are you, young man?' I nodded enthusiastically.

'Well, I have to say, not very good. They've a few good players. Labone's a good young 'un and I've always liked Alex Parker but they need a decent centre forward. They should never have sold Hickson to Liverpool, you know. Bobby Collins is good but he's too tiny. They've got no height now Hickson's gone. They'll have to find a replacement. I think they might be after Roy Vernon. You know, Tommy? The lad who plays for Blackburn. There's been a bit of talk about him.'

'Has there? Well that'll cost 'em,' suggested my father. 'And now they're out of the cup as well. Not able to beat a third division side. Even Tranmere managed to beat Bradford.'

'And they got beat 8–2 at Newcastle,' I interjected. They both glared at me.

'That would never have happened in my day,' added Bill. He shook his head, his rosy cheeks chomping. My father agreed sadly. 'Out of the cup, nowhere in the league, it's enough to make you want to support Liverpool.' They both chuckled.

I seized my chance. 'But Liverpool have just got a new manager, Bill Shankly, haven't they?' I interrupted. 'Is he any good? Did you know him?'

'Aye, I did actually. He was a good player. I played against him, you know, quite a few times before the war. He was a right half. He was only young then but he was a hard player, gave me a tough time more than once, he did. He was playing for Preston in those days. They had a good team then, you know.'

'Did you ever play against him when you were playing for England?'

'No, I don't think I did,' he replied, trying to cast his mind back.

'I never won any caps after 1932. But he's a real Scotsman. Loves his country.'

'Do you think he'll be any good?'

'For Liverpool? Oh, I hope not. You should be supporting Everton, you know, like your dad.'

'Shankly used to live next door to the wife's uncle in Huddersfield, that's why he's interested,' chimed in my father. 'I think he saw him there once and he got him some autographs.'

'Oh, I see,' he replied, warming to the conversation. 'Well, I'll let you into a secret,' said Bill, leaning across as if he was going to whisper in my ear. 'I think he'll be a very good manager. You see, he's committed, he loves football. He's just what they need at Anfield.'

He turned to my father and with a twinkle in his eye added: 'But remember, I never told you that. They'd have my guts for garters if they found that out at Everton. It's a pity we haven't somebody like him. Can't see Carey doing anything.' He smiled and put a finger to his lips. 'Must be off, now.'

At this point, you might have thought that I would be ecstatic. But no, far from it. I was, it is true, a little mesmerised, but the fact is that I was really half kicking myself. I had wanted to ask him if, some day, I could see one of his international caps or even those boots, the ones that had scored sixty goals. I could at least have asked him for his autograph. I had just spoken to the greatest footballer ever, even better than Stanley Matthews or Tom Finney. But he was gone, the door slamming in the wind as he left. All those questions, still unanswered. They would have to wait for another time, if indeed there would ever be another time.

But what did intrigue me was his prophecy that Liverpool had, as I suspected, found a saviour, a Messianic figure, a man I'd actually met. If Dixie Dean thought he was good, then he had to be good. It was time for me to make contact with the man again. The following day, I raced home from school, having spent most of Mr Ball's geography lesson composing a letter in my head, instead of studying the difference between the Tropics of Cancer and Capricorn. My mother was out, but I found some of the purple-scented paper I had bought her for Christmas and began to scribble my letter.

Dear Mr Shankly,

I don't suppose you will remember me but my Uncle Horace used to live next door to you in Huddersfield when you were the manager there. I saw you in the garden one day and my dad took a photograph of us. You also very kindly agreed to get the autographs of the Huddersfield Town players for me and sent them to me a few weeks later. I wanted to welcome you to Liverpool. I hope you will be very successful. This evening a friend of my father's came to see us. His name is Dixie Dean and he said he had played against you when he played for Everton. He told me tonight that you will make a great manager for Liverpool. So, I wanted to wish you the best of luck.

Yours sincerely,

Stephen Kelly

I didn't expect a reply. And it was certainly not with any such motivation that I posted the letter. I just wanted him to know that Dixie Dean reckoned he would be a good manager for Liverpool. I forgot about the letter almost immediately but I did vow to go and see Liverpool as soon as possible. Well, I thought, it's the least I could do. 'You could pop in after the game and say hello to him as well,' suggested my mother.

The game chosen was the last of the season, the visit of Sunderland, still a giant of a club and 'the kind of fixture that should be gracing the first division', my father declared, as we strolled up Everton Valley towards Anfield. 'I don't think we should go in the Kop,' he warned, 'it might be a bit of a crush in there.' Well, my father was rather short and never the fittest of men and in truth I was even shorter. So we duly took up our place on the Kemlyn Road terrace, moving into the corner of the Kop as Liverpool shot towards that goal in the second half. It wasn't the most memorable of games and I didn't even see Billy Liddell but I did remember the surging runs of the two front players – Hickson and Hunt. They were difficult to tell apart at times, their blond hair sweeping behind them as they powered towards the Kop goal. Liverpool won 3–0 with both Hickson and Hunt grabbing a goal, while young England international Jimmy Melia bagged the final one. It was hardly the game to inspire but the size and sound from the Kop did at least catch the imagination. It was far from crowded that day but it was singularly the largest terracing I had ever seen, much bigger than anything Goodison, Leeds Road or Elland Road had to offer, the only other major grounds I had been to. Even Dad was impressed, telling me that he liked the look of Hunt. 'Could do well,' he said.

Maybe Mr Shankly realised I had been to the game, maybe not. Whatever it was, it was a mighty coincidence. A fortnight later, on the Saturday morning, my mother came pounding up the stairs to my room, clutching a letter. 'It's for you,' she said, handing the neatly typed white envelope to me. I was puzzled but not for one moment did I imagine it would be a reply to my letter. It was headed:

Liverpool Football Club Ltd., Anfield Road, Liverpool 4.

Telegraphic Address: Goalkeeper.

Dear Stephen,

Thank you for your letter and your good wishes. I do remember your Uncle Horace. Please give him and his wife my regards when you next see them. It was kind of you to pass on Bill Dean's remarks to me. He was a great player and I value his comments. He is still a good friend but being an Evertonian he would never of course admit such things to me personally. We are doing our best at Liverpool and I am hopeful that next season we shall win promotion to our rightful place in division one. If you ever come to Anfield do drop in and see me.

Yours sincerely,

W. Shankly
Manager

'Tom, come and see what's he got,' shouted my mother excitedly when I showed her the letter. Father was impressed. 'That's very good of him to write to you,' said my mother. 'Such a busy man as well. Do you think he wrote it himself?'

'Of course, he did,' insisted my father, 'look, you can see, the typing's not that good.' I smiled, returned the letter to its envelope, placed it under the bed and settled down for another half-hour's sleep. 'Well I never,' I thought to myself, instinctively feeling that I was on my way to becoming a Liverpool fan.

three

Tonky Tales

'I've just got some great new programmes,' shouted Peter, as he wandered into the back yard, clutching a bulky, well-creased envelope. 'Here, look at them, ' he added, knowing I'd be green with envy. Five years had passed since Peter had moved in and we were still avid programme collectors.

'Where did you get them from?'

'From my Auntie Madge in Manchester. Some bloke gave them to her to give to me. There's about twenty here. And there's a cup final one.'

I opened the envelope and began to flick through them. They were mostly Manchester United, hence Peter's interest, but there were a couple of Liverpool ones, a few Manchester City and an Everton. Mostly they were league games but there were a couple of European matches, including United against Anderlecht, United versus Bilbao, and United against Real Madrid. Plus, there was a programme for the 1950 FA Cup final, Arsenal v. Liverpool.

'Wow,' I said, 'wanna do some swaps?'

'Maybe,' he replied, 'depends what you want and what you've got.' I already knew what I wanted.

'Well, I wouldn't mind this,' I said, picking out the cup final programme.' I already had a few cup final programmes but not one as far back as this. And it was Liverpool.

'No way, it's the only cup final programme I've got.'

'Arr, go on,' I pleaded. But it was no use. He was insistent.

'Well, what about these?' I said pulling out the three European programmes.

'Not Real Madrid, in fact, not any,' he said very firmly. 'I'm keeping them. They're all the Busby Babes team, before the crash.'

'Wow,' I said, flicking through the pages, 'just look at these players, Di Stefano, Kopa, Gento, Mateos. What a side. And there's all Spanish writing on the front.'

'Yes, well you can keep your hands off that,' he said snatching it back. 'You can have this one, though, it's Wolves against Honved, but I'll want something decent for it.'

Two minutes later we were in my bedroom pulling out the large box from beneath my bed.

'Do you want first division games?' I inquired.

'Mmmm, not really, I've got loads. What else have you got?' He began searching through the box. 'Here, I'll swap you for that England–Hungary.'

'No way,' I replied. 'That was an historic game, that one.'

He flicked through a few more. 'Well, I want an international.'

'How about this Scotland one?'

'Who are they playing?'

'West Germany.'

He pulled out the programme and examined it. 'Nah, it's a bit mucky. 'Anything better?'

'What about this, England against Yugoslavia?'

'Depends when it was and who's in the team?'

'It was just a couple of years ago, 1956,' I said, 'and it's even got the score on the front. See? England 2, Yugoslavia 1.'

'Who played?' he asked, turning to the middle pages.

'Ditchburn, Jeff Hall, Roger Byrne, Clayton, Billy Wright, Dickinson, Brooks – who's he? – Johnny Haynes, Stanley Matthews, Tom Finney and Frank Bluntstone.'

Peter looked at me in delight. 'Okay,' he said, 'I'll take that.' The deal was struck and the Wolves v. Honved programme was handed over in exchange. 'I've got six international programmes now and all England,' announced an excited Peter.

'Look, haven't they got funny names,' he said, going through the Yugoslavia line-up. 'Stankovic, I'll bet he smells a bit, and who's this guy Toplak? What stupid names. And there's another one down here in the reserves called Conc.' We both fell about laughing.

I rifled through a few more of the programmes and picked out one of the Liverpool ones. It was against Preston North End and was dated August 1947. I was about to put it aside when I suddenly wondered if Bill Shankly had played. I flicked through it and there on the team page was the name Shankly (4), just below the name of Finney (7). Among the players in the Liverpool side were Liddell, Stubbins, Hughes and Paisley.

'What's it say about Shankly in the pen pictures?' asked Peter when I pointed it out.

'"*Human dynamo of a right half who began his career with Carlisle United. Born Ayrshire. Joined Preston in July 1933. FA Cup-winner 1938, who has now played more than 200 games for the Preston outfit. Scottish international with five caps.*"'

'I wonder who won?' asked Peter.

'I didn't know he'd won the cup,' I said. 'Can I have this one as well?'

'Okay,' he said, pulling out a Manchester United-against-Everton programme from my collection. 'Straight swap?'

'I've met him, you know.'

'No, you haven't.'

'I have, honest. He used to live next door to my uncle and aunt in Huddersfield. I've got a photograph to prove it as well, and I've got his autograph.'

'Go on then, show us.' I ran upstairs. Finding the autographs was no problem but mother was too busy to dig out the family photos. Peter was impressed by the autographs but remained unconvinced that I'd ever met him. 'I wanna to see the evidence,' he insisted.

Peter wandered off back to his house, so I decided to go and tell Billy, up the road, about my new swaps. I was delighted with my deals. I may not have acquired the Arsenal–Liverpool programme but at least I had another European programme to add to my growing collection of English clubs against foreign opposition, the favourite of which was Chelsea against Moscow Dynamo. I kept that in a special wrapper. But more importantly I had a programme of a game Shankly had played in.

Billy was the only other programme collector I knew. He was not that interested in the game but he did have a collector's instinct and his collection was partly enhanced by the fact that his father was Glaswegian and a huge supporter of Rangers, or *the* Rangers, as he always referred to them. Hence Billy had a fair smattering of Scottish programmes in his collection, something that made it different, at least, if not always that swappable. Billy's closest friend was Andy, an equally tall lad, though leaner and more clean-cut with a strong chin. Both of them were a year older than me and attended the same school but, although I was friendly with them, they had little to do with Peter. 'He's a left-footer,' said Andy, whose family were fundamentalist Church of England. 'Me mum says I shouldn't have anything to do with him.' The reference to 'left-footer' was, alas, nothing to do with which foot Peter kicked a football, but was the shorthand for Catholic. Billy's dad especially was filled with terror. The prospect of his son mixing with a left-footer, whose father would no doubt be a Celtic supporter, was too much to contemplate. My friendship with Peter, however, was independent of them and bridged any sectarian divide. Anyhow, Peter knew and understood football better than any of them, even though he did support Manchester United. That was fine by me, even if the others didn't care that much for him and were always ready to poke fun at his god.

Billy was sitting on the wall outside his house with Andy. They were both giggling.

'A tonky? Go 'way,' said Andy.

He looked us both in the face, his eyes bulging. 'Honest!' he replied. 'I found it in me dad's drawer.'

Andy promptly burst into a fit of giggles. 'Yer dad's got a tonky?'

'Shurrup,' yelled Billy, now beginning to regret he'd ever mentioned the damn thing.

'I don't believe you,' argued Andy. 'I bet your mum and dad don't do it.'

'Don't do what?' I asked innocently. Andy explained what the conversation was about.

'Urggh!' I shrieked. 'Imagine your mum and dad doing that.' The pair of them burst into laughter. I wasn't sure whether they were laughing at my innocence or the thought of Billy's mum and dad doing what comes naturally.

'Why's he hide it in his drawer?' I asked once we'd quietened down a bit.

'Well, he's got to keep it somewhere,' answered Billy. 'I'll show you if you like,' he suggested rashly.

'Great, come on then,' insisted Andy, 'let's go and have a look.'

'We can't go now,' answered Billy.

'Why not?'

''Cos me mum's in.'

'We could wave it in front of her,' said Andy beginning a demonstration. 'Here, look what we found, Mrs Edwards. It was in your husband's drawers. What is it? Warra you do with it, Mrs Edwards?' Andy was prancing around dangling an imaginary condom in front of him. At this there was uncontrollable laughter.

I'd never seen a condom and I have to confess that I was faintly intrigued, and a little saddened that Billy's mum should be in the house and our expedition to their bedroom therefore curtailed.

'Nah, I don't believe you,' said Andy.

'Honest, it's true.'

'You'll have to prove it,' I said egging him on.

'Alright,' he replied, 'I will. Me mum's going out later this afternoon, we'll go and have a look then.'

That afternoon we returned to Billy's house. Andy knocked on the door. Billy answered, peering carefully around the door before he invited us in.

'Oh, it's you,' he said. 'Come in. I thought you'd be here earlier. I don't know whether we can do it. Me mum'll be back soon.' Billy was wearing only a pair of underpants. We looked at him. 'I don't know that we've got time now,' he argued.

'Excuses,' said Andy. 'You haven't found any tonky, have you?'

'Oh alright, come on then,' replied Billy, reluctantly.

'Hey, by the way,' asked Andy, 'why are you wearing just a pair of underpants?' Billy looked at us, embarrassed. 'I was just havin' a cack,' he replied.

'Like hell, he was,' sniggered Andy. 'Do you take all yer clothes off to have a cack then?' Billy went bright red and began racing up the stairs. Andy and I followed as Billy pulled on some trousers. We made straight for the front bedroom. I'd never been upstairs in Billy's house before. It was just a two-bedroom terrace house, much the same as ours. Billy made straight for his father's chest of drawers and pulled opened the top drawer. There was a towel inside and he carefully removed it. And there, beneath the towel, was a long, red, rubber tonky.

'Corr!' exclaimed Andy. 'The bloody size of it. Is your dad's dick that big?' Andy grabbed hold of the condom and started swinging it around his head.

'Hey, bloody stop it,' screamed Billy, grabbing Andy by the neck. 'You'll break it.' Andy was laughing and fighting him off.

'So, does he use it every time?' I asked.

'Of course he does,' replied Billy, finally wrenching the red rubber away from Andy.

'How does he clean it?' asked Andy.

'He washes it so as he can use it again.'

'He washes it!'

'Yeah, what's wrong with that?'

'So, who washes it, your dad or your mum?'

'I don't know really, suppose me mum does 'cos she does all the washing.'

'Does she wash it in new Oxydol, the whiter-than-white washing powder?' asked Andy, putting on his best television advert voice.

'I don't think so, I think she just washes it in the sink in hot water.'

'Let's go and try it,' suggested Andy.

And with that we raced towards the bathroom. Andy carefully placed the condom under the tap and Billy turned it on. Water gushed into the condom and it began to swell. Soon it was as big as a football. Andy removed the filled condom from the tap and, holding the end tightly, offered it to Billy for heading practice. Andy leapt from one end of the room to the other. 'And it's Hickson coming in on the far post. Goal!'

'Hello Billy, are you up there?' This was followed by the sound of Mrs Edwards closing the front door behind her.

'Fuck!' shrieked Billy. 'It's me mum! Give us it! Quick! Get downstairs!'

A dog barked as it rushed up the stairs. Digger, a hefty black mongrel, back from his walk in the park, bounded through the bathroom door, delighted to see Billy and his chums, and immediately leapt up to greet each one individually. This was all very well except for the fact that Andy was clinging on to the wet condom. The inevitable happened. The condom, like a greased water melon, slipped form his grasp and bounced onto the bathroom floor, spilling water everywhere.

'Oh, fuckin' hell,' said Billy, not knowing whether to mop up the water that had gushed onto the floor or to pick up the condom and hurl it into the sink. In the event, he did neither.

'William, are you up there?' shouted Mrs Edwards from the bottom of the stairs. At this point she spotted me through the partly opened bathroom door, trying to ease the dog out onto the landing.

'Oh, hello Stephen. What are you both doing up there, William? You're making a lot of noise,' shouted Mrs Edwards.

'Oh, er, just washing our hands,' Billy told her, the panic in his voice all too obvious. 'We'll be down in a sec.' As I peered down the stairs at Mrs Edwards, I suddenly saw her in a different light. She was no longer Billy's mum but rather she had become a sex object. She was a handsome-looking woman with jet-black hair and sharply defined cheekbones. She had a neat, gentle body with a shapely bosom and broad child-bearing hips.

She turned and went back into the dining room. Billy picked up the half-filled condom and lobbed it into the sink. It landed with a heavy splat and lay there gurgling.

'Hey, it looks like we've caught a bloody salmon,' said Andy. 'Do you think it's dead?' he added, giving it a gentle poke.

'Careful, it'll squirt into your hands and jump back down the sink in a minute,' suggested Billy. We all fell about laughing until we heard the intrepid footsteps of Mrs Edwards mounting the stairs.

'Quick, chuck us that towel,' yelled Billy, looking at me. 'Get mopping that water up.' Meanwhile, Billy took the condom out of the sink and, turning it upside down, began to let the water run out. In theory, this was not a foolish idea but in practice, as anyone who has ever filled a balloon with water will know, it takes more than a few moments to empty all the water out. And nor was it helped by Digger, who continually jumped up at Billy, thrashing his powerful tail against everyone in the confined space of the bathroom, while sloshing his muddy paws on the water-strewn floor.

Once Billy had finally emptied the condom of most of its water he began trying to dry it on his pullover, but this wasn't working too well. He pulled a grubby handkerchief out of his pocket and wrapped the condom in it before patting it in the hope of getting rid of all signs of liquid. 'Oh fuck! There's water everywhere!' he yelled, pitifully.

'Christ! This is all your fault,' said Billy, not knowing what to do. He quickly stuffed the dripping condom more firmly into the handkerchief and shoved it into his pocket.

'Oh, are you here as well, Andy?' said Mrs Edwards, poking her nose around the bathroom door.

'Sure am, Mrs Edwards,' he replied, with all the appeal of a snake charmer.

'What have you been doing, boys?' she inquired nosily, 'there's water everywhere.'

'Er, just spilt some water, Mum,' replied Billy, unconvincingly. Mrs Edwards glared at him, not believing a word he'd said.

'Well, get it cleared up and then I think you boys ought to go home. It'll soon be teatime.' She disappeared out of the door and we all breathed a sigh of relief until we realised she was making for the bedroom.

Andy was the first to comprehend the full significance of this. 'Oh Christ! I think we left the drawer open,' he said. Billy's jaw hit the bathroom floor with a thud. It was going from bad to worse. But when things are at their worst your only hope is that some messenger from heaven will arrive to rescue you from further crisis. Our saviour announced himself with a loud knock at the front door. 'I'll go,' shouted Mrs Edwards, making her way out of the bedroom door and down the stairs. To a man, we all promptly raced into the bedroom. The drawer had remained open but presumably unseen by Billy's mum. Billy hurled the wet condom into the drawer, stuffed the towel back on top of it and, heaving a sigh of relief, slammed it closed. We all calmly walked out and down the stairs. It was Peter at the door, wondering if I was there.

'Hi Pete,' we shouted and like a shot we were all out of the door, rolling over the front wall and sniggering like girls before finally dropping to the pavement and clutching our stomachs in exaggerated response. Peter looked at us in total bemusement.

'What's going on?'

'You wouldn't understand,' said Andy.

'Why not?'

''Cos Catholics don't use tonkies, so you wouldn't know what one looked like,' said Billy. We all burst out laughing again.

'I'll bet your dad hasn't got any,' said Andy. Peter looked at us puzzled.

'Hey,' said Peter, once we had stopped laughing. 'I came to tell you something.'

'What?' we all asked.

'Liverpool have just signed a new player. It's in tonight's *Echo*.'

'Who?' I asked.

'Someone called St John.' We started laughing.

'St John? They'll need more than fucking St John. They'll need St Paul and St Peter as well if they're ever going to get out of the second division,' said Andy.

'Ha, ha, ha,' I replied sarcastically.

'They'll need bloody Jesus Christ, as well,' suggested Billy, who was never that interested in football but was quick to spot an ideal opportunity to poke a bit of fun.

'Are you having us on, Peter?' I asked.

'No, honest,' he replied. 'He's called, I think, Ian or Eamon, or some bloody name, but his other name is St John. I remember that and they've signed him for thirty-five thousand pounds from some Scottish club.'

'Blimey, that's a lot of money,' I said. 'Is he any good?'

'Dunno, but he ought to be for that price,' said Peter.

It was May 1961 and for the umpteenth time Liverpool had narrowly missed out on promotion. 'They're fine until Easter,' Dad had warned me, 'and then they go to pieces.' In the past five seasons they'd finished third, third, fourth, fourth and in the season just ended, third again. Shankly had been there a season and a half and was beginning to ring the changes but still Liverpool remained trapped in the second division. Everton, meanwhile, had just enjoyed their best season in years, finishing fifth in the first division. Peter and I had been across to Goodison a couple of times that season, most notably to see them thrash Newcastle United

5–0. We cheered new signing Alex Young's every graceful flick. We'd also been to Anfield, this time on our own. Yet despite Shankly's letter I hadn't been totally converted. It was difficult. Money-bags Everton were still the headline-catching club although Shankly was outsmarting his counterpart, who was about to be given the sack. Second division football did not hold a great deal of attraction: it was still a case of Scunthorpe, Lincoln and Swansea, little better than Tranmere really. But there was a rumbling, a feeling that something was going to happen. 'Ballocks,' said Andy, 'they'll still be there in five years' time.'

For days thoughts of Mrs Edwards haunted me as teenage sap began to rise in my loins. She had become my fantasy. I could barely stop thinking about her long, slim legs and the things she must have done with a tonky. Football had taken a back seat as wave after wave of illicit introspection took over. I tried looking the same at Andy's mum, even Peter's mum, but they still seemed the same as ever. They were just mums. But Billy's mum was different. When I called at Billy's house a few days later I was in a sweat in case she answered the door. I half hoped she wouldn't be in but when Billy opened the door I was immediately disappointed. He called me in, leading me towards the kitchen, then disappeared upstairs to get a coat.

In the kitchen Mrs Edwards was kneeling, cleaning the floor, her back neatly arched and her rear pushed pointedly upwards. Her dress was pulled slightly above her bare knees, exposing a flash of warm thigh. Her arms were naked and tanned.

'Hello, Mrs Edwards,' I blurted. She looked up and in doing so unveiled an expanse of bare bosom. Her milky white breasts rocked gently to and fro. 'Oh, hello Stephen.'

'What are you doing?' I asked. She looked at me, puzzled. I could barely take my eyes off her bosom. 'I'm washing the floor,' she replied although she might just as well have said, 'What the hell do you think I'm doing?' My eyes remained transfixed.

'Dandelion and burdock,' she said.

'Dandelion and burdock?'

'Yes, it's all over the floor. That stupid dog has just knocked a glass of it over.' She paused. 'Are you alright Stephen?' She must have realised that my eyes were rooted to her breasts. She adjusted herself and stood up, though not before her face had turned ever so slightly red. Thankfully, Billy appeared at that moment, and as his mother emptied the bucket into the sink he skilfully secreted one of her cigarettes into his pocket, and we hurriedly exited for the park.

It was our final carefree summer together. Billy and Andy were already working at Cammell Laird while Peter and I had just left school. We made the best of it, puffing on cigarettes in the park hut or being initiated in the science of kissing by willing girls in the long grass. We also played endless football tournaments for make-believe cardboard trophies on a stretch of field that had once housed an eisteddfod. Peter was the star, a skin-and-bone winger who could squirm past any defender. He not only played for his school but had also represented the town. Everyone wanted him on their side and given that nobody ever wanted to pick me for their team, it was always down to Peter to choose me. He never let me down and as a consequence I usually ended up on the winning side. Yet despite my endless hours of practice alongside him my footballing skills barely developed. Nothing had rubbed off. More often than not I was the goalkeeper. I may have been small but I was agile and not afraid to fling myself about. Sometimes it was instinct, occasionally it was good luck but once or twice it was sheer brilliance. At least, I liked to think it was. Plus there were accolades and considerably fewer complaints about my goal-keeping than my defending. When I did play outfield I was usually a goal-hanger. That way I was less trouble. I could lurk about the opposition goal area awaiting the arrival of the ball, and even if just one strike in five was successful, it would win me a pat on the back. Peter, on the other hand, drifted his way through entire defences, smashed in shots from any angle, and set me up for countless chances, if not goals. What's more, he never complained when I missed.

It came as little surprise later that summer when he spotted me one afternoon and came racing across the road. 'Hey, guess what?' he said. 'I've got a trial with Manchester United.' His freckled face was beaming.

'You're kidding?'

'No. Look at this.' He pulled out a letter on Manchester United headed notepaper. It was from a Mr J Crompton, someone we'd never heard of, but apparently a trainer at Manchester United. Peter was to go for a trial the following week.

'How did they find out about you?' I asked.

'Me dad and one of our teachers wrote to them. I'm going to stay with my Auntie Madge in Manchester,' he continued, hardly able to spill the words out. 'Me dad's coming as well. We're going the night before on the train. Me dad's going to take the day off work. Maybe Matt Busby'll be there or even Bobby Charlton?' he added, showing me a few fancy footwork turns with a tennis ball. 'If they are, I'll get you their autographs. Come on, fancy a game of headers?'

I was genuinely pleased for him, even though it was Manchester United, but in those days there was never the hostility towards them as there is today. In fact, the very opposite: everyone remembered the Busby Babes with admiration and the Munich Disaster was still a short, frightening memory away.

The day after the trial he was back, looking subdued and bouncing a ball against the yard wall.

'How did it go?' I asked enthusiastically.

'Don't know. I only got about ten minutes on. They had a game going and they kept pulling people off and putting others on. It went on for about three hours and I came on right at the end. It was bloody scorching.'

'Well, how did you play?'

'I only touched the ball about twice. Me dad said they were nice touches but I never got a decent run at anyone.' That was the end of the conversation. 'Fancy a game of headers?' he asked.

Peter received the rejection letter a week later. He was in tears. I found him sitting on the yard step, head in hands. He didn't want to talk to anyone all day. 'They could have given him another chance,' said his dad. 'He only had a few minutes. It was so hot. You can't tell what anyone's like in ten minutes. Even Matt Busby.' But it never quashed Peter's love for United. Not long later Burnley, then a first division club with an impressive record in youth development, were knocking at his door. They'd seen him play for Birkenhead Boys. Would he like to come for a trial? No, he insisted to his dad, it had to be United or no one. 'Go on,' I told him, 'it's worth a try, you could always go to United later for a six-figure transfer fee.' He bucked up at that thought and decided to give it a go. A few weeks later, following his trial, they offered to take him on. He thought about it long and hard. 'So, are you going?' I asked.

'Nah,' he said. 'It's a long way.'

'Ah, come on, you've got to,' I pleaded. 'It's no farther than Manchester. You could become a famous footballer one day.'

'Nah, I really wanted to go to United. Anyhow, there's a chance of a job at Ford's in Halewood. They're just opening up and they're looking for loads of people and they pay well.' It was true that Ford were set to open a factory on a new site at Halewood, near Speke, and it was being heralded as a major jobs boost for the area. What with the docks running down, it was certainly needed.

'So, what job would you do there?' I asked.

'I really fancy being an electrician but the only problem is that I'm colour-blind. Me dad's been told you can't work there as an electrician if you're colour-blind.'

'What difference does that make?'

'It's to do with knowing the colours of the wires. Anyhow, if they won't give me a job as an electrician I'll try and get on the production line. There'll be plenty of jobs there as fitters.'

'And warra bout the football?'

'I'm sure they'll have a side at Ford's, so I'll try and play for them. I might even have a go for someone local like Tranmere or Chester.'

Our mundane schoolboy years were about to end. Ahead of us stretched the terrifying but lucrative prospect of work, although at that stage we didn't realise just how mind-numbing it would be as well.

As for me, I'd long fancied being an architect. Well, ever since the art teacher had pinned my drawing of the Sagrada Familia onto the classroom wall. I'd enjoyed the hours spent on that, sizing up those Gaudi façades and tracing its twelve-spired bell towers. But becoming an architect was out of the question. I might have attended a grammar school full of its own self-importance but architects were hardly tripping over each other at the annual alumni. Horizons were limited and at best the brightest became teachers. You had to go to university to become an architect and no way was I in that league. When it came to academic ability I was lingering in the lower reaches of the third division north.

Anyhow, I'd had enough of the school, with its pomposity, crude punishments and Latin conjugations. So, for me, it was the next best thing. Well, not quite. The next best thing would probably have been a naval architect or a quantity surveyor. Instead, I settled for a further rung down the ladder of ambition: a draughtsman, or to be more specific, a ships draughtsman. Peter was off to Ford's, I was heading for Cammell Laird, builders of ships, the town's largest employer, and where Andy and Billy were already well into their apprenticeships. But first of all I had to pass the exam.

'I'll come down with you if you like,' offered my father on the morning of the examination. 'I've got to go down town.' I'd never had cause to visit the shipyard, apart from going to see the launch of that prodigious post-war aircraft carrier, the *Ark Royal*, and barely knew where the place was. I wasn't going to argue.

'Used to employ twenty thousand when I worked there during the war,' he told me. 'I don't suppose there's much more than ten thousand now.' We made our way through spiralling July rain, past the Mersey Tunnel entrance and down alongside the gas works where he now worked. 'Are you nervous?' he asked sympathetically. I didn't answer. I just strode ahead as usual, he lagging behind with his busy bow-legged walk. 'Just be yourself, you'll be fine,' he added, as we approached the gigantic rolling gates of the Cammell Laird shipyard. My father took off his watch and handed it to me. 'Wear this,' he suggested.

'No, I don't need it,' I argued, but he insisted. 'It'll look better. Here, put it on. I'll meet you back here at one.' The gateman checked my name on a list and then accompanied me across to the drawing office where I was to sit the company's entrance exam to become a ships draughtsman. My father stood waving at the gate, looking almost as nervous as me.

The drawing offices were housed on the first floor of the main office, an insipid-looking building, entered, for the first and last time in my six years at the shipyard, via the swing glass doors at the front. In future, entry would be restricted to a wooden side door. It might have been drab on the outside but inside a century or more of maritime history spread out before me. They obviously wanted to impress someone: model ships in gleaming glass cases, oil paintings, brightly polished brass, shag-pile carpeting and a quiet air of achievement. Well, that was downstairs. Upstairs, where I was taken, was less peaceful. Dozens of equally nervous, spotty-faced juveniles were milling around, each clutching a pencil case and a letter. And yes, we were all here with one purpose. I didn't recognise anyone, not that I expected to. God forbid. Becoming an architect might have been a tad ambitious for my school but a ships draughtsman was undoubtedly downmarket, a little too close to the greasy world of engineering. We didn't get our hands dirty at Park High Grammar School.

The morning was to comprise a one-hour mathematics examination, followed by an interview. The exam proved to be well within my capabilities while the interview with a kindly looking gentleman known as Mr Atkinson seemed a mere formality. I hitched my sleeve up and deliberately displayed Dad's watch. Mr Atkinson must have been impressed. A week later, a letter duly arrived offering me a five-year apprenticeship as a ships draughts-man, commencing on 1 September for the princely salary of three pounds and four shillings per week. My father seemed more delighted than my mother. After all, I was, to some degree, following in his footsteps. My mother had hoped for more, convinced that I was being influenced by Andy and Billy. But she was, at least, thankful that I hadn't accepted the offer of a job as a cartographical draughtsman in London. There was little doubt that I would accept the job at Laird's and within months of leaving school and having purchased an expensive set of German-made drawing instruments, courtesy of my father, I found myself ensconced in the drawing office beginning what amounted to a prison sentence. If only I'd known.

four

Giraffes, Cows and Elephants

I was awakened from my daydream, the first of many, by the abrupt voice of the man sitting opposite. 'Christ, you look bored already and you've only been 'ere a fucking day.' It was that uncomfortable Liverpool mix of friendliness and sarcasm. He was a balding, ashen-faced man and even though he was only in his late twenties, beads of sweat clung to his forehead. I must have looked startled. Being spoken to in such a way had not been a part of my culture. Outside of a football ground, I'd rarely heard any adult swear. I offered a bleak smile in exchange.

'Who d'ya support?' he asked in a gummy Liverpool accent.

'Eh? Warra you mean?'

'Which football team? Don't wanna sit opposite a fuckin' bluenose every day. Der's enough of dem in 'ere already,' he said, raising his voice as a short, thick-set lad wandered past. 'That's Frank, otherwise known as Bluenose,' he added.

'Oh, er, Liverpool,' I replied, a little less half-heartedly.

'Dat's good den.'

This was tribalism, something else I'd not much encountered. The people I'd known might have favoured one team or the other but they never voiced any real hostility to the opposition. But this was different, genuine vitriol. I wasn't sure that I liked it. After all, Dad supported Everton and there was a certain W R Dean to think about. The man opposite was, you can take it, a Liverpool supporter, and despite his apparent acrimony and abruptness, turned out in time to be an upright and civilised sort. He told me his name was Phil.

'D'ya go to the games?' he asked, thinking he might have a partner in crime here.

'I've been to a few,' I stuttered, realising that perhaps it was time to make a more genuine commitment if I was ever going to survive in this office, and added as a quick afterthought: 'But I'd like to go to more.'

'This season'll be good, might even get promoted, you never know. I think the man Shankly's doing a good job. Warra'ya reckon?'

And with the mention of Shankly, I spotted my cue. 'He used to live next door to my uncle in Huddersfield,' I told him. 'He wrote to me not so long ago.' He looked at me, quizzically and, dare one say, even with a little respect. That was it, I'd hooked my man, and at the same time publicly announced my commitment. We were soon gabbling about football. And that was much the way every day would be for the next few years or so, the conversation twisting and turning around the game, Liverpool, Everton, Shankly, Catterick, Ian St John, and that much overrated Everton striker, Alex Young, the Golden Vision, or as Phil called him, the Bronze Shite.

I soon learned that the office's other Evertonians were the twins, Al and Joe. They were a couple of years older than me yet still dressed identically every day, and usually in blue pullovers. 'Which one is which?' I asked my new-found friend Phil.

'Dunno,' he replied, 'I still can't tell dem apart.' It was true. Six years later I still struggled to tell the difference.

The Ships Drawing Office, where I was employed, was the size of a football pitch with long horizontal wooden drawing boards neatly positioned, each large enough to take the gigantic rolled-up plans of a ship, sometimes a dozen feet in length. There must have been a hundred or more draughtsmen, including some fifty apprentices aged between sixteen and twenty-one. And just starting, a dozen fretting sixteen-year-olds, plucked mostly from the secondary schools of Merseyside, about to embark, supposedly, on a lifetime of devotion to ships.

The office was divided into various departments or sections, such as Ventilation, Pipework, General Arrangement, Steelwork and Admiralty. The latter worked exclusively on naval vessels and was considered a cut above the rest because all its staff had to sign the Official Secrets Act and regularly entertain gold-braided sailors of high ranking.

Farther down the corridor were the real elite, the Design Office, where the naval architects worked in a studious calm that befitted their lofty position, and then the estimators, not quite as grand as the architects but certainly more consequential than we mere draughtsmen. But if we were the poor relatives, spare a thought for those in the Engine Drawing Office and the Electrical Drawing Office, whose members toiled over plans that not only looked exceedingly boring but were largely indecipherable except to a small minority.

The one ray of sunlight in our office was the tracers, four young women who cavorted together at the top end of the office, labouring throughout the day tracing onto an ozalid material so that the plans would be indestructible and could be utilised as a master copy. Wendy, Sheila, Jenny and Pam were their names, every one of them in their early twenties and as pretty as English roses but, of course, not in the least interested in any of us spotty-faced first-year apprentices. But at least we could ogle and fantasise from a distance.

I found myself assigned to the smallest of these departments, the mysterious animal world of Ventilation with its safari park of cow vents, elephant vents and giraffe vents. There were just four of us working there.

Keith Hollins, the section leader, was a cheery middle-aged man, with a neat quiff of dark hair, who could thank marriage for his prominent position. It didn't take him long to point this out to me, probably thinking it best to warn me in advance in case I made any untoward remarks about his Uncle Arthur, no less a figure than the Almighty himself, or as he was officially known in the office, the Director of Shipbuilding and Design.

Arthur Rowlands was a bully of a man with a face as wrinkled and leathery as a walnut and a tiny head that sat rigidly on broad shoulders. He carried with him a fearful reputation and judging by his winged collar and gold-chain pocket watch had probably been terrifying apprentices since ships shifted from sail to steam. When he appeared from out of his office, which thankfully was not too often, there was widespread panic. He was General Paton and the Emperor Napoleon rolled into one. Newspapers would be hurled into drawers, conversations would be rudely cut short, heads would hit the drawing boards. The toilets emptied faster than a nuclear warning could ever have cleared them. In a matter of seconds the word spread. Arthur was on the warpath. Usually it was simply a case of him wanting to pay a visit to the toilet, if you could indeed believe that a man as exalted as Rowlands ever needed to go to the toilet. But if he did, it was in the safe knowledge that it would be to the executive cubicle to which Uncle Arthur and a small elite held the key. Private health care, company cars, free televisions, free books, free newspapers, even free football seats; I've had them all as perks but never, *never*, the key to the executive loo.

Pity anyone who might be hanging around the toilets, especially if they were doing something they shouldn't be doing, such as smoking, or worst of all, washing cups in early preparation for lunch. Although smoking was strictly forbidden in the office, the toilets were deemed safe and were always entered through a haze of deep-blue smoke. But if Uncle Arthur wasn't on his way to relieve his bladder he would invariably stand outside his office door and bellow for whoever he wanted. Silence would promptly descend, everyone praying the call wasn't for them. And usually it wasn't for us minions. It would be one of the departmental leaders he wanted.

Opposite the genial Keith sat Stan Watson, the senior draughtsman in our team. It was Stan who taught me my first lesson: how to sharpen a pencil. Now this may seem obvious and trivial but to a draughtsman it was the first, and probably most important, task of the day. Sharpening a pencil would never be quite the same again. There was a skill. For a start it had to be carried out with a particularly sharp knife. The trick was to delicately carve the wood away, leaving a long point of lead. The lead then had to be shaped on a file, flattening two sides and levelling the end. Sounds easy but this was a skill that would take me months to master. It was one of the few skills Stan ever taught me. I also had to learn the litany of pencils: 4H for fine work, 2H for drawing, H for hardening, HB for lettering.

Tall and wretchedly thin in his buttoned-up waistcoat and starched collar, Stan's profile resembled that of an ill-bred battery hen. And with his sleeves rolled high up his arms, his bony elbows revealed the scars of a draughtsman. I would soon learn that the office was divided into those who wore waistcoats and those who didn't. Those who didn't were usually less formal while those who did were officious, frosty and bullying. Stan had all the hallmarks of a Uriah Heep. It was 'humble I am Mr Hollins and humble I always will be!'

And finally there was Bob, in his early twenties, recently qualified as a draughtsman, the joker of the office, always a smile, and the voice of a natural crooner. But sadly nobody, bar us, ever listened to Bob, except at Christmas, when he became the singing drunk and would entertain an entire pub with his song, 'And I Say To Myself, What A Wonderful World'. Between us we designed, ordered and monitored the installation of ventilation equipment on each ship. Not the most glamorous of tasks, I'll agree, but if you sit in the cabin of a ship somewhere in the steaming tropics you'll soon realise the importance of decent ventilation.

Undoubtedly the most prestigious section was Steelwork. The bourgeoisie of this department designed the superstructure of the ship: plates, bulkheads, decks, doublebottoms and so on. Make a mathematical error here and the ship might finish up at the bottom of the ocean instead of at Singapore. But they were an insipid bunch, managed appropriately by the aesthetic Frank Wellbeck, a bachelor who had the ungracious habit of visiting each of his draughtsmen and apprentices once a day to spend some time examining their plans critically. His visits were hardly greeted with enthusiasm as they normally revealed the lack of progress since the previous day's call. As an antidote to these visits, schemes had been painstakingly devised over the years to distract Frank. The secret was to carefully sidetrack him onto the subject of one of his many favourite pastimes, chief of which was hill-walking. Others included archaeology, Egyptian hieroglyphics and photography. In fact, Frank seemed to know a lot about a lot of things. He was the kind of man who could bore you with a lecture on the history of the stapler or which fly was most suitable for a chalk river. 'I was just wondering, Mr Wellbeck, about the wording on the tomb of Ramesses the Third, did it say . . .?' Neatly pencilled illustrations explaining the differences between certain hieroglyphics or detailing the pig-track route up Snowdon adorned the corners of many a plan that emerged from the Steelwork Department.

The focus of the office was an area commonly known as the 'safe'. It was, as its name suggests, a secure vault where the Admiralty Department stockpiled their top secret plans overnight. But it was quite unlike any safe I had ever seen, being as large as our living room. The proprietor of the safe was a man known as 'Hoss' simply because his sizeable girth resembled that of a character in the American TV western series *Bonanza!* 'Hoss's stoutness might have been even more vast if it was not for a substantial leather belt that helped restrict his mighty girth to a reasonable 46 inches.

The safe also doubled as the stationery cabinet. Along with the top-secret plans, it was the storeroom for pencils, erasers, elastic bands, paper and so forth. It even had a counter. Hoss acted as storekeeper and was as miserly as any storeman Dickens might have dreamt up. As far as he was concerned the cost of each pencil might just as well have been coming out of his own pocket. 'Let's see what's left of the old one,' he demanded when I finally plucked up courage and made my first approach for a new HB. I showed him the one-inch butt of pencil that remained. He glared in disbelief. 'Bugger off, you've still got an inch of that left,' he yelled. Hoss was a storekeeper, not a draughtsman; had he been he would have realised the impossibility of drawing anything with a one-inch butt of pencil. And if he did grudgingly give you a pencil then it was noted in a large register – Kelly, one HB, 4 August 1961. Inevitably when you pleaded for a new pencil he would check back in the register and grumble at the fact that it was only five weeks ago since you had the last one. 'For fuck's sake, what do you do with them?' he'd demand before returning to his cubby hole in the safe and his collection of pornographic postcards.

On day one they had sussed out my football allegiance. On day two I was approached by a square-shouldered man with a stab of a beard and reeking of pipe tobacco. He had been talking to Stan, then sidled over to me with a welcoming smile. Taking out his pipe, he eased himself onto the empty stool next to mine, pulled out a long thin pipe cleaner and with deep concentration began to poke the cleaner up the stem of his pipe before announcing that his name was Vince and that he was the union representative. 'Thought of joining the union?' he asked after shaking my hand.

'Er, well, I don't know much about it. Do you have to?'

'Well, it's advisable,' he replied. 'Most people are in the union. In fact there's only one or two not in.'

'Which union is it?'

'It's the draughtsman's union, DATA.' It didn't mean anything to me.

'How much is it?' I asked. Such an unprincipled question but I was only sixteen. He reeled off a list of benefits, chief among which was weekend schools. 'All the lads go, weekend away in Blackpool in the autumn, nice hotel, all meals provided, only costs one pound or so. We also publish technical pamphlets very cheaply.'

'Can I think about it?' I suggested.

'Sure,' he sighed, handing me a bundle of leaflets. 'You've got 24 hours. I'll talk to you again tomorrow.' And with that he strode off, poking the unlit pipe into his mouth, and headed towards the toilets.

'Should I join the union, Dad?' I asked that evening over tea. He'd been a lifelong active trade unionist and I knew that he was something big in his local branch but didn't fully understand what.

'Of course son,' he replied. And that was it. The next day I duly signed up. My education was about to begin, but in more ways than one.

Three days into the office and Eric Richmond, barrel-chested and with a wild orange beard, was leaning over the desk talking to Phil. They were roughly the same age. Eric who could easily have been taken for an Australian bushranger, was the office genius as well as being a Liverpool supporter. He wore thick bottle-bottom glasses and had the dishevelled look of a man deeply in need of a wife. He was commonly known as Eric the Red. I'd like to think that genius and supporting the Reds went together but years of standing on terraces have taught me otherwise. Eric had served a five-year apprenticeship, studied naval architecture at university, and was now back where he began, earning less than he would have done had he stayed. But that was the way of remuneration in the shipyards. One of the senior apprentices, George Martinez, was chatting with them. He was a tall, slim lad, aged about 20 and smartly dressed in a two-piece suit and crisp, white shirt. His coal-black hair and swarthy looks betrayed his Spanish origins. His real name was Jorge but we all called him George, sometimes even Spanish George. They were all laughing.

'Could you take this plan to the shipwrights?' asked George. 'I've had a word with Keith, your boss, and he says it's alright.' I glanced towards Keith, who gently nodded his approval. Well, who was I to refuse? I'd only been there a couple of days. 'I want you to take this plan, give it to them and they'll give you a long stand, is that okay? You'll get it from the foreman. If he hasn't got one, then he'll suggest who might.'

'Yeah, sure,' I stammered. 'Where do I find the shipwrights?'

'Over there,' he replied, pointing out of the window in the general direction of the Mersey. 'Just ask.' And so I set off on my first exploration of the Cammell Laird shipyard, a nervous, naïve sixteen-year-old.

I soon found the shipwrights, first shed on the right, and entered a Fagin's den of templates and dark wooden shapes. The ship-wrights were the aristocrats of the yard, the oldest of all trades, and acted with all the arrogance of having history on their side. I found the foreman's office at the top of some steep wooden stairs. The foreman himself was huddled over a batch of plans. He looked up at me disparagingly, took a sip of tea and rolled out the plan that I had handed him, then gruffly told me to go and wait in the outer office while he found someone to have a look. Twenty minutes later he called me back in. 'We haven't gorra long stand,' he said. 'We don't stock dem any more. Your best bet is to try the welders. They're over the far side of the yard.'

Well, it was a pleasant day, the sun was glistening on the water, and apart from the smell, it seemed a better idea to be out than in. I may not have been connecting with work too well but the Welding Shed made the Ships Drawing Office seem a haven of peace and decency. The noise was relentless: overhead cranes hauled gigantic iron plates threateningly above my head while the blinding glare of welders lamps fizzed everywhere. It was not the kind of place for an ex-grammar-school boy. The shipwrights might have been the aristocrats but the welders were a new breed of proletarians who didn't take much to my fumbling and stumbling across their steel plates. You had to shout to make yourself heard. I had already been warned not to look too closely at anyone welding otherwise I might get welders' eye, which I was told left you feeling as if a bag of sand had been thrown in your face.

The foreman welder called me into his office, hung his traditional bowler on a peg, and brutishly told me never to walk under a swinging iron plate again. 'Now, what is it you want?' he asked grumpily. I showed him the plan. 'Hmm,' he said and shouted to someone down the office. 'Have we got a long stand?' They seemed amused by the notion. The general consensus, after some debate, was that they might but I'd have to wait while they looked. 'Stand over there,' I was told. 'Someone'll go and have a look.'

Thirty minutes later he came over shaking his head. 'Sorry, we haven't got one.' But he suggested that the riveters might. So, it was off to the riveters. Now, if the Welding Shed had been alarming the Riveters' Shed was bedlam. You couldn't hear yourself think for the piercing noise and vibration that shook the entire building. Just walking across the floor was terrifying, and making yourself heard above the racket was impossible. 'The foreman's office?' I repeatedly asked an elderly boiler-suited man sitting on a large steel plate. 'Where is it?' He put down his newspaper and cupped a hand to his ear. After I had repeated the question a half a dozen times, he pointed to some stairs at the end of the shed. The offices overlooked the entire floor. I was told to 'close the bloody door' when I walked in. The foreman was a muscular, ruddy-faced man who must have been nearing retirement age. 'What is it?' he snarled, in a strong Welsh accent. I showed him the plan and told him that I'd been sent from the welders.' He laughed quietly to himself, then called someone over. ''Ere, take this lad down to the floor and see if you can sort this out,' he said, pointing to the plan. 'Go on, follow him,' he said. Back down on the floor we criss-crossed a series of girders and plates being riveted together. 'What's that smell?' I asked, becoming increasingly aware of an appalling aroma that was hanging around everywhere.

'It's the abattoir next door,' he said, 'it's always like that on hot days. It's the rotting carcasses and all the blood. Cows eyes and intestines. Lovely isn't it.' It was a smell I would become more acquainted with over the years. 'Wait 'ere,' he added and disappeared into a small cabin decorated with pin-ups. I stood around for what seemed an age, my head bursting from the racket, my stomach turning with the smell, and with only a half-sight of a few naked breasts to entertain me. Eventually he reappeared, only to tell me that I'd have to go to the Engine Shop as they'd run out. I was off like a shot.

The Engine Shop stood next to the fitting-out basin where ships, once they had been launched, would be moored for fitting out. In time it was to become my second home but my first visit left me confused and floundering. It was vast, with small departments dotted here and there going by such names as the Machine Shop, the Brass Shop, the Lathe Department, the Coppersmiths and so on. It was here that Andy and Billy worked. Being older than me they'd already been employed for just over a year and were both serving their apprenticeships as fitters, or engineers, as they preferred to call themselves. I sauntered down the main aisle of the shop, eyes watching me from every lathe machine, when I heard a shout.

'Steve, over here!' I looked up to see Andy, in a pair of dirty overalls, waving to me.

'What you doing in 'ere?' he asked.

'I've got to take this plan and get some kind of a stand,' I told him. I've been bloody dragging around everywhere. I've been to the shipwrights, the welders, the riveters and I'm getting a bit pissed off 'cos nobody seems to have one and they just tell me to hang around while they look. It's been taking them an age, then they send me in another bloody direction. And now they've sent me here. Is this where you work?'

'That's my machine over there. Let's have a look at that,' asked Andy, taking the plan in his greasy hands and rolling it out.

'Ha, ha,' he began to laugh. 'Hey Marty,' he called to the lad on the next machine, 'seen this?'

They gathered around the plan and all laughed.

'Who gave you this?' asked Andy.

'Some bloke in the office,' I replied, 'told me to go and get one from the shipwrights.'

'Bit of a piss-taker is he?' asked the lad called Martin, with a Buddy Holly hairstyle and sideburns. I looked puzzled.

'Stevie,' explained Andy, 'this plan is for a long stand.' I looked at him, puzzled.

'I know.'

'A long stand.' He repeated it again. 'A long stand. You know, standing around for a long time.' Suddenly the penny dropped.

'Oh, shit,' I said. 'I hadn't a clue, it was all double-Dutch to me.'

'You've been *had*,' he explained. 'It's a joke, they always do this. Down here they always send the apprentices out to find a left-handed spanner.'

'Well, I suppose you could go back and tell them you're having one made up especially,' said Andy.

'Best thing is to hang around and go back late. The whole office will know. As soon as you walk in they'll all be laughing.' Oh God, I thought, how humiliating. They'd well and truly taken the piss out of me. Sadly, it wouldn't be the last time.

'Happens to us all,' said Andy, realising that I was looking a tad depressed.

'Where've you been?' asked Stan, when I finally strolled into the deserted office, his face looking more pinched than ever. 'We've been ringing all over the yard for you. What happened?'

'Well, I was dragging from one place to the next. It's taken me ages, and then I guessed I was having the mickey taken.'

Stan was not amused. The joke had backfired. 'I've missed my bloody bus now, having to hang around for you.' He pulled his jacket on, grabbed his battered briefcase and stormed off without even a goodbye. But at least I hadn't had the entire office gleefully awaiting my arrival. It might have been half past five but I'd saved myself a load of blushes.

Had the set-up in Ventilation remained as it was, it might have been fine, but within months of my arrival the Ships Drawing Office was thrown into chaos. 'Hollins!' bawled Uncle Arthur one morning, standing outside his office. Keith looked up, grabbed his jacket and went scurrying down the aisles, pencil in hand, past drawing board upon drawing board, watched discreetly by the entire office. He might just as well have been naked. Usually Uncle Arthur just wanted to talk about theological matters – he was a deacon of his local church, where Keith, too, was a lay preacher – and Keith would return five minutes later, a faint smile on his face and jokingly tell us that, 'he just wanted to know if we were coming over for tea on Sunday.' But this time it was different. The section leader of the General Arrangement department had fallen under a bus. It necessitated a major reorganisation, and Uncle Arthur was about to tell his favourite nephew-in-law that he was to take charge of the more prestigious General Arrangement department. It raised a few eyebrows, not least when Stan won surprising promotion as well by stepping into Keith's shoes.

It was the making of Keith but for Stan it was to prove a disastrous appointment. Even I could have told them that. Stan was never the man for the job: he was a nervous wreck, incapable of taking decisions, unable to delegate, a consummate worrier. He became a workaholic – crusty, paranoid and uncommunicative. He simply went to pieces. A year into the new job his insides imploded under the stress. Liver, kidneys, gall bladder, spleen, blood, it all went up in smoke as the engine of his body overheated. One morning, out of the blue, he disappeared. 'I'm going down the ship,' he told us, as he pulled on his white overalls. They found him hours later wandering around the yard asking the way to the drawing office. They sat him down in the shipwrights, gave him a cup of tea and called the doctor. I was asked to accompany Stan home in a taxi to his leafy suburban house, though quite what I was supposed to do, apart from smile at him occasionally, I didn't know. Stan stared out of the window through narrow veiny eyes for the entire journey.

It was nine months before he reappeared. In the meantime Bob was told to keep the ship afloat as best he could. It should have been a challenge, and indeed it was for a while, until the newly appointed Chief Draughtsman, Mr Leonard T Woolton, decided to interfere. Lennie, as he was generally known, had just taken over from the affable Ernie Smith, who had recently retired. Ernie was a tall, straight-backed man, who was always smartly dressed but never wore a waistcoat. He had been unceremonious, easy-going, and simply let us get on with it. Lennie was the very opposite: a small, bony bantamweight and the busiest of busy-bodies. He criticised everything, insisted on counter-signing all documents that left our department, and paid us a visit at least twice a day. Maybe he was testing Bob for the big job; whatever, Lennie was out to undermine us, subconsciously, if not consciously. Bob gradually learned to loathe him. His crooning became more restrained, his infectious laughter dried up, even his bride-to-be nagged him. 'I'll get that bastard one of these days,' he muttered to me as he returned from another meeting in Lennie's office. Bob was out for revenge.

five

Cousin Janet

'I could meet you at the ground, outside the Kop,' suggested Barry. 'There's a pub just opposite, called The Park, warra bout in there, two o'clock?' When I arrived it was heaving; bodies were spilling out onto the pavement, the noise was overwhelming. Eddie Cochran blared from a jukebox in the corner while warm beer sloshed down parched throats. I found Barry squeezed up against the bar. We ordered a couple of pints and edged our way into a corner, though not the one with the jukebox. We were still underage but nobody seemed bothered.

Barry was a decent sort, Old Swan born and bred, Catholic, and a year-one apprentice like myself. He was cumbersome, shy with a unique shot of white hair on an otherwise totally black head of hair, and wore unflattering glasses. His mother was Irish and his father worked down the yard as a boilermaker. Barry had started coming to Anfield early that season and had spent the last few months trying to persuade me to join him. Eventually I acquiesced

Conversations floated past; the talk everywhere was of football. Yeats this, St John that. There was a sense of occasion but maybe it was like this every week.

'I've met Bill Shankly, you know,' I told Barry. 'He used to live next door to my uncle and aunt in Huddersfield. He was manager there then.' Barry looked at me as if I'd just revealed to him that I was the secret love child of Elvis and Alma Cogan. I could see he didn't believe me. 'In fact I've even got a photograph of us together. I'll bring it into work and show you sometime.'

Someone pushed their way towards us and tugged on a man standing close to me. 'Der's a huge queue outside the Kop,' he told him. 'I think we berra be goin' in.' And with that a small gang sank their pints and made a quick exit. I looked at Barry. 'Warra y' reckon?' This was, after all, our D-Day: Liverpool versus Southampton, Saturday, 21 April 1962. A win today and Liverpool would be promoted to the first division.

Football fever had swept the office. Even the Evertonians, egged on by Bluenose, were faintly optimistic about their team's prospects, although, much to the amusement of everyone, Bluenose had inadvertently arranged his wedding day for the penultimate Saturday of the season. He told us that when he had explained to his bride-to-be that Everton were at home that day she had told him they wouldn't be winning anything, so it didn't matter. Showing an inconsiderate lack of concern for his predicament, she had then added in unambiguous terms that he had a simple choice: her or Everton. Bluenose, much to the surprise of everyone, chose her and thereby demonstrated where his true love lay. As fate would have it, Everton were lying third in the table only a handful of points off the top spot. After an appalling start to the season, when they had lost five of their opening seven fixtures, they had become unstoppable. We teased Bluenose that if Everton's nearest rivals were to collapse dramatically in the next two weeks, then there was the possibility (albeit slim, although we didn't say that) that his side could be at Goodison Park playing for the league title as he walked up the aisle. He wasn't much amused by this suggestion.

In the Red camp, Eric and Phil had been ranting on about how Liverpool would be playing in the first division the following season and what they would do to Everton. August holidays were already being cancelled and switched to June and July in anticipation.

Liverpool had been top of the table since the season kicked off and there had never really been any doubt that they would be promoted. Shankly had swept into Anfield and inside a year or so had revolutionised the club. From a sleeping giant they were emerging once more as a major force in football. The talk on Merseyside no longer focused on Everton alone. There was still some way to go but there was little doubt that Shankly's magic was rubbing off. It had been time for me to pay another visit to Anfield.

'Yeah, I think we'd berra go,' replied Barry, gulping down his pint. I sipped a little more then discreetly left my half-filled glass on the counter. It was just as well. The queue now snaked all the way along the high bricked wall at the back of the Kop. I'd never seen so many people in my earlier visits to Anfield. We must have spent half an hour in the queue as we painfully edged our way closer to the turnstile gate, praying that the door would not slam closed in our faces as we reached it. A policeman manoeuvred his giant of a horse to pin the queue against the wall, bringing yells of complaint from everyone. And, just as the rain began to descend, with a final lunge we were in. For a moment there was a brief respite, a sudden calm. We caught our breath, bought a programme, paid a traditional visit to the toilet and then clambered up the open staircase at the back of the Kop. Unbeknown to me, a ritual had been born. From the top of the Kop, we could see the rooftops of neighbouring houses and sprawling back yards bursting with washing and yelping dogs, while in front us we peered down on a vast, swaying rabble of people. Barry led the way into the mob, taking us down and into the epicentre, criss-crossing aisles, ducking under barriers, pushing past thick-set men until we reached a barrier halfway down and to the left of the goal. We had landed on what he called his 'usual spec'. He adjusted his glasses and grinned.

This was the Kop, a clannish gathering of like-minded folk. 'Here,' chuckled Barry, 'is where your true Liverpool fan watches the game.' I was about to become captivated, a fully signed-up member. It didn't take long. Within half an hour after kick-off the unpredictable Kevin Lewis, deputising for the injured Ian St John, had put Liverpool into an unassailable two-goal lead. We were in raptures. The rain rattled down relentlessly from a dismal grey sky but the world could not have been rosier. There was Louis Armstrong playing the Philharmonic Hall and Gene Vincent over the water at New Brighton. And we were about to go back into the first division.

At the final whistle, the ground erupted. The players danced their way off the sodden pitch, greeted by Mr Shankly, and then disappeared down the tunnel. We wanted more and nobody was ready to move until we had it. Some in the stands drifted off but not so on the Kop. An ear-splitting round of clapping emerged from the vast terracing, ringing to the tune of a song that had recently topped the hit parade: Liv-er-pool, clap, clap, clap. For ten minutes we stood our ground until the Liverpool chairman T V Williams announced over the tannoy that the players were already in the bath but they were doing their best to hurry them out and back onto the pitch. We cheered. Then Mr Shankly came on. 'This is the happiest moment of my managerial career,' he told us. We cheered even louder. 'We want the Reds,' we chanted. And then, one by one, in the distance a handful of half-dressed players emerged, some barefooted, some in trousers, some wearing red Liverpool shirts, one or two fully dressed and wearing ties. Gradually more appeared until the entire team was on the pitch. The Kop roared its approval. In the distance I could see Mr Shankly applauding the crowd, like a benevolent Mr Khrushchev, before urging the players on a lap of honour. Down towards us they ran, waving and acknowledging our cheers, admittedly slightly embarrassed by their sudden fame but in time they would get used to it. Yet they had hardly run twenty yards before hundreds of youngsters raced onto the pitch to overwhelm them. A young woman plonked a straw hat in Liverpool colours on Ron Yeats's head and gave him a kiss. We pleaded for the team to do a second lap of honour but Mr Shankly knew you can have too much of a good thing and the occasion was in danger of turning into chaos as more fans piled onto the pitch. As we finally spilled out of the Kop and tumbled down the stairs onto the Walton Breck Road and into the April rain, we knew that we had seen something special. It was called success and it had left us with a taste for more.

As for Bluenose, he was duly married. Everton failed to win the title, finishing up in fourth spot, and as Bluenose pledged his future to his bride his team enjoyed their best win in years, trouncing Cardiff City 8–3. The marriage didn't last long.

'Hey, what were you doing on Easter Monday?' Barry asked Bluenose when we got back to work.

Bluenose looked at him thoughtfully. 'I was on me honeymoon. I was in the Isle of Man with Pat.'

'Oh aye? Are youse sure? 'Cos someone broke into Anfield after the game on Easter Monday and blew open a safe and made off with four thousand pounds. All the gate receipts. I'll bet it was some bloody bluenose, like you.' We all laughed.

I quite liked Barry. He was never as prejudiced as the others and it wasn't long before we were regularly meeting up in The Park before going to Anfield. His dad, who frequently dropped in on us in the office, was a bit of a comedian as well.

The following season, back in the first division, Barry and I stood together in the Paddock at Goodison Park and cheered as Liverpool squeezed a last-minute draw in the first derby game in a decade watched by over 73,000. The game had captured not only the imaginations of football fans on Merseyside but of fans everywhere. This was the biggest derby game in the country – bigger than United/City, Arsenal/Tottenham, maybe even bigger than Rangers/Celtic. 'Here, after eleven long years,' read the programme, 'is the game we've all been waiting for.' Within 24 hours of going on sale, every ticket had been sold.

Ian St John was the only doubt. 'Ah, poor Ian. He's got a poorly toe,' mocked Bluenose on the Friday before the game. We ignored him but had a nagging feeling that a poorly toe was not much of an excuse for missing this, the most important game in years. But we had our own back. When we arrived at Goodison Park there was a mist of cigarette smoke and autumn. The crowd already hugged the touchline and there was a noise like no other I had ever heard as both sides swapped chants. The word was that jokers had sneaked into Goodison Park in the dead of night and had painted the goalposts red. It was true. Staff were still repairing the damage, making sure that the fresh coat of white paint had dried before kick-off. 'I wondered where me dad was last night,' said Barry. I didn't take him seriously but at the same time I wouldn't have put it past his father. There was a streak of insanity in the family.

The match began almost disastrously when the Liverpool keeper, Jim Furnell, fumbled the ball in the first minute for Roy Vernon to pounce on and poke into the back of the net.

Fortunately the referee disallowed it and we all breathed a sigh of relief. But 24 minutes later things turned sour again as the ball brushed the arm of Gerry Byrne. This time the referee was not so forgiving and pointed firmly to the spot. Vernon ambled up: 1–0 Everton. 'Ev-er-ton, clap, clap, clap,' mocked the Gladwys Street end, mimicking our chant. Cheek of it. We whistled back at them. Thirty-five minutes on the clock. Callaghan chips the ball into the area and Kevin Lewis, bless him, is there to level the score. Half-time and it was still 1–1. But in the second half Everton piled on the pressure and eventually scored through, of all people, the ex-Liverpool winger Johnny Morrisey after Jim Furnell had bungled yet again. But even then there were doubts. Had the ball really crossed the line? Had a Liverpool boot just managed to get there in time? We, of course, disputed that it had ever gone over the line but the referee got it wrong once more. And so the score remained until the final minute, when a long ball pumped into the area was nodded down by Kevin Lewis and Roger Hunt nipped in to beat Gordon West to it . . . 2–2.

We had stolen Everton's glory. They had been abruptly halted in their celebrations. Many of the fans had already made off to the local pubs to begin their festivities. Now they were drowning their sorrows. The echo of 'Liv-er-pool, clap, clap, clap' rang around us as we piled out of the ground and into the autumn evening. It was a moral victory to us. 'Can't wait to see Bluenose on Monday,' said Barry gleefully. A gentle autumn rain was beginning to tumble from grey skies as we made our way back across Stanley Park. Kids on the swings shrieked; a covey of blackbirds answered back.

'I honestly thought they'd had it,' I told Barry.

'Nah, always knew we'd do it.'

'Ballocks, you were as miserable as sin. You were slagging off St John for having a bad toe and not playing and Hunt for not getting involved enough.' But Liverpool had kept going until the final whistle, always believing that one last effort might reap rewards. It was all about optimism, about believing in yourself. There was a lesson there. But as usual I never heeded it.

Bluenose was not at all happy but he had the last laugh. Although we were back in the top flight, eventually finishing eighth, Everton of course would have to go even better and win the league title. It seemed we were cursed forever to live in the shadow of Goodison Park. Phil and Eric sat opposite me and whined bitterly throughout the steaming summer as Bluenose rubbed it in. Fortunately, we didn't have too long to wait to gain our revenge.

'Hey,' muttered Barry one day, 'you said ages ago that you were going to bring in a photo of you and Shankly.'

'Oh yes, I'd forgotten about that.'

'More like you haven't got.' When I reached home that evening I asked Mum about it. 'I think it'll be in the album,' she said. 'I'll go fetch it.' She brought down the large red album with gold lettering on the front and I began to search through it. But there was no photograph of me and Shankly. 'Have we got any other photos?' I asked.

Well, there's a box up there with mainly my family's pictures in,' she suggested. 'But I wouldn't have thought it would be in there.' Nevertheless I decided to look. I spent most of the night going through it but there was no picture. 'Maybe it's got lost,' said Mum. I thought it best not to mention anything to Barry.

When I wasn't trekking up Everton Valley on a Saturday afternoon, another routine had kicked in. I would take the train across to Liverpool with Andy, Billy and Martin and spend Saturday mornings wandering around NEMS record shop or gawping at Gibson guitars, along with dozens of other would-be pop stars, in Frank Hessy's music shop. Being unable to afford a Gibson, Andy had set his heart on a gleaming red Fender Stratocaster guitar, which to be honest wasn't that much cheaper. Week after week he caressed it sensually in the shop, holding it as if it were a small child and running his hand up and down its thin neck while his fingers danced along the frets.

'He'll never bloody buy it,' predicted Billy, as we waited upstairs in Hessy's one particular Saturday. Andy strummed on a Gretsch he'd suddenly taken a fancy to and Martin sat astride a set of drums.

'I wonder if I should buy an acoustic rather than an electric,' he wondered. 'I can't afford an amp as well.'

'But that *is* an electric,' I replied. 'You'll still have to buy an amplifier.'

'Yeah, but it is a semi-acoustic and at least with this I can hear what I'm playing without an amp.' I have to confess that I had no great opinion on the matter.

'We'll still be coming here in three months' time,' muttered Billy under his breath. But I knew Andy better. His heart was set on it. Quite where the money came from I'll never know. He claimed he was working overtime but I saw little evidence of it and he still seemed to have plenty of spare cash. 'Our easy terms are easier,' boasted the advert in Hessy's window but the deposit alone was twenty-five pounds and then it was a case of two pounds ten shillings a week until Tranmere won the league and cup double. Well, not quite, but you get the sentiment. Nevertheless, it was mainly Hessy's credit deals on guitars, amps and drums that kick-started a whole music revolution in the city. Without it nobody, least of all Andy, would have been able to afford any equipment.

'How are you ever going to be able to pay it off?' asked Billy.

'I'll join a band and then start to pay it off with the earnings from playing gigs,' was his instant answer.

'You should buy it now, ' said Martin, ''cos you'll never have to pay it off, anyhow.' We all looked at him.

'How's that?'

'Well, we'll probably be into World War Three next week.' It was true. President Kennedy was flexing his muscles with the Soviet leader Nikita Khrushchev over the siting of missiles in Cuba and a deadline had been set for their removal. The idea of a guitar that would never have to be paid for was tempting to Andy but alas he couldn't even stump up the twenty-five pounds deposit. Through-out the following week little work was done. Nervousness gripped the nation as well as our office as we discussed the possible end of the world.

'I know where I'll be going,' said Eric.

'Where's that?'

'On 1284, in the basin. It's equipped with an entire shut-down in case of nuclear war. You'd be alright on there.' Twelve eighty-four was a guided-missile destroyer that was awaiting commissioning, whence it would become known as HMS *Devonshire*. In the event, Khrushchev backed down, the missile bases were removed and World War Three did not break out. As a result, Andy's guitar was reinstated onto the agenda.

As Andy's birthday approached the four of us, accompanied

this time by Andy's father, who had to sign the agreement, made the final trip to purchase the coveted instrument. Andy had a final strum on the Gretsch, then glanced enviously at a Gibson Everly, the sort so loved by the Everly Brothers. We pulled him away and Andy's dad signed the relevant forms committing his son to two years' payments of ten shillings per week. The Fender was his. After that we didn't see Andy for months. If not working overtime he was usually stuck in his bedroom fingering his new treasure. Thankfully he wasn't able to afford an amplifier – well, thankfully for his mum, who would never have been able to live in the same two-up, two-down with a Fender Stratocaster and an amplifier.

After Hessy's, most Saturdays we'd usually wind up in one of the many dark and mysterious coffee bars in Bold Street. The Liverpool music scene was just beginning to take off and coffee bars like the El Cabala and the La Bussola played a not insignificant role in the low culture of the city. They were our version of Greenwich Village, Soho and the Left Bank.

On one particular Saturday we were sitting in the El Cabala sipping our cappuccino, or 'frothy coffee' as we called it, waiting for a Liverpool poet or a pop group to stroll through the door. The only trouble was that had they done so we would never have recognised them, anyhow, especially given the lack of light. Usually it was some unknown actor drifting down from the Everyman Theatre or, as was the case this Saturday, a group of giggling girls taking a coffee break from one of the shops.

'Hello, Steve, what are you doin' in 'ere?' I turned around, startled.

'Hello Jan, you alright?' It was my cousin. 'I'm 'ere with the lads havin' a coffee. Warra bout you?'

'Oh, I'm just having a late lunch break. I work in town on a Saturday now at Blacklers.' I remembered my mother having mentioned it to me with an addendum like 'Why don't you pop in and say hello to Janet one Saturday.' Of course, I never did, certainly not with the lads around.

'Who's your friend den?' asked Martin.

'Oh, this is Jan,' I said, 'me cousin. She lives in Tuebrook.'

'Hello Jan,' they each echoed as I introduced her before she wandered off to a table with a group of other girls.

'She's not really your cousin is she?' asked Andy furtively.

'Yeah, of course she is.'

'You're a bloody dark horse. Never mentioned her before, have you?'

'Haven't I? Anyrate, why should I?'

''Cos she's a bit tasty. You've been hiding her.'

'Yeah, I wouldn't mind givin' her one,' muttered Martin, who always had an eye for the girls.

'Eh, that's my cousin you're talking about. You keep your eyes off her.'

'No harm in looking.'

'Well, make sure that's all you do.'

'Ooh! Ger 'im, being all protective about his cousin.'

'She's got a few nice pals as well,' noted Andy, eyeing their table from afar.

'Stop starin' will you,' I pleaded.

'Eh, come on, let's go and chat them up on our way out.'

'Go way.' But it was too late. Coffee cups had been drained and Martin was up, following the scent, with Andy not far behind. Reluctantly I fell in line.

Martin fancied himself as something of a ladies' man and I have to admit that, with his dark, jaunty looks, sideburns and jet-black Buddy Holly hairstyle, he did not go short when it came to girls. To be more honest, they flocked around him. Despite the bow legs, which were the butt of much humour from us, he had considerable charm as well as gall, not a bad cocktail when it came to girls. He was already joking and laughing with them by the time I had paid for the coffees and reached their table.

'This is Karen, who works at Blacklers with me on a Saturday,' said Jan, introducing me, 'and this is Christine and Sheila, who both work here.'

We had soon ascertained that the four of them were going to the Cavern the following evening.

'The Beatles are on,' said the one called Karen, whose stilettos added at least another twelve inches to her already impressive height.

'Do you like the Beatles?' I asked.

'Yeah,' they all chorused.

'Have you got the new record?'

'No, I'm goin' to buy it later this afternoon before I go home,' enthused the short mousey-haired one known as Christine.

'I got it yesterday as soon as it came out,' I told them boastfully. They were impressed by that.

'What's it called?' they asked.

'"Love Me Do". It's great. I think they're really good.'

'They've got a new drummer, haven't they?' said Jan.

Andy nodded. 'Yeah, they've got this guy who used to be with Rory Storm and the Hurricanes.'

'I used to like the old drummer,' said the other girl, Sheila, who sported a neat beehive. 'He was dead cute.'

'Nah, he was crap,' said Martin, who not only fancied himself as a ladies' man but as a drummer as well. We all laughed.

'So why did they get rid of him?'

'I've told yer, 'cos he was crap,' repeated Martin.

'They're playing at the New Brighton Tower next Friday with Little Richard,' said Karen, the stiletto blonde, accepting the cigarette that Martin was offering.

'Yeah we're thinking of goin', should be good. I really wanna see Little Richard. The Big Three are playing as well.'

'Are the Beatles goin' to back Little Richard?' asked Billy, suddenly awoken from his slumber.

'Bound to be,' I told him.

'Any of youse lot in a band?' asked Sheila, the beehive.

'Er, no,' I answered.

'I play the guitar, though,' butted in Andy. 'And I'm hoping to be joining a band soon.' We all looked at him.

'Since when?'

'Since now like. Ginger at work, he's starting a group and wants me to play in it. Lead guitar.'

'First I've heard of it,' muttered Martin.

'Hey dat's good,' said the girl with the mousey hair, beginning to swoon at the prospect of a guitar-plucking hero. 'You could be like the Beatles one day.'

'Why don't you come with us to the Cavern tomorrow?' suggested Jan, turning to me. Andy and Martin immediately took that as an open invitation and gave me an encouraging look. Four of them, four of us, what more could you ask?

'Have you been there before?'

'I've been a few times,' I replied. 'I'm a member. I went to see Lee Curtis and the All Stars there the other week.'

'Oh God he's gorgeous, he's my favourite,' interrupted the beehive.

'And I've seen the Beatles and Gerry and the Pacemakers there as well.'

'So, do you fancy coming tomorrow?' asked Janet again.

'Aye, okay. Are you all going?' They nodded enthusiastically.

'Alright, we'll see you in there,' said Andy.

'Give my love to your mum and dad,' shouted Jan, as we left convinced that we had just conquered the world.

Not only coffee bars but clubs as well had been springing up everywhere in the city. The best known was, of course, the Cavern, which had been going for years. It had been a trad-jazz venue down Matthew Street, which most nights featured groups like the Merseysippi Jazzmen and the Swinging Blue Jeans, with an occasional visit from the nationally known bands of Kenny Ball, Terry Lightfoot, Acker Bilk and Ken Colyer, or the delightfully named Johnny Duncan and the Bluegrass Boys. In the spring of 1961, the club began to experiment with a few 'beat' groups. Although trad jazz was still popular, it was hardly drawing a huge teenage audience and the club was losing money hand over fist. The club's new owner, Ray McFall, much against his preference for jazz, was finally persuaded to give beat a try. But it would only be for one night a week. First up were Rory Storm and the Hurricanes, featuring one Ringo Starr on drums. The jazz aficionados shunned the new development and kept well away but the teenagers flocked in their hundreds. Further beat nights were organised and before long jazz had been pushed into second place and then out of the door altogether. A legend was born.

But the Cavern was not the only venue. There was the Iron Door, the Grafton, the Jacaranda, the Mardi Gras, the Peppermint Lounge, the Black Cat Club, the Locarno and half a dozen others in Liverpool alone. A club in Birkenhead called the Cubik had also opened. It was in many aspects similar to the Cavern, perhaps not as large but it was a genuine cellar, dark, sweaty and noisy. The Beatles never played there and nor did many of the top-rated

Liverpool groups. The owner was far too mean with his money to pay the going rate for bands like the Beatles or even Rory Storm. So instead, we suffered a variety of second rate, usually rookie, groups glad of the experience rather than the money. The Cubik nevertheless became a regular haunt for Andy and me.

Almost above the Cubik was another venue, the Majestic, formerly a cinema and now a dance hall, and attracting the top groups on Merseyside. It was far more elegant, even boasting a balcony, glittering lights and a large dance area. The Beatles played there regularly. Ironically, their last appearance was on the day 'Please, Please Me' topped the charts. I stood upstairs that night and watched as the compere introduced them as Britain's new number one group. They were never seen at the club again; it was the last time I would ever watch them perform live.

The name of the Beatles had been known to us for some time. They may have only just released a record but they had already gained cult status among the city's youth. I had my first glimpse of the group who would in time be known as 'the Fab Four' at the Tower Ballroom in New Brighton one Friday evening. The Tower, which stood next to the site of the former New Brighton Tower Football Club, had become a major Merseyside venue for what we fashionably called 'beat concerts'. It was by far the largest venue on Merseyside and the Beatles had made a number of appearances there before their extravaganza with Little Richard. I was impressed from the start.

Billy had barely said a word the whole time we were talking to the girls. Sadly, he had been all but lost to our gang. He'd found romance and was forever taking his new love – known as 'Maggie' to us but 'Margaret' to him – to the pictures. Even worse, he was rumoured to be simply staying in to hold her hand on the couch. She was Thelma to his Bob. Andy, Martin and I continued to play the field and the Cubik was as good a market as any. Maggie would not have been seen dead in the elegant Tower Ballroom, let alone the Cubik or the Cavern. Stomping the night away was not her idea of fun, although with Maggie it was difficult to know what exactly was her idea of fun.

'That's alright, isn't it?' said Andy, as we walked down Bold Street. 'Warra stroke of luck. I could quite fancy your cousin.'

'You bloody watch it,' I replied, knowing full well what Andy was like. 'She's my bloody cousin, remember? I don't want her mum complaining to my mum.' But the fact was that Andy and Martin had clearly decided who they were having. I seemed to be at the back of the queue.

'Warra bout you Billy? Which one do you fancy?'

'I don't think I can come,' he blurted. 'I'm supposed to be goin' to Margaret's for tea.'

Miss Beehive

At times, it was easy to feel schizophrenic. My social life seemed to have been sharply divided into two. On the one hand, I was following the fortunes of Liverpool FC, often with Barry, although not always; on the other, I was a frequent visitor to the various clubs and music dens of the city. Getting Andy and the other lads to go to football matches had proved near impossible. None of them were great football fans. Andy paid the occasional visit to Anfield but had never got hooked the way I had. Martin, a handy footballer, despite his bow legs, avowed no interest whatsoever in watching the game, while Billy's attention was, more often than not, fixed on Maggie and shop windows most Saturday afternoons.

Sometimes I would meet up with Barry, but, if need be, I was happy to go alone. Barry's elder brother came with us a few times. But then he went off on a six-month visit to one of Her Majesty's institutions. Barry wasn't in the least bit ashamed. 'Silly bugger nicked a car in our street,' he told us all one lunchtime. 'It was the only car in the street.'

'So how did he get caught?' we asked.

'He drove it to me gran's in Knowsley and left it outside her house. He went in and had his tea with me gran, a few beers and then forgot all about the car. When he came to go home, he just caught the bus. Then me gran spots this car outside her house and after a few days she tells the police there's this car been parked outside her house for days. So, the police came, examined it and later that day came back to tell her they'd found the owner and that he lived in Lloyd Street in Old Swan.

'"Oh, that's a coincidence," says me gran, "me grandson and his family live der." Well, it didn't take the police long to add two and two together. So he's finished up inside and all thanks to me gran. God, she was mortified. But he still writes to her from Walton.'

There was a camaraderie about the Kop. No matter where you stood, no matter who you stood next to, conversation was inevitable. As bodies plunged and swayed one way, then another, you soon found yourself clinging to someone or heaving yourself up on their shoulders as a corner kick flew into the box. It immediately invited a fraternity with the man next to you or even in front of you. It was probably much the same at football grounds elsewhere but the exaggerated swaying of the Kop and its singing made this a particularly special community. And even if you did go with someone the chances were that you would soon lose them as you spilled backwards and forwards throughout the game. It was not unusual to end up thirty yards or more from where you'd begun, minus a shoe. And nor was it a good idea to put a packed lunch in your pocket or forget to relieve yourself on the way into the ground.

Barry, loved all that but, on the other hand, rarely ventured into club land. With his thick-set, heavy features and beer-bottle glasses, he was not one of life's naturals on the dance floor. Hence he happily shunned it in favour of the pleasures of the Kop. He was not without charm but was certainly lacking in chat. When it came to clubbing, it was Andy and occasionally Martin who were my companions in arms.

Billy opted out of the Cavern trip but promised he would come to the Tower to see Little Richard. One night out in a week was more than enough for him. We argued with him, pointing out that we would now be three and the girls would be four. But his mind was made up. As it happened, it didn't make any difference.

Condensation was already dribbling down the walls of the

Cavern by the time we had queued, paid our five shillings and squeezed down the narrow staircase. In the depths of the dark tunnel, the thermometer, as usual, was ready to burst but that was no excuse for taking off your coat. Everyone seemed to be of the same mind as well as the same dress. Black was the predominant colour; black polo-necked jerseys, topped by heavy dark duffel coats – or black dresses for the girls, to go along with their Connie Francis looks. Beatle haircuts, Chelsea boots and winkle-pickers were in evidence everywhere. Never mind the heat, feel the fashion. It was that Left Bank look. The place was heaving, with barely any room to dance. Close to the stage resembled the worst conditions at the Kop, sweating bodies, groaning and swaying with the Beatles' groupies in residence and not to be shifted by anyone.

'Christ! It bloody stinks in 'ere,' sniffed Andy.

'Yeah,' mumbled Martin, putting his fingers to his nose. 'It smells of disinfectant and stale onions. And it's bloody 'ot.'

We soon spotted Janet and two of her pals.

'Where's the other one?' asked Andy, barely concealing his interest. Janet nodded towards the dance floor where it was clear that the mousey-haired one was in big demand and looked well on the way to a night of sublime romance. Who were we to interfere?

'I'd quite fancied that one,' muttered Andy into my ear above the din of the group on stage. Undeterred, he was soon up and dancing with Janet while Martin was shuffling with tall, blonde Karen. I was left with the beehive one who reminded me that her name was Sheila. Not that I discovered much else. In the bowels of the Cavern it was impossible to hear anything anyone said unless your mouth was pinned against their ear. And when the music did stop you had approximately thirty seconds to get in your line of chat before it started up again. Your only chance of successful chatting-up came in between sessions as one band left the stage and another moved their equipment on stage. There were no curtains to hide the changeover, just a cramped, bare rostrum, and even then compere Bob Wooller would be playing a record or two. The noise was relentless and must have left a generation of Scousers hard of hearing in later life.

On stage were the Big Three, an immensely popular and accomplished band who, for just three people, could make as much noise as any Merseyside group. Dressed in black leather, they played the usual mix of R & B and rock and roll with a heavy bass line from Johnny Gustafason. Sadly they would never quite receive the national acclaim that they deserved. Chuck Berry, Gene Vincent. The Coasters, Jerry Lee Lewis, Little Richard; these were the sounds and artistes most revered by those at the Cavern.

'Where do yer work?' asked the beehive one when we finally came to a break in the noise.

'Cammell Laird,' I told her. 'I'm a draughtsman.'

'Ooh, that sounds like a good job.' I didn't say anything.

'What about you? Do you work in the El Cabala all the time?'

'No, only on a Saturday. I work in a solicitor's office with Janet during the week. I'm a secretary, like her.' I'd guessed that she was a couple of years older than me and seemed quietly confident. She had a calm face, grey eyes and a nice figure. The chat followed the usual line and I reckoned I was doing rather well. So were the other lads, especially Andy, who was in the process of mauling my cousin alive. When the Big Three finished their session, the six of us ended up in one of the alcoves.

'I'm surprised at you,' said Janet, casting me a glance.

'Why?'

'Well, dancing with an Evertonian.' I looked in horror at Janet. The beehive one threw her an angry glance.

'Yer not an Evertonian are you?' I asked.

''Fraid so,' she said. 'Youse a Liverpool supporter?' I nodded, vaguely.

We both knew instinctively that that was the end of a beautiful relationship. It was like confronting the religious divide. There used to be adverts in the local papers in Liverpool: 'Are you courting a Protestant?' they asked, before telling you that mixed marriages were always risky. For confidential advice you were then prompted to write to Father Ripley at the Catholic Information Centre. No doubt Father Ripley would then warn you to steer clear of all bluenoses. It might just as well have been the same with football. 'Marrying an Evertonian? For confidential advice consult Mr W Shankly before proceeding!'

'With a job like yours I suppose you've gorra season ticket then,' she said. I shook my head. 'No, I go in the Kop. Warra bout you?'

'The Gwladys Street end,' she replied. It was a bit like, 'So which church do you go to? Oh, Our Lady of Lourdes, warra bout you? Oh, Laird Street Baptist.'

Catholicism had never stood in the way of my relationship with Peter but it got in the way of a lot of other relationships. If it wasn't football, it was religion or, as in my case, which side of the tracks you were born. The city was still riddled with sectarianism in the fifties, although by the 1960s it was on the wane. At the beginning of the sixties it was reckoned that there were just over 250,000 Catholics regularly attending mass. By the turn of the century that number had dropped dramatically to a little under 90,000. Most catastrophic of all for the Catholic Church was their inability to attract men to the priesthood. In 1960 there were five hundred priests in the city, but a steady decline over the next four decades saw that number drop to just three hundred. Much of this was to do with a simple collapse in the population level. The city's populace had peaked in 1931 at 856,000 but by the late 1960s had dropped to 650,000. When the Pope made his triumphal pilgrimage to Liverpool in 1981 it was down to 510,000 and by the turn of the century it had fallen even further, to 450,000 – almost half its 1931 level. Mixed marriages, among other things, had further weakened the church's grip on Catholics, along with a growing self-confidence that found people more ready to question the church's values and edicts.

The number of Catholic schools had also slipped, from a peak of 338 in 1975 to 263 a quarter of a century later. More kids were going to state non-denominational schools, which in turn led to a gradual erosion of their Catholic beliefs. It was also claimed that the Catholic Church in Liverpool had never really recovered from the crisis of the 1970s, when dozens of leading members of the church left to marry. It was ironic, really, the church's own leaving to get wed; nobody has ever revealed how many of them married Protestants. What would Father Ripley have said to that?

'Did you go the derby game?' I asked. Her attitude had now changed. She had been coming on strong before, but now she was withdrawing. So was I, for that matter.

'Course I did. You were lucky. That goal was well into injury time. Yer didn't deserve it.'

'Go way. You had two jammy goals. A penalty that was never a penalty and a goal given that didn't even cross the line. How much did you pay the ref? You're just a cheque-book club. All you do is go out and buy players. Look how much you spent on Alex Young.'

'Yeah, but he's worth it. He'll win us the title.'

'What about Roy Vernon, Jimmy Gabriel, Gordon West? Money, money, money, that's all Everton are. It wouldn't surprise me if you bribed the refs as well.' It might have been gentle banter but Janet now realised she should never have said anything. Of course, I'd have found out sooner or later and that would have been that. I was happy to be liberal-minded when it came to religion but not when it came to football.

There was a time when the city's football clubs were closely associated with religion but it was always confused and never on the same scale as Glasgow football. Certainly in the 1940s Everton were regarded as the Catholic club and there was some evidence to suggest an element of truth in this. At the time they boasted not only a Catholic manager in Theo Kelly but a plethora of upstanding Irish Catholics in Peter Farrell, Tommy Eglington, Mick Meagan, Jimmy O'Neill, Don Donovan and Tommy Clinton. There again, Kelly probably just signed the Irish lads because he had good connections across the water. Once Kelly went, however, the Irishness gradually evaporated from Goodison Park.

In its early days, Liverpool had been associated with the stamp of Protestantism. Its founder, John Houlding, was a staunch tee-totaller – strange for a brewer – and also an Orangeman, but any allegiance to the Orange order or to Protestantism ended with Houlding's death. There were of course those who, for one reason or another, wished to cultivate and exaggerate the sectarian divide by linking one or other club with a particular creed. By the 1960s, any religious affiliation had, thankfully, gone out of the window, although there were those like Phil in the drawing office who liked to poke fun by always referring to Frank as 'Bluenose'.

Miss beehive and I had a few more dances. She was a good dancer, I'll give her that much, notwithstanding her flailing stilettos. Frankly, on the cramped floor of the Cavern, you could have been dancing with anyone. In fact, you hardly needed a partner – the Cavern stomp offered enough contact for the preliminary ritual of mating. But despite the easygoing smile and demonstrative touch, it was all over before it had begun, torn apart by football allegiances. I wouldn't have minded if she had just been a fan. I could have forgiven her that but this girl was committed. She went to most games and was clearly a fanatic. That, in itself, was a rarity, as not many girls went to football matches. I could hardly start dating an Everton fan. By the time the Beatles were on stage it was an excuse to quit dancing and watch the spectacle. I'll not bore you with the details as anyone who has ever seen the Beatles perform live will be well acquainted with their abilities. Suffice to say that their closing number, 'Twist and Shout', was as good as anything I have ever heard from any artiste anywhere since.

Andy and Martin melted into a dark corner with their respective partners and stealthily snogged the rest of the night away, although I maintained a discreet, but sharp, eye on Andy to make sure he wasn't up to no-good with my cousin. The Beatles were all but ignored by them.

'We'll beat you in the league,' she said as we all stumbled up the narrow stairs and out of the unimposing doorway of the Cavern into Matthew Street before making our way towards James Street underground station.

'Ballocks,' I replied, smiling, although privately I had to admit that she was probably right. Then as the others made their appropriate goodnights in the shadows of Queen Victoria's monument, she grabbed hold of me in the middle of the road and gave me a deep longing kiss, just to let me know what I might have been missing. I was taken aback. In a way, I quite liked her. She could give as good as she got, and she certainly knew her football. She could dance as well.

'Money, money, money,' I joked again as we left the girls at the top of Lord Street to catch their bus back home to Tuebrook.

In the event, she was right. Everton romped to the title and Liverpool ended up in eighth spot, a creditable performance on our behalf, considering that we had only just been promoted. But it still left me envious of Everton.

Andy and Martin were ecstatic. 'Your Janet says she's going to give us a ring this week,' said Andy, as we bounced into the empty lift that would take us down, creaking, into the bowels of the underground. Martin was also on cloud nine. 'Are yer going to see yours again?' they asked.

I shook my head. 'Nah, I don't think so.'

'Why not? She's quite nice.' I didn't answer.

Later that season, Everton snatched a draw at Anfield. I thought of her that day and wondered if I might see her, but in a crowd of 56,000 there wasn't much chance. I'd even gone a bit early and hung around but it was silly of me to even think that I might. If only she'd been a Red rather than a Blue.

seven

A Weekend in Blackpool

'Do you fancy coming on one of these union weekend schools?' I asked Barry a year or so later, pushing a leaflet Vince had handed me under his nose. 'They're dirt cheap and Liverpool won't be at home that weekend.' I reminded him that it was FA Cup semi-final day and as we were no longer in the competition we wouldn't have a game. Barry groaned in response, ran his fingers through his hair and muttered something about our exit from the cup in the previous round. 'Swansea were crap,' he argued. 'How could a less-than-average second division side beat us at Anfield?' I wasn't going to attempt a considered answer to that question but I did mutter something about 'Liverpool concentrating on the league title'.

'Apparently, there's plenty of others going from the office,' I told him, trying once more to get him to focus on the matter in hand. In the hope of tempting him further, I added that I had also been informed that there was usually a gang of tracers from English Electric at these dos. Barry's eyes lit up at that thought.

By this stage, and with my father's enthusiasm, I had become involved in matters industrial. I'd looked at the way the office was run and audaciously informed Vince that there was total mismanagement. I expected him to laugh but to my surprise he painstakingly removed his pipe from mouth and nodded vigorously. 'You've hit the nail on the head, young man. That's precisely what we in the union have been saying for years.'

And so, on a Saturday morning in March, a dozen or so of us gathered outside the Cammell Laird gates in watery sunshine before piling into four cars to make our way towards Blackpool, hopeful of combining the mundane business of union affairs with more satisfying pleasures of the flesh.

The Norbreck Hydro was down the north end of the prom, a mausoleum of a hotel, characterless and meandering. It might not have been five-star grandure but it far exceeded anything I had ever encountered. A room of my own, waitress service, silver cutlery, starched tablecloths, and even a glass of beer with lunch. This was P&O luxury. The only drawback was that following this copious lunch we had to sit and listen to union business. The theme for the weekend was 'Nationalisation: the way forward'. It was to be introduced by Jim Cage, a national official from the union's head office. It didn't sound particularly inspiring, especially given that I wasn't even sure what nationalisation meant, but that was the price we were paying for our cheap weekend.

I had just settled into my room and was unpacking when there was a furious banging on the door. It was Barry. I'd only left him a minute ago. 'You won't believe this,' he stammered. 'Guess who's here?'

'Where?'

'In the hotel.'

'I don't know. Who?'

'Liverpool.'

'What do you mean, Liverpool?'

'Liverpool. Liverpool Football Club. The team, the whole fucking team's here, and Bill Shankly. I've just seen them. They're in the dining room having their lunch.'

'You're kidding?'

'No, honest, come and have a look.' We were off like a shot with our noses soon pressed to the glass doors of the dining room. Sure enough, there in a quiet corner of the largely inhospitable room sat the players and, what I presumed were, the staff of Liverpool Football Club. They looked different in their trousers and shirts but it was still impossible not to recognise most of them instantly.

Ron Yeats was such a giant he would have stood out on a foggy day. And there was Ian St John with his round bubbling face, young Tommy Smith, that slim whippet of a winger, Peter Thomson, and Tommy Lawrence, with his mop of curly hair. Most of them were seated around a large table enjoying their lunch. And there, on a separate table, sitting with a few others who I did not recognise, was the manager himself, Bill Shankly. I could barely believe what I was seeing. 'What are they doing here?' I asked.

'I dunno,' said Barry, almost frothing at the mouth.

'Of course,' I realised, 'they haven't got a game 'cos it's the semis this afternoon, so they've probably come away for a break.'

'Stop gawping,' said Bill.

'I'll have to get their autographs,' I said.

'Not now, though, we've got all weekend.'

'You still think they'll be here tomorrow?'

'I suppose so. We could ask the girl on reception.' A sweet rosy-cheeked girl at the reception desk smiled at us when we enquired. 'Yes,' she assured us, 'they're here until tomorrow, leaving after lunch. But they have asked to be left in peace and quiet.'

'Do they come here often?' I asked, trying to make some kind of conversation with her.

'Well, they were here last year, if that counts as often.' She turned away and continued writing in a leather-bound ledger.

'Come on. Let's go and have something to eat,' I suggested to Barry. We found a table as close as we could to the players and throughout lunch could barely take our eyes off them, observing their every move, what they ate, whether they took a drink, smoked or even swore. None of the other Laird's lads seemed particularly bothered to be in the presence of such august company.

We saw them again that evening on the same tables.

'Hey, who won this afternoon?' I asked Barry suddenly, remembering the semi-finals.

'Christ, I'd forgotten all about that.'

'Go and ask them, they'll know.'

'No, you.' I looked across but didn't fancy it. 'Go on,' urged Barry. I got up and walked over to the players' table.

'Er, excuse me. I wondered if you knew who won the semi-finals this afternoon?' There was silence. Ron Yeats scowled at me. I wanted to crawl away. It probably wasn't the most diplomatic of questions, reminding them that they weren't in the semi-finals.

'West Ham and Preston,' came the short reply from Tommy Lawrence, quickly returning to his food. I noticed he was wearing crocodile-leather shoes.

'Christ! West Ham beat Manchester United,' I told Barry, retreating to our table. 'They're playing Preston in the final.'

'That's a turn-up for the book.'

'That's Shankly's old club, no wonder he's looking pleased,' I said, casting a glance in the direction of the manager.

'Where are we going tonight, then?' I asked, as we assembled at the bar after dinner. I was trying to play the man-about-town. George Martinez, as ever, was wearing a two-piece suit, a white shirt with a sharp starched collar and loud tie. You could always rely on George to be dressed for the occasion. Always the same occasion. It seemed he'd been wearing a similar suit and shirt since the day he sent me on a wild goose chase around the yard looking for a long stand.

The twins, as usual, wore identical black corduroy drainpipes and blue pullovers. Barry, who had just ordered a round of drinks, was looking particularly dapper in a suit sharply cut at the lapels and with a neat flap covering his breast pocket as well as black suede chisel-toed shoes.

'Thought I'd better make an effort,' he said, when he saw me staring at his attire. 'You never know who you might meet.' I noticed he'd left his glasses off as well. The smell of cheap aftershave wafted in my direction. Spanish George was also impressed by Barry's elegance, whose white patch tonight was gleaming beneath an excess of Brylcreem.

'Hey, I've always meant to ask you, where did you get that white patch in your hair?' asked George. 'Were you born with it?' Barry looked at him as if he'd just been asked if his granny had sex every Saturday night. I grimaced.

'No,' he replied. 'I got it when I was about fourteen. Me dad took me to Anfield for a trial and after the trial we saw Bill Shankly and he patted me on the head. When I woke up the next morning I had this white patch on my head where he'd patted me.'

'Ger away.' I looked across at Barry, but he kept a straight face.

'Aye, yer fuckin' kiddin' me aren't yer?' said George.

'No, it's true, honest.' But Barry could contain himself no longer and burst out laughing.

'No, it's not, yer a fuckin' liar, you are, yer 'avin' me on.' Well full marks to George for asking. I'd always wondered myself, and a few days later I made my own enquiries. 'I told you, I got it when Shanks touched me,' he replied. I never did find out more. But back to the evening's entertainment.

'We're starting here and then going to Yates's for a few more but there's talk about going on to the Tower Ballroom after that,' said Barry.

'The Tower Ballroom!' I exclaimed. 'What happens there?'

'You dance, dummy.'

'Oh really, I would never have guessed.' He smirked back at me. 'Listen,' I continued, 'I'm not going bloody waltzing with you lot.'

'Nah, don't worry, they have groups. The Merseybeats are playing there tonight.' I was up for that. I liked the Merseybeats. They were a typical Liverpool group. They hadn't quite made it to the top in the wake of Beatles hysteria but they were a decent, honest Liverpool band who had been around a good few years. They weren't particularly original but they did play all the R&B numbers and a bit of rock and roll that was good for dancing; you always had a good night watching the Merseybeats.

The wind ripped down the prom as we made our way out of the Yates's Wine Lodge, sending what few sorry light bulbs remained from the illuminations rocking and clinking in the dark. The sea pounded against the prom wall, cascading into the sky. Silly girls in the queue outside the Tower Ballroom screamed and giggled as they escaped its spray. Ten minutes and ten bob later we were inside, smothered by sparks of dancing lights from a cumbersome revolving globe overhead. On stage a local warm-up band was doing its best to impress a small bevy of local girls who squealed and cooed at their every crass remark and hip-hip shake. Around the perimeter of the dance floor, groups of lads, glasses in hands, stood watching their every movement, fantasies flashing across their minds. This was the cattle market.

'I'm not dancing to this crap,' I told Barry. Thankfully, the local band brought its act to a swift conclusion before we had a chance to debate the question further. Over in a corner an electrical merger of some sorts looked to be on the cards as we spotted the lads from Plessey smooth-talking the tracers from English Electric. From behind the stage curtains we could hear the tuning of guitars and the roll of a drum. It was the turn of the Merseybeats. There was a sudden burst of noise.

> *'Wop, bop, a loo bop a lop bam boom!*
> *Tutti frutti, oh rutti,*
> *Tutti frutti, oh rutti.'*

The curtains flew open, drums pounded, guitars screeched and with a cheer the dance floor was immediately invaded. Girls began to sweat and bounce to the thumping sound of the bass guitar. Four smart-suited lads had taken control. The tracers were being pulled onto the floor by the Plessey lads.

> *'I got a gal, named Sue, she knows just what to do,*
> *She rocks to the East, she rocks to the West,*
> *She's the gal that I love best, Tutti frutti . . . '*

'Do you think we should muscle in?' I asked Barry, half-heartedly.

'Nah, I think we're at the back of the queue. They're nearly all taken.'

'Come on, let's give it a go,' I pleaded, 'they can only say no.'

'That's what I'm worried about,' he said.

'Warra bout those two there, dancing around the handbag. I spoke to one of them this afternoon. She seemed okay. She works at English Electric on the East Lancs. Go on, I'll take her.'

Barry wasn't keen. 'I can't see them properly,' he said. 'I left my glasses off. I can't really see, especially in this light. I need to get a bit closer.' We elbowed our way through the gyrating bodies until he was close enough the see the girls.

'Nah,' he said, 'I don't fancy her. She's a skinny minny.'

'Well, I'll have her then.'

'Nah, I don't fancy the other either,' he snarled. It was back to the drawing board. That's the trouble with draughtsmen; always planning, never doing.

'Warra bout those two there, then? You can have the one in the blue cardigan.'

'Nah, she's another boney moroney.'

'Christ, Bill, I think you need to put your glasses back on. You're clearly incapable of telling one decent bird from another.'

By the time we'd debated who were going to be the lucky girls the number had drawn to an end and everyone was drifting off the floor for a well-deserved rest. Barry was squinting and looking edgy. 'Let's have another drink,' he suggested.

An hour later we were still weighing up the possibilities.

I'd like to say that I marched forcefully onto the dance floor to take command of the situation, but in truth it was more of a shuffle, a sideways glance and then a hesitant request to dance. The two girls we'd finally chosen were, as far as we knew, tracers. What we didn't know was where they were from. Appropriately, I finished up with the short one while Barry took the tall one. They didn't say 'no' but, there again, they didn't say 'yes'. They simply acknowledged our presence by making the slightest shift in our direction and carrying on as if nothing had happened. The music was far too loud to engage in any kind of intelligent conversation but mine was a good dancer. As soon as it stopped I plucked up the courage to talk to her. Typical. 'Where'y from?'

'Gatley.'

'Where?' I could barely hear, as the noise was still ringing in my ears.

'Gatley.'

'Where's dat?'

'Manchester.' I'd never met a girl from Manchester before.

'Are you up for the union weekend?'

'Yes,' she replied.

'So am I.'

'Yes, I saw you this afternoon.' Ah, an encouraging sign. She had noticed me.

'D'ye fancy a drink?'

'Yes, a port and lemon'll do,' she replied, a little too eagerly. I looked for Barry but he'd disappeared. By the time I'd returned from the bar mine was back in the corner with some pals. They looked at me scornfully as I arrived with the drinks. Pardon me for forking out for a port and lemon. I was being sized up and I didn't reckon I was doing too well.

'What d'you reckon to the Merseybeats?' I asked, desperately trying to make conversation and stake my claim. After all, I'd just bought her a drink.

'They're alright,' she replied. Over her shoulder I spotted Barry dancing and smiling with one of the other English Electric tracers, one he'd earlier rejected as being too skinny. He'd obviously now got a closer look. She was tall with a mop of bright auburn hair. The little bugger, I thought. He was clearly making more headway than me.

''Ave you seen them before?' I asked Miss Port and Lemon.

'Who?'

'The Merseybeats.'

'No.'

'I have. I've seen them at the Cavern a few times,' I said, thinking this might have impressed her, leading her to maybe ask if I went to the Cavern regularly. But, no, silence. She wasn't exactly Miss Talkative 1964. Instead she turned to one of her other pals. I felt like a spare part in a garage. Thankfully the music stopped and Barry came meandering over. He asked how I was doing, took a sip of my drink, and was off onto the dance floor again with his new-found love.

'D'ye fancy another dance?' I asked Miss Gatley, as soon as the music started up again.

'Er, maybe later. I'm a bit tired at the moment.' Well! If that wasn't the bum's rush I don't know what is. I promptly made my excuses, claiming I was going for another drink, and left them to themselves.

The rest of the lads didn't take much finding. They were sitting in a dark corner around a table stacked with empty pint glasses and still discussing who to dance with. As I've said, that's draughtsmen. I don't think any of them had ventured onto to the dance floor all night.

It was midnight by the time we slunk back to the hotel, womanless and weary. The foyer was in near darkness and the rosy-cheeked girl on reception had been replaced by a shadowy figure with tired eyes. He looked at us. 'Is the bar still open?' we asked. He nodded apathetically.

'Come on, let's have a nightcap,' suggested George Martinez. The fifth-year apprentice who had so kindly sent me on a walkabout on my first day at work led the move into the bar. I dutifully followed, hoping that I might spot a player or two slumped over their pints. Instead, George spotted Jim Cage huddled together with a group of union officials in a quiet corner. They looked up as we walked in. 'Hey, be careful: there's commies around here. We'd better not sit near them,' whispered George, pulling up some chairs closer to the bar. Bluenose, who'd been to the toilet, came striding through the door, his eyes beaming. 'Bloody hell, guess what?' he said, eager to tell us his news. 'I've just seen Barry sneaking up the stairs with one of those tracers.'

'Gerraway,' said a startled George, 'which one?'

'That tall one with the red hair. He must have copped off with her at the Tower.'

'Yeah, he was dancing with her,' I told them. 'The cheeky sod, he said he didn't fancy her.'

'She's a bit of alright,' said Bluenose. 'Shall we give him ten minutes and go and bang on his door?'

'No. Don't be mean.'

George was looking over towards the group of union officials across the room. 'What a load of ballocks he was talking this afternoon,' he said, nodding in the direction of their table. 'If you ask me, I don't think the union should be getting mixed up in politics. It's not right. Too many communists in our union. All that talk about nationalisation. I mean, what good would it do if they nationalised the shipbuilding industry?'

'It won't happen, anyhow,' said one of the twins. I think it was Al.

'Well, it might,' I said. 'We could have a Labour government soon. I can't see the Tories getting re-elected. Alec Douglas-Home's an old fart. They've been around too long.'

'Didn't that Wilson used to be a communist?' said George.

'Well, if he was he's certainly not any more.'

'Ballocks. Once a commie, always a commie,' replied George.

'I don't rate that Wilson. Too much of a smoothie. Have you seen the way he sits there cocking his little finger and rubbing his wedding ring?' said Albert.

'He's a dead clever man, though. He went to Oxford.'

'Too clever, if you ask me,' said George.

'But nobody's asking you, George.' We all burst out laughing.

'Hey, is it true your dad was a fascist?' asked the other twin, Joe. We all knew that George's father had fought with Franco's Republicans in the Spanish Civil War. In fact, George had told us countless times.

'No, he wasn't a bloody fascist, he was an anti-communist,' said George. 'There's a big difference. And, what's more, thanks to the likes of my dad, we don't have communists in Spain any more.'

'No, they've all been shot,' I muttered. 'Eh, and you want to watch it you know,' I added in a whisper. ''Cos I've heard that Jim Cage's dad was killed in the Spanish Civil War, fighting for the communists.' George looked at me, startled.

'Come on, are we having another drink?' I suggested, a little more loudly. But there wasn't much response. George was warming to his subject and wasn't going to let it go.

'Pity they didn't bloody shoot his dad before he got round to starting a family. Him and the rest of them. They were going on this afternoon about wanting *more* nationalisation. There's too much already, that's the problem. They don't know how to run industries. Look at the bloody dockers, always striking, always wanting more money. For fuck's sake, they've got a job, what more do they want? There's a bloke lives over the road from us, he's a docker, he's never at work. You see him in the garden in the summer. He's got a better sun tan than me. The country's going to the dogs. There won't be any ships coming to Liverpool soon, they'll send them somewhere else.'

'Yeah, and the less ships, the worse it'll be for us,' chipped in Joe.

'But some industries have to be nationalised,' I suggested.

'Like what?'

'Well, coalmining.'

'Yeah, that's another one. They stick some ex-government minister in charge and expect it to run like a proper business.'

'Yeah, but it's an awful job. Who'd want to be a miner?'

'Go 'way! It's not half as bad as it used to be. They get free coal and free houses these days, you know. They think they're the fucking bee's knees, the miners. Always wanting to be a special case.'

'But it's dangerous. People get killed down the mines.'

'I'll bet you there's just as many people killed in shipbuilding,' said George. We all laughed.

'Ballocks. When did you last hear of anyone being killed at Laird's?'

'There was a bloke killed last year, when that steel mooring rope snapped and cut him in two, remember?'

'Aye, but that's only one.'

'No, it's a fact. There's just as many killed in the shipyards.'

'And where did you get that fact from?'

'I read it somewhere, some newspaper or other. No, I'm telling you, it's a fact and a fact is a fact. There's no disputing it.'

'It might be your fact, but it's not one of mine,' I said.

'Go 'way. If you ask me, it's a cushy number being a miner these days.' George, who was now well into his stride, was suddenly cut short by a gruff voice from behind us.

'Jesus Christ, lads! Is that what you think of miners?' I almost spilled my drink. The voice was unmistakable. It was Bill Shankly. I hadn't noticed him sitting in a high-backed chair turned away from us at a nearby table. He'd clearly been sitting there by himself taking in our every word. We all gulped.

'I used to be a miner myself, you know,' he said, pulling himself out of his chair and walking towards us. 'I worked in the Ayrshire coalfields and I can tell you it's a hard life, as hard a life as you could ever imagine. Underground, in blackness, all day long, breathing in nothing but coal dust. You choke when you get home at night, you know. All night long, every time you cough you bring up black dust and when you blow your nose your handkerchief's covered in black. Awful.'

'Don't they get a disease from it?' I asked.

'Aye, it's called pneumoconiosis. Many a miner I knew died of it. You can't breathe properly with it. There's a miner's rest home just up the promenade from here. It's full of miners from Scotland, young and old, and all with pneumoconiosis. Wheezing all night long. Ah, it's terrible. You should go up there and listen to it. When I worked down the pits in Scotland all I dreamed about was the end of the shift. I just wanted to get away from the blackness, see daylight again, breathe in fresh air.

'You know, I never had a bath until I was fifteen years of age. They didn't provide baths or showers at the pithead in those days.

And we didn't have a bath at home. So I never got to have a proper bath until I was a teenager.'

'But that's got nothing to do with nationalisation,' suggested George.

'I beg your pardon, son, but it has everything to do with nationalisation. When they nationalised the mines after the war they provided showers and baths so that the men could go home clean and respectable. Before that they had to wash in the kitchen sink, strip down to their underwear, in front of the family, just to get themselves clean for their evening meal. Humiliating. They never even had nursing homes like the one up the road when the mines were privately owned. They just let you die. No such thing even as dignity. I've known many a family who didn't get any compensation, and I've seen families kicked out of their homes if they had a house owned by the coal company. When the father died, they just gave you a couple of weeks to pack up and leave. They threw you out.'

George was beginning to regret having taken him on. I listened in awe.

'Best thing that ever happened to the coal industry was the day it was nationalised,' continued Shankly. 'The coal owners were only ever interested in profit, they didn't give a damn about the miners. It was the union that fought for nationalisation. Don't you forget that. You lads are here for a union school, aren't you?' We nodded.

'Well, you should support your union. The union is important to the working man. There isn't much else to represent him, so you be careful, lads. I know you're only young, but don't go arguing about things you know nothing about. Find out the facts first.'

And with that, he bade us goodnight. George was smiling uneasily at him. From my seat I could see Shankly walking slowly up the stairs by the reception. There was silence.

'Phew,' said someone.

'Ah well, he's only a fucking football manager,' said George. 'What's he know? He's another bloody communist.'

I wanted to rush after Shankly and thank him. He'd put George in his place, really shown him up. But I never had the courage. I decided to go to bed, wondering where all the players were.

*

Not everybody turned up for breakfast. One or two tracers appeared, shamefaced, as though they didn't want to look certain people in the eye; feeling that everybody knew who they'd been with the night before. Usually they did. Others wore ashen faces, and tired looks. Barry was just about the only person tucking into the full English breakfast. Nobody wanted to sit near him as he gnawed into his sausages, tomato, beans and two fried eggs.

'So what happened to you last night?' I asked.

'Oh, I came back and didn't see anyone in the bar, so I went up to bed.'

'Like bloody hell you did.' I replied, drawing up a seat next to him. 'Well, you might have gone to bed, but you weren't alone.' He looked surprised. 'You were spotted, sneaking upstairs with that tracer.' He looked even more surprised now. 'I would never have thought that of you, Barry.'

'Ah, it was all innocent,' he said a smirk on his face.

'So, how did you make out?'

'I'm not bloody telling you.'

'Did y'do alright?' He raised an eyebrow but wasn't saying any more.

'Hey, you missed something last night.'

'What's that?'

'Shankly. We were talking to him.'

'You're kidding?'

'No. He was in the bar, sitting just by us, but none of us knew. Old George was really giving the union and the coalminers what for when Shankly gets up and starts giving it to George. Tells him he should think before he speaks and tells us how he used to be a miner and how important the union is. He was fantastic.'

'Christ, you're kidding?'

'No. You should have seen George's face.' There was a pause as a look of disbelief spread over Barry's face. 'Serves you right for going off with girls,' I added teasingly. 'Anyrate, how did you make out?'

'Bloody hopeless, she wasn't having any of it. We had a bit of a neck and that was it. Fucking hell, you mean I missed Shankly?'

''Fraid so. Have you seen him this morning?'

'No. I haven't seen any of them.'

'Fucking amazing it was. Shankly speaking to us. Christ, he

really put George in his place.' Barry was looking very down-in-the-mouth at the thought that he had missed this once-in-a-lifetime exchange.

'I never knew he used to be a miner. I thought he'd always been a footballer. Fancy him being so left wing.'

'George kept going on about him being a communist. Any sign of George this morning?'

'Yeah, he came down earlier. He looked bloody awful. He was as white as a sheet. He took one look at the breakfast and made a quick exit. I haven't seen him since.' We both smirked.

'Ay up, here's the new love of your life,' I said, poking Barry as the tall red-head walked past us. Barry smiled faintly at her.

Partway into the morning session we broke into groups. I was put in a bunch with half a dozen tracers from English Electric, including Barry's red-head, and some lads from the Marconi plant in Liverpool. Barry carefully avoided our group. We were asked to discuss whether our respective industries might be suitable for nationalisation and to report back. Nobody seemed keen to speak, so I opened up.

'I work at Laird's,' I told them. 'And I have to say we might just as well be nationalised, because the government keeps the yard going, anyhow, by ordering destroyers, frigates and submarines. If it wasn't for those Admiralty orders the yard would never survive. And when the government's paid out all that money, the company makes a profit and all those people who have invested in it get a rake-off. So, you, the taxpayer is putting money into their pockets.' I quite liked that logic but it was met by blank faces, particularly from the girls.

'I don't think nationalisation ever works,' said a plump-nosed lad, who I guessed was from Marconi. With that, I was off.

'Well, look at coalmining,' I argued. 'All those miners suffering from disease. It's called pneumoconiosis or something.' Jim Cage, the national official ambled over and decided to sit in on our group. I began to regurgitate everything Shankly had said the night before. 'And the other thing,' I said, as I came to a final conclusion, 'you people are working in electrical industries where technology is important and where you have to be one step ahead.' The tall red-head crossed her legs tantalisingly. I tried not to notice but couldn't help but see a flash of white thigh. 'If you were nationalised think of all the money the government could pour into developing new ideas and new technologies. That way we'd be able to compete with the Japanese and the Americans.' Jim Cage smiled, the tracers sighed.

At lunch, Jim came over and sat next to me. He was a stoutish man with greying temples and hands heavily stained with nicotine. 'You're at Laird's, aren't you?' he inquired. I nodded. 'Do you fancy becoming a delegate to the union's regional youth com-mittee?' he asked in a quiet, shaking voice. 'We need someone from Laird's, they're one of the biggest firms in the area. And you seem like someone who's sympathetic to the union.' I must have looked at him slightly bemused. I can't say as I'd ever been asked to be the representative for anything before. 'Well, what's it involve?' I asked. He explained that it was a new committee that was being set up to help establish and co-ordinate a national policy for apprentices. 'We need to get all the major companies involved where we've got members. Apprentices get the rough end,' he said. 'We need to do something about it.'

'Yeah, sure,' I said. 'I'll do what I can.'

'Well, after lunch I'm going to suggest that this meeting elects a few delegates. I'll put your name forward, if you like, as the Laird's delegate.' I nodded, flattered that anyone could think that I might have something to contribute. And so, later that afternoon, I was duly elected to represent the Laird's apprentices even though there were no more than a dozen of them there to vote for me. Even George, his face still pale and showing signs of a long sickly night, reluctantly raised his hand.

Life was good. Liverpool on course to win the league title. As the season's excitement gathered momentum, not only was I going to the home games but I was now following them as far afield as Bolton, Blackpool, Sheffield and Burnley, taking the British Rail special or bumming a lift with someone or other. Barry seemed to know plenty of lads with cars, especially his brother, who was now out of prison and seemed to be able to lay his hands on a different car every few weeks.

At Turf Moor, Burnley's ground, we gazed in admiration as Liverpool romped to a 3–0 win. If only Peter had been playing for them. Instead, he was clogging for Ford against BICC. That win left us requiring just one point from the remaining four matches. The title was a foregone conclusion, even for a pessimist like me. But with the final three games away from home, we really wanted to win the title in our next fixture, at Anfield, against the mighty Arsenal. In truth, they were a side living on past glories rather than their current reputation. Nevertheless, it was a mouth-watering prospect.

'Better get there early,' warned Barry, 'they're opening the gates at half twelve.' It was a day befitting a coronation: a crystal-blue sky, a warm glow, and the television cameras of the BBC's *Panorama*.

'They've come to hear us sing,' I told Barry. 'It was in the *Echo* last night.' A commentator stood on the touchline in front of the Kop clutching his microphone. We gave it all we had. 'She loves you, yeah, yeah, yeah.'

'They don't behave like any other football crowd, especially on the Kop,' the man from *Panorama* told his viewers. Behind him swayed the crowd, one way then the other, every one of us looking like a Beatle. 'This is a mystifying popular culture, inventing new words to old known songs. This is Wacker, the spirit of Scouse.' Later that week we watched in awe on television.

Ten minutes in and Anfield has all eyes on the goalkeeper. His name is Tommy Lawrence. He is standing rooted to his line. Eleven yards from him, hands on hips, is George Eastham, the golden boy of cockney football. It's a penalty. 'Just the kind of bloody start we need,' I tell Barry. 'Eastham doesn't miss chances like this.'

I have felt a strong allegiance with goalkeepers ever since watching Manchester City's Bert Trautmann in heroic battle with Birmingham in the 1956 FA Cup final. The tall, blond Trautmann won the hearts of Tommies that afternoon. It was hardly difficult for them to spot and respect the heroism of the former German paratrooper. No matter that we had been fighting the Germans a few years earlier when Trautmann had worn the pale-grey uniform of a German soldier.

Trautmann had been captured and imprisoned in Lancashire where he met and fell in love with a Lancashire lass. They were wed and Trautmann soon found himself goalkeeping once again.

City, to their eternal credit, offered him a chance. Memories were short. 'Why doesn't he go back to Germany and play his football there,' suggested Uncle Les grumpily as we watched Trautmann's heroics on Granny's television.

'Because there's not much football being played there at the moment,' replied my father, suddenly expert on German soccer.

In those days, goalkeepers rarely flung themselves recklessly at forwards. The lesson of Big John Thomson, the famous Celtic and Scotland 'keeper of the 1930s, still loomed large in most players' minds. Thomson it was who dived at the legs of Sam English, of Rangers, and suffered serious head injuries from which he later died. But that afternoon, as the shadows stretched across Wembley, the former German paratrooper twice threw himself at the feet of onrushing Birmingham forwards to save his side's bacon. Twice they picked him up off the ground, and twice he rubbed his neck as if merely swatting some damned mosquito. Little did he know that it was broken. And when the truth of his injuries emerged, Trautmann became a national hero, probably doing more to heal the anger and heartache between the British Tommy and the German soldier than any politician or general.

Eastham, in his white strip, begins his run up with all the deliberacy of a slow left-arm spin bowler. He shows not a sign of hesitancy. He thumps the ball straight at the bottom corner.

Over the years, Liverpool have boasted a lineage of athletic goalkeepers: Ted Doig, Sam Hardy, Elisha Scott, each of them lean and hungry. But not so Lawrence. He was more squat and rounded. He never looked like a goalkeeper should. He was more your portly linesman. But Shankly had arrived and spotted something in the youngster. When the incumbent custodian, Jim Furnell, was injured, in came the lad lingering in the third team. He never went back to the third team.

Yet, for all the look of a linesman, Lawrence could be as athletic as the best of them. He had a natural spring, a command of his box and was fearless. On the Kop they were calling him the 'flying pig'. You had to laugh, but it seemed a tad unfair.

There goes Eastham's shot, like a bullet. Told you so. But wait. Lawrence, with the spring of a fourteen-year-old, has guessed right, flinging himself to the bottom of the post. Although he does not fist the ball cleanly, he does enough to smother its pace and it bobbles behind for a corner. The Kop rises in salute. The Flying Pig has saved the day. Eastham glares in disbelief, a curse on his lips. His team mates console him, though only half-heartedly. Arsenal's chance has gone and they know it. After this, they are pulverised.

Within a few minutes, Ian St John has restored order. By half-time it's 2–0. Then in the second half Liverpool bag another three goals, with Peter Thompson, on one of his loping runs, blasting two identical shots into the same corner in the space of five minutes. Roger Hunt adds a fifth on the hour and the rest of the afternoon is a carnival. Liverpool caress the ball from player to player. The Kop oohs and ahhs at every glorious twist, cheers like a bullfighting crowd at every delightful pass, and mocks the southerners with a version of 'London bridge is falling down, poor old Arsenal.'

A body is passed unconscious above our heads, making its steady way from the heights of the Kop to the touchline below where the St John ambulancemen are waiting. Ten minutes later, it is returned from whence it came, this time showing more signs of life.

The championship is won – Liverpool's sixth and their first under Bill Shankly. The chant goes up for the manager and, as he had some years earlier, he appears like a benevolent Mr Khrushchev applauding the crowd. The players surround him, then trot towards us to receive our cheers. But there is no trophy. 'You might have thought they'd have anticipated us winning it and brought it here,' I tell Barry. 'It's those bloody bluenoses,' he replied. 'They're hanging on to it, it's at Goodison, they won't let it go.' Ah yes, I remember, Everton still have the trophy from the previous season. But somebody produces a mock trophy and Liverpool go off on a famous lap of honour. Long shadows stretch across Anfield and the sun dips behind the old gabled stand.

That afternoon Tommy Lawrence went where others feared to go. He charged out at corners with arms and legs flying. And woe betide anyone who got in his way. And when the shots rained in on him he was as good as any on his line. On the advice of Shankly, he became the last line of resistance, pushing upfield as the forwards advanced. Standing on the Kop, we thought he had gone crazy. 'El

Laurens', like most keepers, was always prone to a touch of madness. But that afternoon he ventured further upfield than any goalkeeper we had ever seen. And when the long ball came hurtling down towards him we held our breath, expecting the worst, only for Lawrence to return it with the tenacity and grunt of a modern-day baseline tennis player. The teutonic Trautmann might have been your picture-book hero but Tommy Lawrence, from Ayrshire, was your ordinary 'Tommy' – crafty, resilient and effective.

eight

Red All Over

It was clear that a head of steam was building up. For months the union and the shipbuilding employers had been haggling over the annual pay deal. Little progress had been made, apart from the union slamming on an overtime ban, which had now been going on for a month or more. Thanks to my being newly elevated to the role of union representative I was well attuned to all ongoing negotiations. Vince took me aside one day; negotiations had broken down yet again, with the union storming out of the meeting when nothing new was placed on the table. Vince had been convinced that the employers would finally back down and pay up but now he wasn't so sure. 'It's getting nasty,' he said. 'They didn't up the last offer by a penny. I don't know why they bothered calling the meeting. Something's going on, but I'm not sure what. See if you can get anything from Keith,' he suggested. 'Maybe Rowlands tells him something when they're at prayers together!'

Keith, of course, had the ear of his Uncle Arthur, but whether Uncle Arthur whispered the inner secrets of the Cammell Laird boardroom to his nephew-in-law was debatable. Uncle Arthur was too shrewd an operator to let much slip. Keith often stopped off at my desk when he was going to see Stan. He was a decent man, always interested in how the apprentices were doing. I was eating my lunch and reading the latest edition of *Merseybeat*.

'What's this?' he asked. 'I've never seen this before.'

'It's a newspaper about the Liverpool music scene,' I explained. He picked it up and started looking at it.

'How often does it come out?'

'Once a fortnight.'

'There must be some market to sell a paper like this.'

I explained to him that the Liverpool music scene was indeed huge with plenty of groups besides the Beatles. He smiled, then picked up a copy of the union magazine, which was also lying on my desk. I seized my opportunity.

'What's going to happen with the pay dispute?' I asked hesitantly.

'Depends,' he said, pulling up a stool. 'Depends on the order book. I think they'll pay up if we get this order for two oil tankers from Shell. But it doesn't look good.' Keith had now moved into the estimating office and was at the sharp end of information concerning new orders. 'We've put in a bid but the Japanese and Swedes are also in and they'll probably be bidding lower. It depends on whether Shell go for the cheapest price or whether they go for quality and keep it in Britain. If we get them everything'll be fine. There's enough work to keep us going for a good year or more. And of course there's Polaris. But it's touch and go.'

'When will we know?'

'Before Christmas, they've promised.'

Vince wasn't so convinced when I told him. 'I just don't think they want to pay up,' he said, 'They're not interested in the fortunes of just one yard. I think they're looking for an excuse so they can have a showdown. And if that's what they want, that's what they'll get. We've given them until 14 December to give us an answer.'

As Christmas approached there was a nervous tension buzzing around the office. Nobody was quite sure what was going to happen. Everything seemed to have gone quiet on the tanker deal and pay talks had come and gone, still unresolved. The company seemed to be playing for time, yet when the explosion did happen it came just when nobody expected it. After all, Christmas is a time of humility and generosity. But not in the case of employers.

Each Christmas it was the job of the apprentices to decorate the office. This was no ordinary task. It was a long-held tradition, almost a vocation, which necessitated an entire weekend's work and even before that weeks of much devoted planning. The office had to be transformed into a grotto focused around a theme. Individuals were allocated various tasks, from design, to painting, to balancing precariously on high stepladders. This particular Christmas the theme was the Wild West. It could hardly have been more appropriate – after all, High Noon was approaching. Posters had to be painted, then erected above appropriate desks, while various parts of the office were to be magicked into something resembling the Warner Bros set for the *Gunfight at the OK Corral*. Cardboard tubes had been painted and glued to the windows of Lennie's office so that it became the Sheriff's office; the safe became the gaol with Hoss depicted as the bow-legged hero of *Bonanza*, sporting cowboy hat, guns and, of course, the keys to the lockup. The sectioned-off Admiralty department became the livery stables, the Estimators' office was turned into the Bank, while the Design office became the Court House. There was also a grubstore, a hotel and a church. Even the door of Uncle Arthur's office had been appropriately decorated so that it resembled a log cabin. A sign pointing in the direction of the Engineering Drawing office simply read 'graveyard'.

Vince had been depicted as the local bandit, a hammer and sickle on his cowboy hat. He found it amusing. He might have been a Labour voter but he was hardly a Red. It was one of the paradoxes of our union. It was, at the time, perhaps the most militant in the TUC, even though its membership was briefcase and brollie. But apart from Vince, you wouldn't have caught many of them putting a cross alongside any Labour candidate in the recent general election. Harold Wilson was anathema to most people in the office and his election had been greeted with apathy at best, disdain at worst. Trade unions were similarly regarded as being beneath contempt – apart from their own, of course, whose chief attributes were that it published technical pamphlets at affordable prices and offered cheap weekend schools in Blackpool. That aside, pay was the only economic issue that aroused any kind of passion in them. They would have died for their status, which was reflected each week in their pay packet. This unfathomable contradiction between economic and political militancy was about to be highlighted.

Following our weekend exertions, on the Monday morning the Christmas decorations attracted admiring visitors from all parts of the yard and in the days before Christmas would be visited by all the foremen and chargehands, who would take off their customary bowlers and enjoy a glass of sherry or whisky with Lennie. A brief air of Christmas jollity had taken over from the weeks of nervousness but the astute watcher of such events might have noticed that Lennie was not his usual self. For most of the morning he'd been locked in Arthur's office and had failed to do his traditional tour of everyone's desk to publicly acknowledge and admire the weekend handiwork and invention of the apprentices. When he did appear it was not to accept the accolades of the visiting foremen, from the welding shop, or shipwrights. Lennie, in a word, seemed preoccupied. And at 11.30 a.m. we discovered why.

It began when all twelve or so section leaders were unexpectedly called into a meeting in Rowlands's office. This was most unusual. Uncle Arthur was not in the habit of addressing the masses, such a thing might constitute democracy. Something was up. Heads were raised from drawing boards and, in the absence of authority, people began to mingle. No thought for a moment that it might be Uncle Arthur serving out the sherry and mince pies. There were puzzled looks and questions. 'Maybe, it's something to do with that order for the tankers,' suggested Phil. 'Could be good news.'

We soon found out. Stan was first out of Uncle Arthur's cubby hole, like a greyhound out of the starting gates. He came marching over and, as we were the closest to Lennie's office, we were the first to know. He had an even more gaunt look on his face and determinedly handed us all a sheet of paper. 'It doesn't apply to you,' he said, still handing me a letter.

I looked at it. Shock! Horror! The letter was official, coming from the managing director of the company.

'As from 11.00 a.m. 10 December, all members of the Draughtsmen's union, DATA, shall consider themselves suspended from work, without pay, until further notice. This action follows the breakdown in negotiations over this year's pay

settlement. We much regret having to take this step, particularly at this time of year, but the continued ban on overtime has left us with no alternative. We hope that this suspension can be lifted as soon as possible once a satisfactory agreement has been reached with the union. We believe that a fair offer has been made and we would urge all draughtsmen involved to accept our generous offer. The offer is detailed overleaf. We would assure all our staff that this is our last and final offer.'

The letter went on to explain at length the various offers that had been made and the economic consequences of any further increase in the offer. It concluded by saying that the suspension did not apply to apprentices, who were expected to continue working as per normal.

'Fuck me,' said Bob, 'what's it mean?'

'You've been locked out,' replied Stan, who didn't seem sure whether to laugh or cry.

'And when do we come back?'

'When the union climbs down and accepts the last pay offer.'

The office was in uproar. Vince was being surrounded, everyone looking to him for answers. But he was as uncertain as anyone. 'It's the first I've heard,' he was telling them. 'I'm going to go and phone head office.' Twenty minutes later all the draughtsmen, the tracers and a few apprentices gathered at the far end of the office, as far away from Lennie as they could get.

'I'm afraid it's true,' Vince told them. 'I've spoken to head office. We've been locked out and so have some of the other yards. The employers have decided to escalate matters. It's a very serious situation.'

'But it's Christmas! They can't lock us out just before Christmas,' pleaded Wendy.

'That's exactly it, though,' said Vince. 'They're doing it now because they think we're vulnerable. They think we'll be back within a few days with our tails between our legs. We've got to show them that we're not going to be bullied around and we're not going to come crawling back just because it's Christmas.'

He had no idea how long it would last but the guess from head office, he told everyone, was that it wouldn't last much into the New Year. He did have one crumb of comfort, however: the union would guarantee to pay everyone eighty per cent of their normal earnings. 'Don't worry, you'll still have a good Christmas. The union intends to fight this to the bitter end,' he added. 'And now I think we should all pack up our things and march out together.'

'But the lock-out doesn't start until tomorrow morning,' said Eric.

'I know, but I don't think much work'll be done here today. And, anyhow, I think we should show them that we're not going to be pushed around. We make the rules here, not them,' answered Vince, rather abruptly. Eric shrugged his shoulders.

And so, off they trooped, the younger ones with grins across their faces, the family men not displaying quite the same degree of cockiness. Mostly they resembled naughty boys off to see the headmaster, morally confident but not so sure what punishment might await them. A day or two off to do the Christmas shopping was the general consensus. 'Keep in touch,' Vince shouted, as he led his army past me and through the main office door. Through the window we watched them marching across the yard, like some workers' soviet making for the Winter Palace. All that was missing was a red flag. At the main gate they assembled *en masse* to form a picket line. Suddenly there was a rare silence in the office broken only by the angry voice of Barry.

'Warra bout the sodding Christmas decorations! I spent half the bloody weekend putting dem up and look what de've done. I've a good mind to pull the bloody lot down.' Needless to say, he didn't.

Instead, we returned to our desks, shell-shocked, leaderless and without enthusiasm. Stan grunted and sighed. As management, he had been left behind, along with a handful of other section leaders. The thought of working alone with him for however long the dispute took to be settled filled me with horror. We apprentices were left for a day or two, nobody quite sure what to do with us. There were still a couple of weeks to Christmas, so we twiddled our thumbs, drank tea and slouched over our drawing boards and even chatted to Lennie, who seemed remarkably relaxed about the whole business. I overheard him a couple of days into the lock-out chatting quietly to Uncle Arthur. 'Forty-two days,' Arthur was telling him. I guessed what he meant. Stan, meanwhile, seemed to be carrying the burden of the entire dispute on his shoulders. It was, of course, his fault and he alone had been left to resolve it and to make sure that every ship would be completed on time, irrespective of the fact that there was no one to do the work. He was heading for a second breakdown. But that was Stan.

The drawing offices always worked at least six weeks ahead of the yard, and with Christmas and New Year almost upon us, the company figured it had ample time on its side. But of course it never works out quite like that. There were always problems to be resolved and the office was now left with only its section leaders to untangle an increasing number of crises. The company could hardly have us apprentices take over all the duties of our fellow draughtsmen, as this would only make matters worse. Equally, the union didn't really want us out of the door as they would have to pay us as well. It should have been a neat stalemate but, trusting that the apprentices were full of seasonal goodwill, the company craftily began to push more senior duties our way. After a further week of unresolved negotiations, I called all the apprentices together one lunchtime and we trooped furtively up to the other end of the office.

'What do you reckon?' I asked. There was silence. 'Do you think we should be doing all the work they're piling on us? We're not exactly helping our colleagues.' Much to my surprise, there was general agreement.

'Yeah, I had to go and see the foreman shipwright this morning,' said one of the twins, 'and work out a re-design. Poor old Frank's snowed under with work. There's only him and a couple of us apprentices left. It's not his fault.'

'And I had to carry out an inspection on 1285. That's not apprentices' work. I had to go and check out all the piping valves on the poop deck. I shouldn't be doing that,' said Terry one of the pipework apprentices.

But when it came to doing something, nobody had much in the way of ideas. No one, for sure, wanted to confront Lennie or anyone else. 'Go and tell Vince,' was the general resolution. 'He'll know what to do.'

At the far end of the office Uncle Arthur, hands on hips, stood outside his door scowling over his half-moon glasses, while Lennie watched from the other side of the office, with a menacing look on his face, his eyes clocking our every move.

Vince was half expecting it when I told him outside the gates that evening. 'It's getting nastier,' he said. 'I thought it might have been sorted by now but there's no sign.' I then told Vince about the conversation I had overheard between Lennie and Uncle Arthur. But he was dismissive. 'Forty-two days? No, don't read anything into that. It'll be over long before then.'

'So what do you want to do about us apprentices?' I wondered.

'No option,' he replied. 'I'm going to have to go in and confront the company with it.'

The following morning a weary-eyed Vince appeared in the office. He was promptly given a quizzical look by Lennie when he spotted him, like 'what-are-you-doing-in-the-office-get-back-to-your-picket-line'. Vince just ignored him and strolled over to my desk. 'I've just been to see the personnel manager and I'm meeting with the company at half two to talk about the apprentices,' he told me. 'Can you come?'

'Yeah, sure,' I answered, wondering what I might have let myself in for.

nine

Lennie Smells a Rat

We were ushered into a sombre, mahogany-panelled room hidden in a maze of offices directly beneath our drawing office. No cheap Christmas decorations down here. Instead, paintings of ships and maritime adventures adorned the wall, Persian carpets covered the polished floor and, on one wall, a drinks cabinet stood half open, displaying some fine cut glass. I imagined the boardroom of a football club would be like this. I hadn't been in this part of the building since the day of the entrance exam and had almost forgotten the opulence of the grand entrance and the shining glass cabinets containing model ships. There was history here, especially in the boardroom, where kings, queens, princesses and other notables had been dined and wined at a hundred different launches. Who knows? I could be sitting in the same chair as King George V, or if I went to the toilet I might sit on the same seat as Queen Mary, or more likely the Queen Mother, who had launched a ship here only a few years earlier. Tempted though I was to ask where the toilet might be, I was instead overawed by it all. Me, an eighteen-year-old apprentice; them, the managers and owners of one of the most prestigious shipbuilding companies in the world.

Five company representatives sat at an opulent table opposite us, the kind that treaties are signed on. They included Arthur Rowlands, Lennie, the company personnel manager and two other company directors I'd never seen before. We were Vince, myself and Jim McGill, the union's full-time regional officer. I'd never met McGill before, although I had heard him speak at a couple of meetings in the yard. He was a larger-than-life Glaswegian, physically impressive, and an orator of some considerable propensity. We were offered, tea, coffee and biscuits by a kindly looking lady in a white pinafore.

Once the formalities were over, McGill opened up, banging his ham fist on the table. 'It's not good enough,' he told them in his baying Glasgow accent, totally unimpressed by their titles, presence or wealth. 'We have a dispute on here and you are trying to draw innocent apprentices into it. They have no part in it.' You could hear and feel the power in McGill's voice. For the first and, I have to say, only time, I saw Rowlands visibly squirm in his seat. There was a time when the old man would have had McGill guillotined for such an audacious statement. McGill turned to me. 'That's so isn't it?' I froze, but managed to unfreeze just in time to nod my head vigorously. The personnel manager looked at me and, with fierce blue eyes, attempted a smile. 'Perhaps you could tell us *exactly* what you have been asked to do?' he inquired.

I could feel the panic ripping through my nerve ends. I was, after all, only a teenager. A tingling sweat was breaking out all over me. I couldn't think, let alone speak. There was silence, a silence that seemed interminable. I was in this too deep, way out of my depth. I thought of Shankly. What would he have done, what would he have said.

Just tell it like it is Steve. Tell them the truth. Don't let them push you around. You have as much dignity as they do. Don't ever forget that. Don't shout, don't get over-excited. Just talk quietly and slowly, that way everyone will have to listen to you. Go on, list the work you've been asked to do. Take your time. Take a deep breath. Remember, it's all about confidence, belief, call it what you like. You've just got to believe in yourself and what you're fighting for.'

The silence went on. Across the table, everyone was looking at me. Rowlands with his furrowed brow, Lennie with his sarcastic smile, the personnel officer with his piercing eyes and the other director with a wry grin slapped across his face. Sensing my hesitation, McGill interrupted.

'Go on, tell them,' he said encouragingly. I coughed nervously and then listed a few jobs that we had been asked to cover. I explained how I personally had been asked to finish off one of Bob's plans and to send it to the contractors, how another apprentice had been expected to crawl along the double-bottom of a ship, and how a couple of us had been asked to work overtime. 'Some of the work,' I added, as my final *coup de grâce*, 'is dangerous because one of the apprentices was asked to carry out a final inspection of the pipework before the ship was to be handed over. He could easily have made a mistake and that could have dangerous consequences.'

There was a general gulp around the table. The personnel officer shifted uncomfortably in his seat. 'Is this so?' he asked, turning to Rowlands and Lennie. Rowlands, in turn, looked at Lennie. Lennie was on the spot. And Shankly puts the ball in the back of the net. 1–0 to us.

McGill eased himself back in his chair.

'But these are the kind of jobs they would always do,' explained Lennie, adding, with a vengeance, 'dispute or no dispute. That's the way they learn.' Well, some of this was true; at times we relished the responsibility. Lennie had equalised from the re-start. 1–1.

'Hold on,' said McGill intervening sharply, his eyes dancing to the challenge. 'We have a dispute here and you are trying to escalate matters by involving apprentices. You should know better, given the situation. You cannot ask apprentices to carry out final inspections. It's potentially dangerous. If the other unions in the yard knew this there'd be a walk-out.' We all nodded on our side of the table; a little too enthusiastically, if you ask me. But McGill's nifty footwork had now made it 2–1 to us. The personnel manager had lost his smile and was shifting the argument by accusing the union of not going through official procedures.

'Don't talk to me about fucking official procedures. You were the ones who locked us out,' roared McGill, nodding us into a comfortable 3–1 lead. I wanted to stand up and cheer. Instead, I shook as McGill swore. I'd never imagined anyone could swear at management like this. I half wanted to hug him and half wanted to hide under the table. 'You've never been a party to official procedure in your life,' he continued. Insults continued to be hurled across the table. McGill was saying the management were 'incompetent' and 'not fit to manage' and 'deliberately engineering a dispute' and so on. They were telling him that they could not afford to pay the kind of increases the union was demanding, that there was a slump in world shipbuilding, that the Japanese could build ships, faster and cheaper than we could and that we had better start living in the real world. The issue of the apprentices seemed to have been forgotten.

'That's because they don't pay their workers,' roared McGill. Yeeesssss! 4–1 to us.

'Perhaps we could have a brief adjournment,' suggested the personnel manager, jumping in as McGill paused for breath. We agreed and were sent outside while they helped themselves to more tea and coffee.

We walked out of the main door and gathered in a sheltered corner where we all lit up. Vince laughed nervously. I said nothing. McGill was dismissive of them. 'If they want to escalate it, fine,' he said. 'We can always bring the apprentices out. That's no problem. I hope what you're saying's right, Steve. Maybe they should be out anyway. How will they feel about it?' he asked looking at me.

'Okay, no problem,' I answered, knowing that things were now getting way over my head.

'Right,' he replied, 'that's our bottom line, a guarantee of no attempts to put work on them, especially final inspections, or they're all out.' We carried on smoking. The glass door swung open and the personnel officer signalled us to come back in. I went to stub out my cigarette. McGill thrust an arm across my chest. 'No hurry,' he said, 'finish your cigarette, let 'em wait.' When we eventually returned, McGill was full of bonhomie, his infectious laughter filling the room as he joked with them.

'Well, we have considered what you have had to say,' began the personnel manager, choosing his words very deliberately, 'and we feel that the tasks that we have asked the apprentices to continue doing are part of their normal practice.'

'Does this mean that you'll expect them to continue doing such tasks?' interrupted McGill.

'Hang on,' continued the personnel manager, his otherwise gentle voice now beginning to rasp.

'It does then,' interrupted McGill, sighing heavily.

'No, not altogether. We are prepared to concede that the apprentices will not be asked to do any final inspections. We agree that this should not have happened and we do apologise.'

'I should bloody think so. Now, what about the other tasks?'

'Well, although we are prepared to make this compromise, we do feel that the apprentices should be prepared to continue carrying out some of the tasks that they would normally carry out as part of their duties. However, we assure you that the apprentices will not be asked to carry out any tasks beyond this.'

'Beyond this! I should bloody hope not,' said McGill, banging his fist on the table again. Lennie's cup rattled in its saucer. 'I'm sorry, but this meeting is not about some hypothetical task that might be suggested in the future, it is about the tasks that the apprentices are being asked to do today. In the light of your response, I have to say that we have not been offered any guarantees, apart from not carrying out final inspections. Are you therefore telling me that the tasks that the apprentices have been asked to carry out over the last week are acceptable to you and that you will continue to give them such jobs?'

'Apart from the final inspections, yes, that is the situation,' intervened one of the directors forthrightly.

'In that case then, you must realise that you have involved the apprentices in this dispute and that you have left us with no alternative.' With that, he shuffled his papers into order, stood up, nodded goodbye and walked out. We followed hurriedly, leaving them open-mouthed.

McGill insisted on speaking to the apprentices himself. Downstairs he had been ruthless; upstairs, in a corner of the Ships Drawing Office, he was calm, warm, and charming. He explained the situation and one by one the apprentices slipped beneath his bewitching spell. It was simple, he said, them against us. This was the only way to resolve the dispute. We held the moral high ground. We had to support our colleagues. 'I know it's almost Christmas,' he added, 'but from tomorrow morning, I'm afraid, you're on strike. But don't worry, you'll get eighty per cent of your pay. Any problems?' We all shook our heads meekly.

When we arrived on the picket line the following morning, we were greeted warmly by our colleagues. We were men, now, never mind that we were a bunch of sixteen- to twenty-one-year-olds, we were all out together, in support of one another. The only drawback was that we had to be on duty at seven to catch the early shift going through the gates. But at least we didn't have to do it every day. There were enough of us to form a rota and at worst we only had one dawn call every four days. At times it seemed worthless. We received little sympathy from the boiler-makers, engineers, shipwrights and other aristocrats of the yard, even though it was the festive season. I guess we had never had much sympathy for them when they were in dispute, so now we were getting a dose of our own medicine. It was a dreary process, not helped by the biting cold. 'It's blowing in straight from Siberia,' claimed Vince. Most of the time we huddled around a burning brazier, our breath heavy in the freezing air, not much to do but talk. Barry and I, along with anyone else who fancied joining in, whiled away the hours quizzing each other from a football records book. What was the highest aggregate score in any English league game? Which ground had the biggest capacity? Which player had scored most goals for England? If the picket line did little for my morale it certainly boosted my knowledge of football trivia.

Christmas turned into New Year 1965 and the cold turned to snow. Huge waves of it drifted down, making the early-morning duty on the picket line a severe punishment. It was dark, miserable and seemed never-ending. But at least we had been receiving strike pay that left us only a few pence short of our normal pay. And even though the loss of overtime meant there was no extra, there was still enough for a football match or two.

To while away the time, I had also helped organise a public meeting in Liverpool in support of David Kitson, a fellow union member, who had been imprisoned in South Africa for what was described as 'revolutionary conspiracy'. Kitson had been imprisoned for twenty years and the union was mounting a campaign for his release. Drumming up support for the meeting among my picket-line colleagues would, I assumed, be no problem. We were, after all, on the front line of political activity ourselves.

'What the fuck do we wanna go to that for?' asked Spanish George. He was in one of his combative moods. I explained that

Kitson had been imprisoned for his belief that apartheid was morally wrong and so shouldn't we be supporting him?

'But they're different,' he said, staring at me through eyes like washed pebbles.

'Who's different?' I asked innocently.

'Blacks, of course,' explained George 'Look, for a start they're not educated. They're pig-ignorant. Did you know they go moon-bathing?' Everyone looked at him. 'It's true,' he insisted. 'They go out at night when there's a full moon and lie on the ground to try and turn white.' When we'd all finished laughing, he continued. 'They don't know how to run things. It's much better to keep them apart. It's the whites who've made South Africa. You can't just take it away from them.'

'Yeah, I've got a cousin out there,' chimed in Billy Wadsworth. 'He says that blacks out there suffer from a terrible bone disease.' I looked at him thinking I was about to get some sympathetic support. 'Yeah, it's called bone idle,' he said. There were hoots of laughter. 'They're all lazy, you know. They won't do an honest day's work, none of them. You can't let them run the country,' he added.

'Yes, it's like trying to ban them from the Olympics and cricket. It's daft. What good does it do? It doesn't help the blacks,' said someone else.

'Yeah, it's the same with having boycotts, not buying their apples. The only ones who suffer are the blacks themselves.'

'But they don't even get a vote, they can't live where they want to,' I said.

'Quite bloody right! Why should they?' argued Norman Gobbett. Norm, as he was occasionally known (a name that he strongly disliked), or Gobbo, as he was generally known (a name that he intensely disliked), was a short, stocky lad with a square face, thick lips, and a crew-cut that contrasted sharply with the plethora of Beatle haircuts that adorned most of us apprentices. But it was his sharp ears and pointed nose that had earned him the name of Gobbo, the most feared enemy of little Noddy. He was in the same year as me, with a reputation for a temper on a short fuse. The argument was beginning to get a bit heated and I wasn't exactly getting much support for my seemingly revolutionary opinions. I had never imagined my views were that extreme but suddenly I was beginning to discover that I was somewhere on another planet when it came to politics.

'So why's this Kitson guy in jail?' asked Gobbo. I explained. He was a leading anti-apartheid member and when he worked in London he had been an active member of our union. He'd then gone back to South Africa, where he was born, and had been involved in a strike.

'Is he black or white?'

'He's white,' I replied.

'Fuckin' idiot. So what did he do?'

'Well,' I explained reluctantly, knowing that I was about to make things worse for myself. 'He was accused of trying to blow up a post office.'

'Fuckin' hell! And you expect us to support him. He could have killed people. Why doesn't he keep his nose out of it, if he's white? Leave it to the blacks to fight their own fight.' Gobbo was beginning to get aggressive. You could see the glare of anger in his eyes.

'You're becoming a fuckin' communist, you are,' someone else added.

'Look, Steve,' interposed Barry, trying to be conciliatory, 'maybe in an ideal world people should live together but we don't live in an ideal world. The whites have built a prosperous country and now you want to take it away from them.'

'It's the same here,' suggested a voice from the back. It was George again. 'This is our country and all these immigrants are flooding in everywhere. I went to Blackburn last year and the place was full of Pakis. All you can smell is fuckin' curry. I had to wind the car window up.' Everyone laughed and started shaking their heads.

'Hey, George, aren't you a fucking immigrant? Anyhow, you're not English, you're fucking Spanish,' one of the twins told him boldly.

'I'm not Spanish, I'm English. I was born here,' he squealed back at them.

'Eh, dat's right, let's repatriate George, send him back to Spain where he belongs. Back with the dagos,' giggled Barry.

'Oh, piss off,' yelled George, pushing his way past everybody as he walked off in a huff. But I wasn't listening any more. I'd given up. I was an alien in my own land. I was hearing that voice again.

'There's nothing wrong with being a socialist, son. It's decency, don't forget that. It doesn't matter if you're an ordinary working man or a rich man. What counts is what's here, in your heart. All men are equal: rich, poor, black or white. And don't you forget who the first socialist was. It was Jesus Christ. He taught men to be equal. I believe in the working man as much as you do. I was a miner once, my father was a miner and his father before him. My brothers were all miners as well. I was brought up to think that what matters is that when you work you do a decent day's work for a decent day's pay. You have to be honest and dignified. Believe in what you think. Don't go along with the pack.'

'Come on. Let's get back to the picket line,' said George. 'The yard'll be knocking off soon.' And there you had it. The neat paradox. Us, well paid, out on strike for even more money and not giving a toss for a nation that didn't even give ninety per cent of its population a vote. But back to the paradox.

The truth, as I was beginning to learn, is that we could just as easily have been talking about Liverpool as South Africa. The religious animosities of the pre-war years had all but disappeared, only to be replaced by an equally unwelcome prejudice. I'd not really encountered much racism up to that point. Down at the YMCA club I'd met and chatted to anyone black, so had my mates. I imagined all Scousers were loyal, decent, principled souls. But no, on the contrary. My eyes were being opened and I didn't particularly like what I was seeing. Of course, there was a black population in Liverpool but somehow you rarely spotted them around town. And if you did spot them you simply assumed that they were itinerant sailors, or 'coolies' as they were more commonly known, sightseeing before they sailed back to their own land. Years later I was told it was because they were never made welcome and just stuck to their ghettos in Liverpool 8. Indeed, in some places in town there was open hostility. You certainly never saw them in the Cavern or any of the other clubs or pubs in town, and certainly not at the football.

In time it would get worse. Even at Anfield, there would be daubings on the Kop wall when John Barnes arrived. And then in 1981 the patience of the black community finally snapped as the city was rent apart in a viscous struggle for respect. It came as a shock to many in Liverpool that torrid summer to discover that there was a sizeable black population living on the edge of the city. Even today there are those who still imagine it was simply a clash between the police and the black community, and fail to understand the role of the white community in this conflict.

Six weeks into the dispute, Vince suddenly appeared on the picket line one Friday lunchtime, a look of disbelief on his face. Just for a change, the sun was shining. We knew he'd been called in to see the company but had assumed it was just another pointless round of talks. Most people had retired to the pub over the road for lunch. 'It's all over,' he announced dramatically to our small group still manning the main gate. We looked at him. 'The lock-out, it's finished. We've won,' he said. 'It's back to work 8.30 on Monday morning,' and then added mischievously, 'so, you're all going to have to get up early every day now.' We all groaned at the prospect. At least on the picket line we'd had a rota.

'What do you mean we've won?' asked one of the senior draughtsmen.

'They've just had us in and totally capitulated,' he explained. At this point McGill appeared, a broad smile stretched across his fleshy face. 'It's true,' he announced. 'They've acceded to all our demands. Totally caved in. There wasn't even a meeting planned. I got a call from headquarters early this morning to say that Vince and I were to attend an emergency meeting with the company. It's a total climb-down. Don't ask me why, but you've got everything you wanted.'

Vince pulled a piece of paper out of his pocket and read out the new pay rates. Even the apprentices were to benefit as we were on a percentage of the draughtsmen's rates. Everyone was cheering, the word was spreading, someone had raced across the road to the pub and dozens were spilling out to hear the news. Vince and Jim were being slapped on the back; they were heroes, the union was a vehicle for success.

As we made our way across the road towards the pub to celebrate, I started doing a calculation. 'Hey, Vince,' I said, 'remember me telling you it would be 42 days? Well, you count. It's exactly 42 days.'

'Well I never,' he replied. 'You're right.' The company had clearly decided to try and see us off. They'd locked us out and given themselves six weeks but it hadn't worked out for them. They'd fully expected us to be crawling back within the fortnight but we'd stuck at it longer than they anticipated. In the end, they backed down and had to pay out a handsome pay increase for all shipbuilding draughtsmen. Now who says industrial conspiracies don't exist?

Handsome pay rise or not, going to football matches was proving expensive, especially given that I was now taking in away games where transport, food and drink came on top of the price of the ticket. Despite the pay rise, apprentices still didn't earn that much, but at least I could supplement my meagre wages with overtime, when we were paid at time and a half, and double time on a Saturday or Sunday. I quite enjoyed working overtime. There was a different atmosphere in the office. It seemed more relaxed, less formal, and naturally it was a great deal quieter.

For Stan, the lock-out had had dire consequences. He flipped for a second time, buried beneath the work that had been thrust on him, and took to his bed. I felt slightly guilty, having left him alone to cope, but Bob assured me that it wasn't my fault. But every dark cloud . . . as they say. Given the crisis in Ventilation, and the backlog of work, there was now ample opportunity for Bob and me to earn a little extra – more than welcome, given that Bob was busily planning marriage to Glenda.

Like all shipyards, Cammell Laird was infested with rats. They were everywhere. You could see them in dim corners of the yard, rummaging, or in more public places, scurrying into their hidey-holes. In the morning you would spot them in the fitting-out basin after they had accidentally slipped in overnight in the darkness and drowned. They would float around in the eddies and the scum, ready for the lock gates to be opened, when a fleet of them would sail into the Mersey and leave on the tide, heading in the direction of Ireland, along with numerous condoms and empty bottles.

It was early March, just a few weeks after the dispute had ended, an evening of biting frost, too cold even for the rats, let alone the mice, to spend much time out of doors. On such evenings the rats would make for the warmth and regularly appeared in our office, racing along the visible steel girders that supported the roof. They would sprint along them from one side of the office to the other, a distance of forty yards or so, scuttle down the piping and disappear between the floorboards. On this particular night, Bob was playing around with his set-square when a rat appeared above him. I nudged him and pointed to it. He quietly lifted his set square and took an elastic band from the box in front of him. He squeezed the elastic band onto the end of the set square, pulled it back until it was taught and let fly. Twangggg! The elastic band hit the rat and sent it scurrying off at an even faster rate of knots along the girder.

'You need a stronger elastic band,' I suggested, and went off in search of one.

We didn't have long to wait before another rat appeared. Bob lifted his set square, again took careful aim, and pulled the fat elastic band back. Twangggg! Whaaaack! The band hit the rat full in the stomach, sending it spinning off the beam and crashing twenty feet to the floor where it now lay with its teeth jutting out. Bob let out a wild cheer. We both tiptoed towards it. The rat must have been eighteen inches in length with a tail just as long.

'What are we going to do with it?' I asked.

'Fuck knows!' replied Bob. 'Do you think it's dead?'

'I think so.'

'Well, I'm not picking it up,' said Bob. 'Get some cardboard and we'll put it on it.' A minute later we were poking the rat onto the cardboard with Bob's set square.

'I suppose we should throw it outside or find a bin,' I suggested.

'Yeah,' said Bob, and between us we gently lifted the cardboard and began to carry it down the deserted office. Everyone had gone home, leaving just Bob and me on our own. As we reached the end of the office, Bob's face lit up.

'Hey, why don't we put it in Lennie's office?' he suggested. 'We could just put it on the floor. He'll never know.'

'Christ, you can't do that,' I said meekly. 'It'll give him a turn.'

'All the more reason,' replied Bob, taking a careful look to make sure there was no one about. Sure enough, the place was quiet and deserted. Bob gently opened the door to Lennie's office and we tiptoed inside.

'Shall we put it down here on the floor by the door?' I asked

'No,' said Bob, 'I've got a better idea. Why don't we put it on his chair?' I looked at him askance, smiled and, carefully sliding the rat off the cardboard, we let it slip onto Lennie's chair. We crept out, or rather fell out, of his office in fits of laughter, and went off home before anyone spotted us, promising each other not to tell a soul and to be in early to catch Lennie's face the next day.

When I arrived at work the following morning, there was a gang staring through the glass windows of Lennie's office. Phil was among them.

'What's going on?' I asked innocently.

'There's a rat in Lennie's office,' replied Phil.

'You're joking?'

'No. Look,' he said.

I peered into the office, automatically looking towards the chair. But no rat.

'Where?' I asked frantically, 'I can't see one.'

'There, on his desk.'

I looked again. Sure enough, there was the rat, sitting mindfully on Lennie's desk. This rat was not dead. It was very much alive.

'Oh fuck,' I thought.

'It's trapped in there,' said someone. 'It can't get out.'

'And it's been eating Lennie's letters. It's made a right fuckin' mess in there. It's shit everywhere,' laughed Phil.

'Oh fucking hell.' I was beginning to get worried. Clearly, the rat had only been stunned by its fall.

By now everyone was clocking on and wandering in. The gang around Lennie's office had grown to a dozen. It was getting hysterical. People were banging on the window trying to attract the creature, which had now spotted the observers and was racing around Lennie's tiny office as if crazed. The word was spreading, people were coming from other offices to look and our office was filling up as more people clocked on. Even Keith Hollins, marching into the office, came and had a look, nobody quite sure how he would react. But Keith chuckled and walked off to his desk wearing a laconic smile. A few other bosses strolled in, attracted by the commotion and also wandered away, chortling.

Bob, as ever, was late.

'Morning,' he said, in his usual chirpy way, as he rolled up to his desk . Then, spotting the mayhem around Lennie's office, added, 'Oohhh shit! I'd forgotten all about that.'

'Well, you'd better go and have a look. You might get a surprise.'

'What do you mean?'

'Well, the fuckin' thing's not dead. It's alive. It's running about his office, creating havoc.' Bob's normally rosy cheeks turned a whiter shade of pale.

'Oh no! Warra we goin' to do?'

'There's nothing we can do,' I said, 'unless you want to open the door and let it out. Anyrate, it's too late now, here comes Lennie.' The office instantly fell silent and all eyes were on Lennie as he manfully strode in through the main office door and headed down the aisle towards his own office.

The gang that had been scoffing outside his office quickly made itself scarce as word of Lennie's encroaching presence became known. Lennie marched on, oblivious to the hundred pairs of eyes spying his progress. He nodded 'good mornings' to a few people as he approached and as usual flung open his door. There was a sudden yell. The rat, wherever it had been at that moment, suddenly finding its new territory invaded, did a quick circuit or two of the office, sending more of Lennie's possessions flying, and then darted out of the door faster than if it had been chased by a fierce cat. Lennie stood frozen, his umbrella raised high above his head, and then let out a second cry.

'What the heck . . .?' he roared. But anything further he might have said was drowned by the screams of two tracers who at that untimely moment were strolling casually into the office just as the rat flew past them. Jenny leapt onto the nearest chair, while Pam cowered against the wall as if she was about to be attacked by some giant man-eating tiger. All hell was let loose. Lennie's freeze was momentary. A second later he was bellowing. Never a man to swear, he had suddenly discovered another side to himself.

'A rat! There's a fucking rat! Where's it gone? Where's it come from?' he screamed, spinning round outside his office like a whirling dervish, his body barely co-ordinating with his brain. The rat, glad of its sudden freedom, was not hanging around to soak in the fun and had made off down the corridor towards the toilets and Design Department. It was probably a great deal more petrified than anyone else, but you would never have guessed it. Pam, still shrieking, was being consoled by Albert, eager to seize this God-given opportunity of comforting his heart-throb, while Jenny was threatening to put her coat back on and walk out. Meanwhile a rabble, led by the twins, had set off in the direction of the toilets to discern the whereabouts of the rat. Bob was unable to contain himself, indeed nor were most of us, though nobody knew quite whether to laugh out loud or hide behind their hands.

Then suddenly there came, from the direction of the toilets, further commotion. The rat was on its way back. The swing doors flung open, there were more squeals from the tracers, and the rat began a circuit of the office chased by half a dozen apprentices wielding set squares – no mean feat, considering a circuit must have been all of three hundred yards. Round and round they raced like greyhounds hungry for the hare, in and out of the aisles, from one department to another, twisting, turning and sliding their way between the desks. They tried to cut it off but the rat was too clever. They lobbed small weights, erasers, protractors, steel helmets, anything they could lay their hands on. But the rat was far too cunning for their artillery. The entire office joined in the chase. Those who couldn't run stood on tables, stools, anything where they could get a better view of the proceedings. It was like the Waterloo Cup. There was cheering, screaming, someone was taking bets, Lennie was like thunder, Sheila and Pam were crying, Albert was smirking, Bob was in tears and Jenny and Wendy had stormed out.

The hullabaloo only ended with the appearance of Uncle Arthur, the noise having eventually penetrated the mahogany panelling and luscious carpeting of his office. He stood, mouth agape, hands on hips, outside his office viewing the chaos and hubbub with some horror as Lennie explained to him what had happened. Once his presence was noticed by the marauding gang, there was a quick return to desks. The rat, seizing its opportunity, shinned down a drainpipe and was off under the floorboards, lost to the visible world within a moment.

The office gradually returned to normality but the smirks and laughter continued for most of the morning. Lennie retreated to his office, slammed the door and wasn't seen for an hour or more. Towards lunchtime, two men in brown apron coats strode into the office. One, wearing the traditional bowler hat that marked the office of a foreman, was the tall muscular figure of Barry Jones, head joiner. Lennie showed them into his office and for the next hour the two chippies rummaged around attempting to discover the route via which the rat had entered. Furniture was removed, filing cabinets were wheeled out and every nook and cranny was explored. But by the end of lunchtime the joiners were as baffled as anyone; there was no obvious sign of entry, no hole, through which anything the size of a rat could have crawled. Some extra beading was nailed in and the skirting board firmed to the wall but in truth it was decorative more than anything. It made Lennie and the joiners feel that at least they had taken some measures. Bob and I sat back smugly, convinced that at the very least we had ruined Lennie's day.

The first inkling I had that something was up came later that afternoon. Lennie had called Bob into his office. I assumed that it was simply something to do with work but when he had been in there for twenty minutes I began to suspect that all was not right. From where I sat I could just see into Lennie's office. Bob looked agitated. A heated conversation was clearly taking place behind firmly closed doors. Lennie was glaring at him, a flume of red-hot vitriol spilling out and slamming into Bob's face. I guessed Bob wasn't getting the best of it. Phil glanced over his shoulder towards Lennie's office and confirmed it. 'Something's up,' he said nonchalantly. Others were pointing their noses in Lennie's direction. 'What's going on?' asked Eric, ambling over. Phil and I shrugged our shoulders but I was slowly beginning to worry that it might be something to do with the morning's events. Bob was in there for half an hour and came back to his desk looking very sheepish. We looked at him quizzically. 'He wants to see you now,' he announced, before adding the words that I most feared and which I had already begun to suspect: 'He knows.'

For a moment I froze. 'Go on, there's no point in denying it. You'd better go and see him,' he added.

ten

On Her Majesty's
Secret Service

I knocked on Lennie's door. He was on the phone but he waved me in, quickly finished his conversation and told me to close the door. And that's when the shit hit the fan.

'I take it you're not going to deny having put a rat in my office last night.' I shook my head meekly. By now Lennie was on his feet, his squeaky voice rising to a new pitch.

'Good, well at least we've got that bit out of the way. What a stupid thing to do. Stupid. Stupid. Think you can take the mickey out of me do you?' he yelled. 'Well you can't. This is a serious disciplinary issue. Don't think I don't know what went on last night. You were spotted, you see. Didn't know that did you? Oh no, thought you'd get away with it, thought you'd take the mickey out of me, eh? Well, we'll see about that.' He opened his filing cabinet and took out a file. My name was on the top of it. It had never occurred to me for one moment that he would have a file on me. 'I've had enough of you,' he said, flicking through the file. 'You've failed your exams, and that was after repeating them. You're not making much progress here. You just don't seem to want to concentrate. What's wrong with you? You're not taking drugs or anything like that are you? '

I shook my head, wondering how an earth he could have drawn such a nonsensical conclusion. He immediately answered my unspoken question.

'I hear you go to clubs in Liverpool. You always look half asleep. I suppose you're up late at night. I've heard about these clubs, dens of iniquity they are, full of beatniks. You're supposed to be serious, you're supposed to be a draughtsman. I mean, look at your hair. Isn't it time you got a haircut? It's almost down to your shoulders. And as for your work.' He sighed heavily.

'I've been looking at it closely these last few weeks. It's just not good enough. I don't think you're suited to this office, so I'm arranging for you to be transferred. You're going to the Polaris office. You start there on Monday. Understood?' I looked at him in disbelief, almost in a state of shock. 'Go on, you can go back to your board now,' he said, flinging my file onto his desk.

I was gobsmacked, and almost in tears. Polaris! The Gulag Archipelago of the drawing offices, the place no draughtsman wanted to go. It may have sounded ever so exciting but, in truth, it was a *cul de sac*, a dead end. If I ever imagined I had a career in the Ships Drawing Office, it was over now. I was Alexander Solzhenitsyn, sentenced, without trial, to the Polaris archipelago for the unforeseeable future.

'Christ,' said Bob, when I got back to my drawing board, 'you're white. Are you okay?' I nodded but I wasn't. I was almost too shocked to speak. I went off to the toilet, found a cubicle, locked myself in, sat down and burst into tears.

'Fuck them,' I thought. 'I'll stay in here. What's the point of coming out.' I stayed there for half an hour. I was livid. Angry that I'd been found out, angry that he should have treated me with such disdain. I was shaking. The little twat, the officious little git. How would I explain it to everyone? I couldn't. And what would my parents say? I churned it over and over. Eventually, Bob came into the toilets and shouted for me. 'You'd better come out.' Reluctantly, I opened the door. Apart from Bob the toilet area was deserted. Bob could tell I'd been crying. 'Go wash your face,' he said. 'Are you okay?' I nodded.

'He's kicking me out of the office, sending me to work on Polaris,' I said.

'Oh shit!' he said. 'When are you going?'

'Monday,' I replied lighting up the cigarette Bob handed me.

'Well, maybe it won't be that bad. I know the work's not that interesting but there's some decent guys over there.'

'How about you?' I inquired.

'He gave me a right bollicking. Says it's going on my record. He's a cunt, he is. Even worse, he's going to bring someone else in to run the department.'

'Shit, who?'

'Dunno.'

'How the fuck did he find out?' I asked.

'Someone saw us,' answered Bob. 'I suspect there must have been some people still working in the design office or the estimators'. If I ever find out who it was snitched on us, I'll bloody kill them.'

'Yeah, let me know and I'll help you,' I said. One or two people strolled into the toilets and looked pryingly at us. We finished our cigarettes and walked back into the office. I could feel the eyes following me down the aisle, the whispers, the humiliation. They'd all know my fate soon.

'I hear you're coming to work for us,' said Harry, the deputy section leader of the Polaris department, turning round in his seat. It was a couple of days later. I was sitting in the canteen about to eat lunch. Harry was seated at a table behind me. I nodded. 'We could do with a few more apprentices,' he added. 'We're a bit short.' He could see I wasn't too excited at the prospect. 'Don't worry, it's not all that bad,' he added. 'And you won't have Lennie to contend with.' I smiled and he gave me a knowing wink back.

Cammell Laird had won a contract to build two new Polaris submarines for the Royal Navy; Vickers, in Barrow, would construct the other two. Each submarine carried sixteen Polaris missiles, each armed with enough power to blow half the world, including Lennie, to smithereens. Good old Supermac and JFK had hatched the deal between them one sunny Sunday morning in Nassau. I say 'good old Supermac' because it was a multi-million pound order that would take five years to complete and guaranteed the survival of shipbuilding on the Mersey for a few more years. British shipbuilding was still in the doldrums. Competing with the Japanese and Brazilian yards was proving even more difficult, and one by one British shipbuilders were feeling the pinch. Over the next ten years the entire industry would collapse. But at least this deal had bought us some time.

I had to admit that life in the Ships Drawing Office had proved to be tedious. The only saving grace had been union work. As the elected spokesman for the apprentices, I had some leeway to wander around the office talking to the other apprentices on alleged 'union business' when in fact I was just nattering, usually about football. When I wasn't on union business I would be out in the yard, as far away from the office as possible, usually visiting a ship when it was in the fitting-out basin, where there were always pipe and ventilation cowls to be checked. Most of all I loathed venturing onto the slipways where danger lurked at every angle. The ship would be little more than a bare hull of rusting plates and half-constructed bulkheads, along with pipes, wires and rickety ladders. At every corner riveters and welders lay in wait ready to drill your head off. It was a health and safety inspector's nightmare. You could barely tell one ship from another: liner, destroyer, cargo ship or tanker, they all looked pretty much the same silhouetted against the bleakness of the slipway with the grey Mersey lapping behind them. And the wind. It ripped across the river, raw and biting. Little wonder men died prematurely. But a trip down to the yard did at least allow me the chance to drop in on the lads in the Engine Shop and waste another hour nattering.

Harry's friendliness was more than welcome, and I began to feel a touch more enthusiastic at the prospect of escaping Lennie and the formality of the Ships Drawing Office. So much so that I had decided to put my own spin on it. Far from being dispirited, I told everyone I was glad to see the back of the drawing office. Polaris was where the future lay. It was high technology, relaxed, run on a less formal basis, more in tune with the modern world. But Lennie's intentions to send me to the Polaris office did throw up a dreadful dilemma. It was almost as if Lennie had done it deliberately. In the aftershock of his announcement, I had not fully realised the predicament.

It was George who was the first to draw it to my attention. He was blunt and to the point. 'I hear you're going to work on Polaris,' he said, carefully sharpening his pencil in the way that draughtsmen do. He looked up at me. 'Now, I don't mean to be rude, but you're a bleedin' communist, you are. They can't have you working on Polaris. Has anybody told them you're a commie?'

'Well, if they haven't I'll fuckin' tell them,' chipped in Jake, in his usual sour manner.

'You'll be selling all our secrets to the Russians,' continued George, sniggering. 'Anyhow, how come you're going to work on our nuclear deterrent? I thought you were a CND supporter. I thought you were opposed to nuclear weapons.'

Ah yes, well, I guess I was, but then I didn't want to continue working in the Ships Drawing Office with this bunch of deadbeats. 'I haven't got much fuckin' choice,' I snapped back.

'What about your principles?' sniped Jake. 'If you were really against nuclear weapons you wouldn't go there under any circumstances.'

'Well, the union's in favour of it,' I replied, trying to conjure up some kind of justification. 'And you're always telling me they're a bunch of communists.'

'Ah, bloody typical,' said George. 'When it comes to the crunch you and the union's just the same as the rest of them. Bloody politicians, especially Labour politicians. Opportunists. Hypocrites. Out for what you can get.'

So I reminded him about the nice little pay rise the union had won for him a year or so back.

They all had a good laugh at that. I decided I was getting nowhere; a respectful retreat might be the most sensible policy. I didn't like to admit it but, in truth, George had hit upon a genuine inconsistency that was to gnaw away at me.

Initially Vince had been all for taking up the transfer as a union issue. 'It's because you're the apprentice's rep,' he raged. 'They've never had a decent rep in here. Remember the lockout? You helped bring all the apprentices out. You were very forthright at that meeting we had with the company, pointing out about apprentices carrying out final inspections. They won't have forgotten that. But I have to say you were a bit daft with that rat, you handed them the excuse to get rid of you on a plate.'

I told him it wasn't worth fighting about and, anyhow, I didn't have the stomach for a fight. I just wanted to get away from Lennie. 'What do you reckon to Polaris, though?' I asked. 'Not that I've got much choice, but should I be working on it?'

'Why? What's the problem?' he wondered.

'Well, you know, I mean, should I be working on it if I'm opposed to nuclear weapons?'

'Why not? What's the problem? It's going to be built whether or not you work on it.'

'Anyhow, I thought the union was opposed to nuclear weapons as well.'

'Come on, don't make me laugh. We've got to have the jobs. Take Polaris away and this yard'll be in big trouble. You have to be pragmatic. That's what politics is about, pragmatism.'

'Yeah, I know, but I don't have to get involved. Someone else can still do it.'

'But you'd be indirectly involved. Can't escape that. And another thing,' he added, 'we haven't got anyone over there. We could do with someone like you to keep an eye on the union side of things.'

I still didn't feel comfortable but Dad couldn't see a problem. I didn't tell him the whole story about my transfer, I just hinted that the company wanted me to go over there. 'They'll never be used,' he told me confidently. 'It's a deterrent, not a weapon. Anyhow, I worked on submarines during the war.'

'But that was different,' I said. 'There was a war on then, you were fighting fascism.'

'And is the Soviet Union any different? They're just as fascist as the next.'

'I know that. I'm not a communist. I don't support the Soviet Union but I do believe in socialism and I don't believe in nuclear weapons.'

'If you don't go and work on it, somebody else will, so in the long run it'll make no difference,' was his final word. Mum was even more philosophical. 'You say they've got a smart new office, Stephen?' she asked. 'That'll be nice.'

Days later, I was signing the Official Secrets Act and having my security photo taken. A brand-new office, boasting the highest security, had been built to house the project. It was modern, clean, calm and a good deal less ceremonial than the office I was leaving behind. In many ways it suited my style, although I quickly discovered why there had hardly been a rush of people from the Ships Drawing Office to enrol on the project. The work was barely creative. There were no drawings to be done. It was all clerical. Vickers in Barrow were the lead yard and even they were simply adapting the original design plans of the American yard in Connecticut. All they did in the Polaris office was push paper around.

Suddenly I was privy to the nation's topmost secrets. Well, not quite. It felt like I was making history but in fact all that we were doing was ordering material and ensuring that the right bit went to the right place at the right time. But there were compensations. The work may have been tedious but the people were, for the most part, friendly. There were Americans: tall, slim, college boys with crew cuts and button-down collars who strode energetically through our offices and spoke in some southern drawl. And naval officers of the highest rank; educated young men with sensitive faces whose job was to press the self-destruct button when called upon.

But none of them were interested in our trivial amusements. When we turned our drawing boards into Subbuteo pitches every lunchtime they looked down on us disdainfully. Football was a proletarian pastime. It may once have been the prerogative of the public schools but not any more. They were oblivious to the excitement that was going on around them. Liverpool were going to Wembley. It was only the third time in their history that they had reached the FA Cup final and in their two previous finals they had lost both. Now the clamour was on for tickets. There was a conviction that this time it would be different.

When I was young we played a game. We had to see if we could reach the school gates without treading on one of the cracks in the pavement. The school was about half a mile away and nobody ever won. It was too far and invariably meant that we would be late for school. It takes time to avoid the cracks assiduously. The girls made out that if they managed it, they'd marry a prince. I suppose it wasn't that different from the routine I followed to Anfield. Not, of course, that I walked to the ground avoiding the cracks in the pavement. No, I was more sophisticated than that.

I always wore the same socks and took the same scarf with me. I'd take the bus down to Woodside, take the ferry boat across the

Mersey, catch the bus at the Pier Head, and jump off as it groaned up Everton Valley. Then I'd meet Barry in the pub, order a pint of bitter and always leave an inch of beer in the glass before placing it on the bar. I never left it on the table. Then we'd race off to join the queue at the Kop, always going through the same turnstile. I'd go to the toilet, buy a programme and had to have read it thoroughly before kick-off. I even had a routine when Liverpool were playing away. I owned a small, grey portable Grundig radio and at 4.30 p.m. on away days, I'd run a bath, and soak in it while listening to Eamon Andrews reading the results on *Sports Report*. We usually won.

I imagined that I was the only person at Anfield who ever carried out such inane routines, but years later I discovered that most football fans have what could be described as a winning routine. The only problem with having superstitions is that they are pretty pointless if your team is not winning. Why bother? What do you do when you lose? Do you change your routine and adopt a whole new gamut of rituals. Only those who follow a successful team can really be superstitious and I suppose being a Liverpool supporter allowed me that privilege, if indeed it could ever be reckoned to be a privilege. Rather, it was the nervous antics of a neurotic pessimist.

Like avoiding the cracks in the pavement, the end result of all these routines was that Liverpool would win. What's more, it did seem to work. Liverpool had been promoted, they had won the first division title and now they had reached the FA Cup final. And all because of me, leaving an inch of beer in my glass every other Saturday at The Park.

I'd followed Liverpool through most of the cup rounds. It had been a rocky road. I'd been at Anfield as they scraped a draw against Stockport County and had given them up as dead only for them to win the replay 2–0. And I'd been to an exhilarating quarter-final replay against Leicester. Now they were facing Leeds United in the final at Wembley.

Getting a ticket for the final was hopeless. It seemed everybody on Merseyside was after one. When they went on sale at Anfield there were only fifteen thousand of them. Most of them went to season ticket holders and a small number went to anyone who had a voucher from the programme for the Stoke City game bearing certain numbers. I looked eagerly in the *Echo* but my number never came up. There was little I could do.

I had been in something of a quandary, anyhow. Billy, bless his cotton socks, had decided to get married on the same day as the FA Cup final. That was typical of Billy, no sense of history or even of getting his priorities right. Even though the wedding date had been agreed a year earlier he should have known this was going to be Liverpool's year. Andy had foolishly agreed to be the best man and I was down to be an usher. But even if I couldn't get a ticket, which seemed more than likely, I was still going to watch it on television. I told Billy straight that I couldn't come to the wedding but I would go to the do in the evening, especially if they won. He was not too impressed by my attitude while his bride-to-be simply disowned me. Getting the cold-shoulder from Maggie was a bit like slamming up against an iceberg. I was down-mouthed about the whole business: no ticket, friends who didn't understand. I had resigned myself to watching the game on television.

'Why don't you try writing to him?' suggested my mother.

'Write to who?' I asked tetchily.

'Bill Shankly, of course. He did say if you ever needed any tickets to get in touch.' I'd forgotten that.

'That was years ago, Mum. He won't remember me. Anyway, there was something in the paper the other day about how all the players have been besieged for tickets.'

'It's worth a try, though. Nothing ventured, nothing gained,' she replied. It didn't make sense. It was a long shot. It wasn't worth the effort.

'You could use your new typewriter,' she said. The typewriter had lain in the wardrobe gathering dust ever since she had given it to me as a Christmas present. She had picked up on a throwaway comment I had made one day when I was writing out some union letters, about how I could do with a secretary. She couldn't afford a secretary, she told me, but a typewriter duly arrived on Christmas morning. It hadn't gone down well, especially as I could think of a million other things I would have preferred, including a new LP by Chuck Berry.

The more I chewed over her suggestion, however, the more I realised there was nothing to lose. Maybe she was right. I could try typing the letter as well. It would be good practice and this was the first occasion I'd had to write a semi-official letter. It was obvious that Shankly himself always typed his letters because they were always full of typing errors. Then, I had a brainwave. I remembered the old programme I had, Liverpool against Preston North End, the one I'd swapped with Peter all those years ago. Why not send him that? He probably wouldn't have it and it was of no use to me. I quickly retrieved it from the loft. I knew it would come in handy one day. It was fate. Later that night I sat down and began to compose another letter to Bill Shankly. With my one-finger approach to the keyboard, it took half a dozen attempts but two hours later I succeeded, producing a letter containing only one mistake. I felt quite proud.

Dear Mr Shankly,

You may not remember me but I have written to you a couple of times in the past. My Uncle Horace and Auntie Gertie used to live next door to you in Huddersfield and years ago you very kindly got some autographs for me of the Huddersfield Town players. I also wrote to you when you became the manager of Liverpool to tell you what Dixie Dean had said to me about you. I have been supporting Liverpool ever since you became the manager. I have been to see both the home cup games this season and would very much like to go to the cup final. Unfortunately I have not been able to get a ticket. I was wondering therefore if it might be possible for you to get me a ticket. I am desperate and will of course pay for it.

I am also enclosing an old programme which I have found of Liverpool versus Preston, a game in which you played. I don't know if you remember this match but I thought you might like the programme as a keepsake. I am also enclosing a SAE in the hope that you might be able to help.

Yours sincerely,

Stephen Kelly

I sat back and waited but never expected to hear anything. 'He'll be too busy,' laughed Peter. 'He's got a cup final to think about.' Andy was equally dismissive. 'Not a chance. He'll be getting hundreds of letters like that.' Secretly, I had to agree with them. I was running out of options. In fact, I'd already run out. I couldn't see any way of getting a ticket. The garage up the road was offering a second-hand car for four tickets. What chance did I have?

Susan didn't have much idea either. Oh yes, Susan. I'd started seeing her after a dance at the YMCA when one of those dozens of hopeful post-Beatles bands appeared on the scene. 'Think of all the money you'll save,' she suggested helpfully. She was right. It was going to cost a pretty penny. But what she really meant was that maybe now I could accompany her to Billy's wedding. She'd also been invited to the wedding ceremony itself, starting at 3 p.m. 'No way,' I told her. 'You'll have to go by yourself. I'll be watching the game on the telly.' She just about accepted that but had promised the bride-to-be that we'd be there for the reception in the evening. Now I had cast a doubt on that and it was not going down well.

'Football! Is that all you think about?' she screeched one night. The coffee bar fell silent. Andy sniggered. Susan jumped up and stormed out. Andy sniggered even more.

Susan could make all the right noises when it came to football but she never wanted to come to a game. She didn't understand. But she was good looking and that made up for a lot. She was a bit of a status symbol; nice dresser as well, what with those sling-back shoes and short skirts. All my mates fancied her. She didn't speak to me all the way home that night. And I didn't make much effort either. I left her on the doorstep, mascara smeared on her face, and walked off in a huff.

'A letter's come for you,' said my mother, as I walked in. She was sitting up waiting for me. I hadn't been home after work that evening; I'd gone straight out. She smiled as she handed me the letter. It was in a brown envelope, marked Liverpool Football Club. I hurriedly tore it open. But there was no ticket inside; just a note from the manager.

Liverpool Football Club Ltd., Anfield Road, Liverpool 4.

Telegraphic Address: Goalkeeper.

Dear Stephen
Thank you for your letter. Although I don't remember your previous letters, I do remember your aunt and uncle in

Huddersfield. I hope that they are both well. Unfortunately, I have been unable to find you a ticket for the cup final. As you will appreciate there is a huge demand. However I am hoping that I may get a few more tickets next week. Could you come to the ground, one lunchtime, after training and hopefully I might have found a spare ticket by then.

I would however like to thank you very much for the programme which you sent. It was very kind of you. As a matter of fact I do remember that game. We didn't do very well, I think we lost 3–0 or 3–1. It was the first game of the season and was played in scorching hot weather. Liverpool had won the league title the season before and there was a huge crowd. It was one of the few occasions I ever played at Anfield. They were good times.

Yours sincerely,

W. Shankly
Manager

I didn't dare tell Susan. I showed the letter to Peter. 'Where did you get the programme from?' was all he asked.

'From you, years ago, remember? Your Auntie Madge sent you a bundle.' He was touched by that, but not so impressed by my uncharacteristic optimism.

'You haven't got the ticket yet,' he reminded me. 'You've still got to go over there and find him, and, anyhow, how are you going to do that?' I'd been wondering about that myself. A weekend wouldn't be much good; it would have to be during the week and that of course posed problems. I could hardly ask for time off from work, and I reckoned it was a bit risky trying it during lunch. I'd never manage it in the hour I had off and even though I could probably wangle an extra half-hour one way or another, it was still too tight. What's more, there was no guarantee that Shankly would turn up at Anfield at 1 p.m. on the dot. I might be hanging around for hours.

'Just take the day off,' suggested Andy, who, as usual, was bent over the bonnet of his car as I wandered up the street towards his house.

'But I've already booked all my holiday,' I informed him.

'Well, when Susan finds out, you won't be going on any holiday anyway,' he replied laughing. 'Anyrate, I don't mean book holiday, I mean, just skive off.'

'I can't do that.'

'Why not? I do it all the time,' he said blowing hard into the carburettor he had just removed.'

'I know,' I replied, suspecting that I sounded a little too righteous. Andy was forever boasting about how he'd taken the afternoon, or even the whole day, off. It was easier for him; he was hourly paid and if he didn't turn up, he didn't get paid. It was different for me. Working in the office meant that I'd still get paid for being absent but I'd have to come up with a believable excuse.

'What's wrong with the car?' I asked, trying to appear interested.

'The carburettor, it keeps getting blocked up. God knows who designed it.'

'You could go for me,' I suggested half-heartedly, knowing full well what the response would be.

'It'll cost you.' That was exactly the response I was expecting.

'How much?'

'Two quid.'

'Two quid! You must be joking.'

'I'd be taking a day off work. I'd be losing that much,' he said.

'Like hell you would. You don't earn that much.' Andy always liked to make out he was earning more than me. Usually he was, but not that much.

'Two quid's as much as it's going to cost to get to London.' I knew I genuinely couldn't afford that. I did a quick calculation.' I'll give you ten bob,' I offered.

'No way,' he replied. I thought it best not to push the haggling any further. 'Why don't you just tell 'em you're ill?' said Andy in a matter-of-fact way. I shook my head.

'Too much conscience, that's your problem,' he said. 'And what are you going to tell Susan if you get the ticket?'

'Dunno, any ideas?'

Andy pursed his lips, sucked in and shook his head. 'More than my life's worth. By the way, if you get the ticket that means you won't be able to go to the wedding do as well,' he said, diving back under the bonnet of the car to escape my reaction.

'Thanks for stating the obvious, Andy. Anyrate, I'll cross that bridge when I come to it.'

'Hey, I've got an idea,' he said suddenly, emerging from beneath the bonnet again. 'Why don't you get Susan to go over to Anfield and see Bill Shankly, get the ticket.'

'Fuck off,' I said and wandered off down the street in the direction of my house, quietly smiling to myself at the thought.

For days I wrestled with the predicament of how to get to Anfield. It was keeping me totally preoccupied. Explaining to Susan that I had a ticket would be nothing compared to getting the ticket. I'd have to make as if I was going to go to work but instead go to Liverpool, maybe while away a bit of time in the shops in the centre of town, then catch a bus out to Anfield, hang around there, and then come back into the city and waste a bit more time, finally arriving home at the usual time. I had it all planned out. It would work perfectly, even though it went against the grain. The following day I would explain to my boss that I had been ill. There'd be no problem with that. I was rarely ill and had had little time off work through illness. And so the great day of the skive approached. But there was one thing that had not occurred to me. The night before as I lay in bed going over the plan in my mind, it suddenly struck me.

How was I going to explain the sudden appearance of a cup final ticket to my parents? I could hardly produce it after tea the next evening. 'Oooh, Dad, look what I've got.' It wouldn't work. They'd read the letter, they knew I had to go to Anfield to see Shankly. They'd want to know when I'd been. Shit! I was so angry at not having worked through my plan. Also time was pressing. There were less than two weeks to the final. Just as annoying was the fact that I'd psyched myself up to having the day off and now I'd have to get up and traipse into work. I lay awake most of the night trying to devise a strategy for getting to Anfield but without having to tell too many tales.

In the end I decided there was only one possible solution. That was to go to Anfield on Friday evening, immediately after work. We knocked off at 4.30 p.m. on a Friday; maybe I could sneak out a little earlier, claim I was going to the dentist's or something, get a head start across the river and get to Anfield well before four. You never know, I thought, he might still be there, especially as they had a home game the next day. It was a gamble, but I had no other option.

Anfield was quiet when I jumped off the bus, just a few old ladies out shopping. I couldn't remember having been there when there was no crowd, no noise, nobody around. It was a warm spring afternoon with only the occasional car on the Walton Breck Road to break the silence. I walked up an entry way close to the Kop, in search of the main stand and the main entrance. That was something else I'd never really seen. Strange that I'd never actually walked all the way around the ground. I'd always come up Everton Valley and gone straight into the Kop. I'd never thought to explore. The entrance to the old gabled stand was modest. I went in and spotted a commissionaire sitting reading a newspaper at a desk. I told him that I wanted to see Mr Shankly. He looked at me as if he had a thousand such requests each day.

''Ee's n' rear.'

'Will he be coming here?' I asked.

'Dunno. He went back to the trainin' ground at Melwood.' The commissionaire turned back to his paper. Oh Lord! What do I do now? 'But are you expecting him back?' I insisted.

'Dunno,' he replied. 'You're not another after a cup final ticket are ya?' he barked. ''Cos if you are you can forget it. Der aren't any.' My heart sank. I'd been sussed. What's more, I wasn't the first. The whole journey had been in vain. No Bill Shankly, no cup final ticket, no trip to London. They'd just have do without me at Wembley.

I began to make my way out into the sunlight. I stood outside blinking for a few minutes not sure what to do, whether to jump a bus straight home or wander around the ground for a while. The latter seemed a pointless exercise but I was feeling so despondent that it made sense, a bit of fresh air before going home. I did it almost without thinking. I was just a fan, just another lad after a ticket. He probably had a hundred such letters like mine every day and probably sent the same reply back. I'll bet his secretary had a pile of them on her desk. And, anyhow, there weren't that many tickets, only fifteen thousand to each club. Every year there were always thousands of disappointed fans complaining about the distribution of tickets. All those little FA officials up and down the country getting their grubby hands on tickets while the real fans had to queue all night and might get one only if they were lucky. It was a scandal, something should be done about it. I began to feel stupid. Why had I even bothered?

eleven

Mr Shankly Delivers

As I reached the Anfield Road, I turned right and was strolling along the back of that end of the ground when a red Vauxhall Viva car came rattling past, veering slightly from one side of the road to the other, before swinging erratically left. It was turning into the space at the back of the main stand where I had just come from. I couldn't be sure, I hadn't really been looking, but was that Bill Shankly I had spied at the wheel? I raced back just as the car pulled jerkily into a parking space and spotted the unmistakable figure of Shankly getting out. I ran as fast as I could and caught up with him just as he was about to go in through the main door.

'Mr Shankly! Mr Shankly!' I yelled. He turned and glanced at me. He didn't seem too happy. He looked older than the last time I had seen him, in the hotel lobby in Blackpool

'Aye, what is it son?' he asked.

I was gasping. 'Mr Shankly, I wrote to you the other week about a cup final ticket.'

'Arh, no, they've all gone son, everybody wants one, you know. People are writing to me all the time. I'm really sorry. I wish I could let everyone have one.' He was almost through the door.

'But you replied saying that if I was to come over you would find one for me. I don't know whether you remember me but my Uncle Horace used to live next door to you in Huddersfield. And I've written to you a few times.' I was talking so hurriedly I didn't think I was making much sense.

'Arhh, yes! You're the lad who wrote to me.' Any irritation he showed suddenly evaporated. His eyes lit up. 'Right. Aye, did I say to come here? Yes, I think I did. Well, let me see. You best come in.' He opened the door and held it for me.

'See you, wait here now. He's okay here isn't he, John?' he called to the commissionaire. 'I'll only be a minute.' The commissionaire glared at me, then sat down and returned to his newspaper. It was a long wait. One minute turned into five, then ten, then fifteen. I thought I'd been forgotten. Then I heard his heels clicking along the corridor.

'Sorry about that son, I had difficulty finding the secretary. Here, I've found one for you.' In his hand he held a five-shilling terrace ticket for Wembley. I could scarcely believe it.

'Wow, thanks ever so much,' I burbled. 'Er, what do I owe you?'

'Seven shillings and sixpence. But it's me who really owes *you* for that programme you sent. I just remembered that. That was very kind of you. It brought back some great memories. I'll always remember that day. The Kop was packed, and the noise, oh the noise. Second only to Hampden, you know. That was a great Liverpool team: Billy Liddell, Laurie Hughes, Albert Stubbins, Bob Paisley, who works with me here now, you know. Great players, all of them.' I smiled faintly at him. 'Aye, and how's your aunt and uncle? I remember your aunt, yes, er, what was her name?'

'Gertie,' I replied. 'Uncle Horace and Auntie Gertie.'

'Aye, yes, I remember them well. Horace was a tall lean man, wasn't he, very well spoken.' I nodded. 'And Gertie, is she well? Nice garden they had.'

'They're both fine.'

'So, do you come to many of the games here?'

'I've been to most games this season and to both the cup games.'

'Well, that's more than me. I missed one of them, you know. I wasn't here for the Stockport game, I was abroad. I c'dnae believe it when I got back to the airport. I saw the newspaper headline, "No Cup Shocks". I looked and saw the score. I said to the man selling the paper, "No cup shocks! Well what the hell's this? Liverpool 0, Stockport 0! That's the biggest shock I've ever heard!" Still, we won through in the end.'

'Do you think we'll win at Wembley?' I asked. It was a stupid question. but I had to ask it.

'Win?' he spluttered. 'Of course we'll win, why shouldn't we?' I beamed, buoyed by his exuberance and over-powering confidence. 'Is everybody fit?'

'Fit? Of course they're fit. They're the fittest team in the country. They're so fit they'd crawl all the way up Wembley Way to play in this game. Now I must go, things to do, you understand. Nice talking to you son. Give my regards to your aunt and uncle when you see them. Enjoy yourself at Wembley.' And with that, he turned and marched off down the corridor, his heels clicking once more. The commissionaire looked at me, not sure whether to smile or glare. I smiled back at him.'

I clutched the ticket, kissed it, and stuffed it into an inside pocket, making sure my coat was tightly buttoned up and that there was no way it might suddenly jump out and fly away. Then I remembered. In the excitement I'd forgotten to pay for the ticket. I'd walked out of Anfield so pleased with myself and so in awe of having spoken to Bill Shankly that I had clean forgotten to pay him the seven shillings and sixpence, even though he'd said that *he* owed me. I turned round and dashed back. What will he think? He'll be fuming. The family's name will be forever blackened. The Commissionaire was still sitting there, still reading the same page of the same newspaper.

'Not youse again,' he said, looking up.

'Yeah, I forgot to give Mr Shankly the money for the ticket.'

'Yer lucky,' he said. 'I was just about to lock up.' I pulled out three half-crowns.

'Best not trouble him any further,' he said, 'just leave the money with me. I'll see he gets it.'

I plonked the three half-crowns on his desk and with a smile and thanks wandered back into the sunlight with only the slightest thought that maybe Shankly would never see the money. But who cares? I was so ecstatic I didn't even think about what I was going to say to Susan. I knew she wouldn't be happy but I never guessed she'd be quite so angry.

'So, I'm going to have to go to the wedding *and* the do without you,' she screeched, placing a threatening emphasis on the word 'and'.

'You don't really mind, though, do you?' I pleaded lovingly. 'I mean, it's only once in a lifetime. They've only ever played at Wembley once before and who knows how long it'll be before they play there again. In fact, they might never play there again.' She continued to glare at me, not believing a word I'd told her.

'I'll contribute to the present, though,' I added, with what I thought was a generous and conciliatory gesture.

'Too right you will! You can buy the whole bloody thing.' It wasn't like Susan to swear. 'What kind of a day is it going to be for me, hanging around all by myself? Who am I going to dance with? It'll be all couples and everyone'll be asking, "Where's Steve?"' She said the latter in a very sarcastic tone. 'What am I going to say to everyone?'

'Just tell them I've gone to the cup final. They'll understand,' I replied.

Shanks would just have told Nessie, 'I'm off to Wembley, love.' She wouldn't have been bothered. She'd have understood. It was said that he once took her to a match on their wedding anniversary. It was to see Rochdale against Southport. He denied it. 'Nah,' he said, 'it was Rochdale *reserves* against Southport reserves!'

But I'm afraid Susan was in a different league from Nessie. 'What if you've lost?' asked Susan. 'You won't be much fun at the party then, will you?' I have to confess, I'd not thought about that; the prospect of losing had never even occurred to me, even though I was the eternal pessimist. 'You know what you're like when they lose, you go around with a sulk on your face,' she continued, realising that she had tapped a raw exposed nerve. 'What are you going to be like if they lose the cup final?'

'But it's the occasion,' I insisted. 'It doesn't really matter if they win or lose, it's the taking part that counts.' I was lying through my back teeth. I knew she was right. How could I possibly go to the party if they had lost. Everyone would be taking the piss, they'd all be bleating, 'Look at all the money he spent on the ticket and train fare, ha, ha, ha.' And as for any Evertonians, all I'd hear from Bluenose and the twins would be 'Liverpool've never won the cup, never will' etc. etc. I knew I'd be miserable, the last thing I'd want would be a wedding do with everybody happy, laughing and joking, and Susan, bloody Susan, wanting me to dance and entertain her.

There was no appeasing her. But I did promise that I'd come straight back from Wembley and see her at the reception later on, no matter what the result. 'If I'm still there,' she hissed. I expected the tears to flow but oddly enough there weren't any. I took that as an encouraging sign.

Dad was really pleased. Mum just smiled knowingly. I went out and bought her a box of Black Magic chocolates, her favourites, as a way of saying thanks for suggesting writing. Andy was just as miffed as Susan. More annoyed, I guess, because he hadn't figured on me getting a ticket. He and Billy would be walking up the aisle while I would be walking up Wembley Way. It was no contest.

'You jammy bastard,' he said.

'It's not what you know, it's who you know,' I replied teasingly. Just for once I'd got something over on Andy. He was always the centre of attraction, always the person everyone wanted as their friend. I didn't mind that because he was my friend as well but just occasionally I wished people would take a bit more notice of me. Getting the ticket wouldn't make much difference in the long run but it made me feel good for a short while.

I told Billy that I definitely wouldn't be going to the wedding and couldn't therefore be an usher. He'd suspected it all along but still acted miffed when I told him. 'It's the most important day in my life, you know,' he whinged.

'Yeah, I know and I'm sorry, but going to Wembley's the most important day in my life as well,' I responded. 'But I will be there in the evening, I promise.'

'That's all very well but what time's that going to be? You won't get back into Liverpool before half nine and by the time you get to the do it'll be well past ten.'

'Yeah, but the party'll still be going on. You're not going off on your honeymoon until the Sunday. You'll still be there.'

'I might not.'

'Warra you mean, "I might not"? Course you will, it's your wedding. Oh, I get it. *You're* wanting to sneak off early, aren't you, with Maggie.'

'Margaret. Her name's Margaret, not Maggie.' I glared at him. As far as I was concerned she'd always been Maggie, never Margaret, and I wasn't going to start calling her Margaret now.

'Bit of hanky-panky aye?'

'No, I'm not going to have a bit of hanky-panky as you so crudely put it,' he exclaimed, not realising that I was having a joke, but he was clearly embarrassed that I'd sussed him. We all knew he was saving himself for his wedding night.

'Look, I promise I'll be there. I'll come straight from the train. I'll get me dad to pick us up and if he can't come I'll even grab a taxi. Honest, I'll be there by ten and the party'll hardly have started. You're not going to be off before then, are you?'

He grunted, but I knew we'd never agree on this one. Maybe I was being a bit mean. After all, I'd known about the wedding long enough. They'd been planning it for more than a year and the date had been etched into everyone's diary for twelve months. Billy had spent most of that time going on about it. Talk about girls being obsessed by weddings, we'd had to go through the rigmarole of who was going to be best man (Andy), who would be the ushers (Martin and me), what suit Billy would be wearing (top hat and tails), which band would play (the Rhythmics or Harry Dixon's Trio), where the do would be (the RAFA Club or the British Legion Centre), who was coming (every Tom, Dick and Harry) and so on. We'd shared every decision. At times it felt like it was us getting married and not just him. I might have moaned a bit to Andy but in Billy's presence I'd maintained a committed interest.

Billy's mum wasn't very happy either. She said something to my mum about how I'd known Billy for most of his life and how disappointing it was that I couldn't be an usher, etc. etc. I hated upsetting Mrs Edwards but my mum never said anything to her. She told me but she didn't pass a comment. I took that as tacit approval. In other words, 'It's your decision, you do what you want.'

As for the bride, I kept well away. When I spotted her strolling into the YM coffee bar I made myself scarce, leaving Billy to inform his betrothed of my decision. But with a week to go I was beginning to have doubts. Susan was fed up, Billy was well pissed off, Maggie was seething, Billy's mum was complaining. Was it worth it? I wondered. What's more, I still kept coming back to the seed of doubt Susan had so kindly planted in my mind: what if they didn't win? Going to Wembley would be all very well but the journey back would be so miserable and I knew that I certainly wouldn't fancy walking into that wedding reception if they'd lost. But could they really lose? Liverpool might have won the league title the previous season but the current season had not been so consistent. We'd never looked serious contenders the entire time. Instead we'd concentrated on the cup. Leeds United were a good side. Admittedly they had been in the second division the season before but they had won promotion and were now challenging Manchester United for the title. They could even win the league and cup double. In Don Revie they had an outstanding manager, a figure almost as revered as Shankly and Busby. There was no doubt that Leeds were an emerging side.

I lay in bed unable to sleep, wondering if I should just sell my ticket. This ticket was causing me more sleepless nights than I'd known in years. I knew I could get a bucketful of money for it; they were like gold dust in Liverpool. But then, what would Shankly say if he knew I had sold the ticket he had so generously unearthed for me. Thankfully, it was only in the hours of darkness when all these deranged thoughts swept through my head that I had any doubts. In the cold light of day there was never any dilemma. I couldn't do it, no, of course not. When I told Barry about my quandary he promptly took a pound note out of his wallet and tried to tempt me, even producing two and then three pound notes later that day. But no way could I bring myself to sell the ticket. Anyhow, this ticket was lucky. If I sold it Liverpool were certain to lose and it would all be my fault. Half a million accusing fingers would point at me. It was incumbent on me to go to the final. I, and I alone, had been entrusted with the sacred key and it was my duty to guard it and use it accordingly. But I wasn't going to tell Susan, Billy, Andy or any of the others that, for a few brief moments, I had toyed with the idea of giving up the ticket and the unique opportunity of going to Wembley.

Dad offered to come to the station with me to buy the train ticket. There were nine trains going from Lime Street, either to Euston, Marylebone or Wembley Central, starting at six o'clock on the Friday evening.

'Some of the lads in the office are going on the 7.50 on the

Saturday morning and going straight to Wembley,' I told my dad. 'I'm going to go with them.'

He stood behind me while I ordered my three-pound ticket but when it came to paying he gently pushed me aside and poked three one-pound notes through the small hole on the counter. 'My treat,' he said. 'But *don't* tell your mother.'

twelve

'Ee-Aye-Addio'

Mum, of course, knew all along. Dad had probably told her, anyhow. He was like that but of course she never let on. The thought that we might lose was now beginning to overwhelm me more than I had ever imagined. I had never been one of life's eternal optimists. On the contrary, I always feared the worst, always picked holes in suggestions, or tried to knock down anyone else's ideas. Supporting a football club was the ultimate test of whether you were an optimist or pessimist. There were those who stood alongside me on the Kop who were certain about the outcome of every game. A goal down with ten minutes to go and they would remain convinced that Liverpool would still win. Me? I was ready to write the team off and get out the handkerchief. Yes, I was one of life's doubters. I might have seen them score enough last-minute goals to ensure that at least I would never leave until the final whistle sounded but not enough to convince me of their infallibility.

But the FA Cup final was different. This was, after all, the biggest one-off game in English football. It was winner take all. It was every sporting cliché you could imagine. Nobody remembers the runners-up or who played in the semi-finals. Being the pessimist that I am, I was convinced that we would lose and I had a vision of tears trickling shamelessly down my cheeks as Liverpool dragged themselves up the steps of Wembley to receive their runners-up medals from the Queen. What would the journey home be like? What would I say to the lads? What would I say to Susan? What would it be like in the office on the following Monday with Bluenose and, no doubt, George and Gobbo taking the piss as well. Bluenose was already at it, reminding everyone that there was a jinx on Liverpool ever winning the cup. 'You know what they say?' he said. 'The day Liverpool win the cup the Liver Bird will up and fly away from its perch on the Liver Buildings. Yer haven't got a hope in hell!' The prospect of Bluenose gloating didn't bear thinking about. But I did, and the more I thought about it, the more terrified I became.

Although I didn't mind going to Anfield by myself, somehow it didn't feel right to be standing at Wembley by myself. This was an occasion, an experience to be shared. As season ticket holders, Phil and Eric had both luckily obtained tickets, although they were tickets for the stands, whereas I was on the terraces behind the goal. But I had arranged to go down on the train with them. Barry was still scrabbling around in search of a ticket but didn't seem to be having much luck. He'd even put up an advert in his local newsagent's. But when I told him that someone was advertising in the *Echo*, offering to totally redecorate a house in exchange for a ticket, he realised he was on a loser. 'Not a chance,' I told him encouragingly.

'You'll probably get a ticket outside the ground, from one of the touts,' suggested Phil one lunchtime.

'D'yer reckon?' said Barry, who didn't seem to have seriously considered that possibility.

'Yer, you'll have to pay over the odds but you'll get one.' Barry looked at him thoughtfully. He took his glasses off and began to wipe them.

'My dad's got a mate who goes to the cup final every year,' I told him, 'and he never has a ticket but he always gets in. He brings me back a programme as well.'

'Yeah, but it'll cost me,' said Barry.

'Well, work out how much you can afford,' suggested Eric, always the intellectual. 'It's worth a try. What have you got to lose?'

'Well der's the three-pound train fare for a start. And then if I don't get in, I won't even see it on the telly.'

'You could take your trannie, listen to it somewhere,' I said helpfully. 'Go on, we'll have a good day out.' Barry still wasn't sure.

'How much do you reckon I'll have to pay then?' he asked, looking at Eric, who was carefully clipping his orange beard.

'I don't know – fiver, tenner, for a standing ticket.'

'Hmm.' I could sense he was warming to the idea.

'I've heard der's always plenty of tickets,' said Phil. 'It's all those small FA organisations up and down the country. Dey get loads and always sell them on to make a bit of money. Dey won't be wanting to go. I mean, nobody in East Cheam'll want to go and see Liverpool or Leeds.'

'Except Tony Hancock.' We all laughed.

Barry suddenly thought of another problem. 'But I might finish up at the wrong end of the ground. What do I do den?'

'You'll be okay. They won't mind, just don't shout too loud,' replied Eric, laughing. We all knew there was little prospect of Barry not shouting too loudly. 'Anyhow, you can always ask a tout for a ticket at the Liverpool end.'

Later that afternoon Barry popped his head round the door and gave me the thumbs-up. 'I'm going.' he said. 'You're right, can't miss this one. I've decided I'll go up to a fiver. Take me trannie as well. I'll get a train ticket on the way home tonight.'

So far it had been an enthralling season. Although Liverpool had never really looked likely to repeat their league success of the previous year, when it came to cup matches they were firing on all cylinders. As league champions, they had entered the European Cup, a competition never before won by an English side. They had begun with an easy enough trip to Iceland but had then drawn the highly rated Belgian side Anderlecht, one of the strongest teams in the competition. Shankly had worried us all when he talked about Anderlecht being one of the finest sides in Europe. He'd been to Wembley to watch the Belgium national side, containing more than half the Anderlecht team, playing England. They'd drawn 0–0 but most newspaper pundits had reckoned Belgium should have won it comfortably. 'A fantastic side,' Shankly told the *Echo*. 'They'll be really difficult to beat.' Then, of course, when Liverpool did beat them, he told the *Echo* that Liverpool were now among the best sides on the Continent.

It was the first time Leeds had ever played in a cup final and in the week before their historic encounter with Liverpool they saw the league title snatched from under their noses. They had lost the league on goal average to Manchester United by just 0.686 of a goal. They were no slouches, this Leeds side. It promised to be an epic match, Lancashire against Yorkshire, the red rose versus the white.

Lime Street station was a glow of red. Fans, dressed in eccentric attire of home-made hats and cloaks, were already making their way along the platforms to the half-dozen trains that stood ready to haul the mighty army southwards. And judging by the number of requests for spares it looked as though half Liverpool was travelling down to Wembley ticketless.

The four of us met up at 7.30 a.m. under the clock as arranged, then sprinted down the platform in search of an empty carriage, sweat already bristling on Phil's forehead. Eric, leading with his barrel chest, barged his way down the corridor, flung open the door of a compartment and threw his bag and other belongings onto the seats to stake our claim. He cut a bizarre figure, his orange beard nestling uncomfortably in his scarf and his long hair poking from underneath a red and white bobble hat. 'Has anyone ever told you, you don't suit red,' said Barry as we tumbled into our seats.

'Yeah, you'd suit blue much better,' suggested Phil. 'Maybe you should become an Evertonian for the sake of fashion.' We'd only been going five minutes when the compartment door was hurled open.

'Got any spurs?' asked a scrawny youth. We shook our heads sympathetically.

Barry decided to give it a go himself but returned half an hour later looking gloomy. 'Not a chance,' he said.

'Well, you wouldn't really expect anyone on this train to have spares, would you?' said Eric encouragingly. We all agreed, and for a brief time it helped lift the gloom that seemed plastered into Barry's face. He fiddled with his transistor radio, trying to find a pirate station that might brighten his spirits, but had little luck.

As the train rattled through the English countryside the compartment door was repeatedly hurled open by a succession of lanky, spotty, fleshy, skinny, podgy youths all asking the same question. When an older balding man opened the door we shook our heads before he had managed to speak.

''As anybody in 'ere lost a ticket?' he asked. We looked at him in disbelief. 'I've found a ticket,' he explained. 'If you know anyone who's lost one I'm in the end carriage but they'll have to give us details of the ticket.' He slammed the door closed. Barry and I looked at each other in astonishment. I could see what he was thinking.

'No!' I said. 'How are you going to prove it's *your* ticket.'

''Ere, let me have a look at your ticket. I could tell him it's in the same section.'

'But you don't know which section this ticket's for.'

'It's worth a try, though.'

'Forget it,' said Phil, 'you don't even know what price the ticket is. He'll wanna know the price, exactly where it's for, and so on.'

'Anyway,' said Eric, 'what about the poor bloke who really has lost his ticket?'

'Aye, what if he doesn't know he's lost it?' said Phil. 'Say he gets to the turnstile at the stadium and goes digging in his pocket and can't find his ticket.' The thought was unthinkable. 'What would you do? Poor bastard.'

'Jesus, you'd go mad, wouldn't you?' Barry was still fidgeting, still churning it over in his mind, trying to come up with a convincing argument.

'No!' said Eric firmly. 'Sit down, forget it.' I tried to change the subject. 'Eh, have you seen this story in the papers? They reckon Manchester City want Shankly as their new manager.'

'Load of crap,' said Barry. 'Shanks won't leave Liverpool, never.'

'Anyrate, in this paper he's laughed at the suggestion. Says it's all nonsense and nobody has spoken to him.'

'It's just newspaper talk, trying to unsettle us on cup final day. Bloody papers.'

'What score d'ye reckon?'

'2–0,' piped up Eric from behind his newspaper. 'Both goals from the Saint. Warra bout you Steve?'

'Er, I think we might sneak it 1–0 or it might be a 1–1 draw.'

'Christ, ever the bloody optimist,' said Barry, now looking more settled.

'3–0 and all three from Sir Roger.' We all laughed.

Roger Hunt, or 'Sir Roger', as we knew him, was our hero; gallant, swashbuckling, one of Lancelot's fair knights. He was unmistakable, his blond hair swept back as he charged forward, his shoulders square and true. 'Cry God for Harry, England and St Roger.' He had a nose for goals. In the season Liverpool won the second division championship he had bagged 41 league goals, an all-time club record. There were those who claimed he lacked skill, though mainly they were newspaper writers from the south. And what did they know? To a small degree they were right, but what Hunt lacked in skill he more than made up for in presence. They claimed he missed more goals than he scored but that didn't bother us or Shankly. 'At least he's in the right place at the right time to miss them,' explained Shankly painstakingly. Well, you understood what he was getting at. In the mid-sixties Hunt's chief rival for the England shirt was Jimmy Greaves. But Greaves was a maverick, a man made to slush around in headlines. He might have had a better strike record than our hero but he was never on the end of the ball as much as Sir Roger. And you don't score any goals unless you're in the right place at the right time and more often than not, Hunt was. Compared to Greaves, Hunt had an old-fashioned, focused, workmanlike approach to goalscoring. When he scored he simply shook hands as he trotted back to the centre circle. Greaves was a showman who played to the gallery. There was no doubt in our minds which of the men we preferred.

At Wembley station the reality of travelling tickletless began to strike home. Dozens were wandering around waiting to pounce on any new batch of arriving fans. Some held up small signs. One read: 'Ticket wanted. Will exchange wife, plus money.' Everyone in the world seemed to be searching for a ticket. Outside the station a faint rain was falling from leaden skies, while cars clogged up the roads. Thousands spilled over the pavements, mostly sporting red rosettes, scarves and hats. There appeared to be hardly any Leeds supporters. We were pushed and bumped along the pavement as the crowd moved gently in the direction of the stadium. The police seemed to have lost total control. Over the road a gang of lads had already given up on ever getting a ticket and had taken up residence outside a television rental shop. Our plan had been to have a few drinks before the game but the queue for the bar stretched into the car park. It was chaos. Fans stood shoulder to shoulder inside the pub while outside others were urinating against the pub wall.

'Forget it, let's go straight to the ground.'

'We'll hang around here a bit longer, see if there's anything going,' said Barry.

'Okay, we'll see you back here after the game,' they said, wishing Barry good luck in his search. Barry and I wandered back into the station out of the rain.

'There's a guy over there in a white mac who's got some tickets for the Liverpool end,' we were told by a Yorkshire lad with freckled skin. For a brief moment our spirits were lifted.

'How much's he want?'

'Fifty quid for a three-pound three-shilling ticket,' he replied.

'Bloody hell, is that how much they're asking?'

'Sounds like the going rate. It's the cheapest I've come across so far,' he told us.

'Friggin' hell,' I muttered. Barry sighed.

'There's no point in hanging around here,' said Barry. 'Let's go up Wembley Way, there'll be more chance there.' You'd think he'd been doing it every year but it was certainly true that there was little or no hope of finding a ticket at our price at the station. My pessimism began to show. 'You'll be lucky,' I told Barry. But he refused to be swayed by my gloom.

Wembley Way was one of the great traditions of cup final day and even in the damp it was enough to lift the spirits. It was heaving with fans from both teams, a glow of red and white and in the distance stood our destination, the twin towers of Wembley. It was the first time I had ever seen Wembley, apart from in newspapers and magazines, of course, and on television every cup final day since 1953. But this was the first time I'd actually seen it for real. And boy, was it impressive! The hairs prickled. This was it, cup final day and I was here. We stood there gawping. It was not difficult to understand why it had become part of the pysche of football.

'Photo,' demanded Barry, pulling out his camera, 'or they'll never believe we've been.' I laughed and clicked.

'Come on, let's go and find a ticket,' said Barry, who having spotted his destination was becoming increasingly anxious. He was like some mountaineer within touching distance of his summit and, no matter what the hazards, was determined to reach the peak. The exhilaration of Wembley and its prospect had engulfed him. But things weren't looking good until Barry spotted an elderly man standing by the road who somehow did not seem to be part of the occasion. He was dressed somewhat more elegantly than the average Scouser and wasn't sporting any team colours. Barry looked quizzically towards him and caught his eye. The man cocked his head and, without emitting any sound, voiced the word 'ticket'. Barry rushed over. 'Have you got any tickets?'

'You looking for one?' Barry nodded. 'Might have, then,' he replied.

'How much?' asked Barry.

'Twenty pound for a twenty-five-shilling seat,' replied the man gruffly.

'What, twenty pound!' exclaimed Barry. 'You're joking. Is that for the seat next to the Queen? How much is a standing ticket?'

'Fifteen,' he answered again. 'Take it or leave it.'

'Fuck off,' said Barry walking away. 'You can stick it up your arse for that price.' The man ignored us.

'Christ,' I said, 'that's a bit steep.'

'Steep, it's bloody scandalous,' said Barry, as we rejoined the swelling throng edging its way slowly down Wembley Way. 'That's twice what I earn in a week.' The usually cheerful Barry sounded disgruntled and pessimistic for the first time that day.

Time was pressing. It was already nearly 2 p.m. and ideally we should have been inside the ground by now. Up and down Wembley Way the Liverpool supporters were singing. 'Ee-aye-addio, we're goin' to see the Queen.' I knew there would come a point when I'd have to leave Barry to sort himself out, and that moment was quickly drawing near.

By 2.15 p.m. we were on the concourse outside the stadium. The fans were beginning to divide, Leeds to the left, Liverpool to the right. I was half excited, half apprehensive, concerned that Barry was going to be left outside unable to see the game.

'There's something going on over there,' said Barry, spotting a small group of lads assembled around a bulky looking man in a trilby. He had a face like a stilton. We wandered over. The man was holding a fistful of tickets.

'Has he got any spares?' asked Barry.

'Yeah,' said a lad much the same age as us.

'How much's he want?'

'Tenner for standing, twenty for sitting.'

'Well, at least it's getting cheaper,' I said, suddenly realising that that wasn't a very helpful remark.

'Arr, come on mate. Can't you drop the price a bit? I'll give you a fiver for a standing,' argued a thickly built man with scaly skin who'd clearly had more than enough to drink.

'No way. Ten. That's the bottom price for a standing ticket. You won't get one cheaper anywhere else here today.' By now, a few more were gathering round, including a man with a conker head that sat smugly on his bulldog neck. His friend was a skinny lad with a square head and hair that looked like it had just had the electric-shock treatment. They reminded me of Laurel and Hardy. There was growing desperation.

'Eh, look. It'll be kick-off in half an hour, you won't get rid of them at a tenner, can't you drop it a bit?' asked a man wearing a tall red hat.

'Go on. Here, I've got five pounds,' pleaded Barry, pulling five notes out of his wallet and proffering it towards the man. But it was falling on deaf ears. The man remained adamant. A tenner or nothing.

'Fucking scum dese touts,' muttered Oliver Hardy at the back of the circle.

'Yeah, fucking cockneys, making a fortune owra us,' agreed the lad standing next to him. It was beginning to turn nasty.

'Come on lads, you telling me you can't afford ten pounds? You haven't been down to Wembley for fifteen years. You've had plenty of time to save up,' he said grinning.

'Cockney bloody barrow boys, spivs, the lotta dem, that's all dee are,' shouted Ollie. 'Should be locked up, the lot of youse.'

'Can you lend us a few quid?' asked Barry quietly. 'I'll pay yer back Monday.'

'Bloody 'ell, Barry. That's daft. Anyrate, I've only got three pounds to last me the rest of the day and I've got to go to a bloody wedding tonight and buy some drinks.'

'Ah, go on, please. I can't come down here and not gerrin. It's going to be fantastic in there, just listen to them singing.'

'Well, I suppose I could lend you two pounds but I think you're mad.' I handed him two pound notes.

''Ere y'are mate, there's seven pounds for a standing, go on,' he said trying to put the money into the tout's hand.

'Sorry lad. Ten, no less.' Barry looked at me. He was almost in tears. I took my last pound out. He grabbed it and smiled.

'Ta. 'Ere, eight quid.'

'No! I've told you, ten. Standing tickets are ten.'

'Come on, dig deep,' he shouted to the crowd that had gathered. They'll be kicking off soon. Don't want to miss the big game, do you?' It wasn't the most sensible thing to say.

'How many tickets have you got there?' asked Ollie.

'Enough,' laughed the tout.

'The prices'll drop as it gets closer to kick-off time,' I assured Barry.

'Ah, come on,' pleaded Ollie. 'We've been saving up for weeks for this game. Go on, I'll give you seven.'

The tout shook his head in disbelief. 'Are you not hearing me? I said a tenner. Right, shove off, then, if you're not going to buy. Let someone else in.' Barry and I turned to go.

'Ballocks. I've had enough of this,' screamed the skinny lad. 'These fuckers are making a bomb out of us football fans. It's not on.' And with one mighty rush, young Stanley Laurel elbowed us all aside and, with almost the same movement, landed a punch firmly on the jaw of the trilby'd spiv. It was as good a punch as the one Cassius Clay had recently landed on Sonny Liston's glass chin. For a brief second we all looked on in total disbelief. The tout staggered backwards, still clutching his tickets – but not for long. With a sweep of his hand, Stanley had grabbed the fistful of tickets off him and was holding his prize aloft like the head of the slain Goliath. 'Anyone want a ticket?' he was shouting at the top of his voice. He must have been waving fifty or more tickets around. 'Free cup final tickets, come and get your free cup final tickets 'ere.' There was a commotion. People were running in from everywhere. Barry pounced into the ensuing mêlée and came out clutching a ticket and sporting the biggest grin I had ever seen. The tout had now recovered his composure. He was yelling and trying to throw punches at anyone in his vicinity. Two policemen spotted the fracas and were making their way towards us.

'Scuffers!' screamed someone. It was the call to disappear. Everyone was off. Stanley raced away, still clutching the handful of tickets above his head and offering them to anyone who wanted one. Ollie was puffing and panting behind him. Likewise, Barry and I decided to make ourselves scarce before the long arm of the law stretched in our direction. Fortunately, it wasn't difficult to lose ourselves in the crowd.

'Serves the bugger right,' said Barry, when we finally stopped running and had a closer look at the ticket. It was genuine enough, a seven-and-sixpence standing ticket, Block C, not that far away from where I was. Barry was giggling. 'Did you see that punch? Christ! He was just a little skinny guy. What a punch! Cassius Clay. He really laid him out.'

'He must have had more than fifty tickets. Blimey, at ten pounds or more each, that's probably a thousand pounds' worth. You could have bought our house for that.'

'You could have bought our entire *street*,' said Barry, still chortling, before adding despairingly, 'I wish I'd thought of hitting him.'

Stanley's punch turned out to be historic. No doubt some old maiden of a magistrate would have sentenced Stanley to twelve months inside if the police had caught him stealing those tickets. The tout would have been seen as the offended. But football fans everywhere would have applauded Stanley. He was our hero. He had made at least fifty people happy that afternoon. It's what Aristotle might have called 'natural justice'. More importantly, touts were never seen on Wembley Way again after May 1965.

Barry pulled his camera out again, and asked a stranger to take our photograph. One arm round each other, the other arm holding our scarves high, liquid grins. Click! I left Barry to make his way to Gate C while I set off for Gate B to join the queue to get into the stadium. The crowd around the gate was chaotic. Everyone was beginning to get anxious as the time edged towards two thirty. People were pushing and tumbling back down the stairs but it was all in good spirits. I even spotted Laurel and Hardy, huge smirks on their face, telling everyone what they'd done.

The community singing, accompanied by the white-helmeted band of the Royal Marines, was still going on as I finally nosed my way into the ground. This was it, my first glimpse of Wembley. I was high above the goal but the pitch seemed a mile off and I wondered if I would ever recognise the players. But the noise, the singing, the atmosphere, was electric. This was something special.

After forcing myself down the terrace a little, where the crush was not so tight, I found myself standing next to a long-haired lad with a flattened nose and an older man who I assumed to be his dad. The crowd sang 'Abide With Me' with quiet dignity but when it came to singing the 'National Anthem' there were catcalls from the entire Liverpool terrace. Instead, they sang 'God Save Our Team'. We all laughed at our disrespect. And then, in the distance, came the two teams, one led by Bill Shankly, the other by the former Manchester City deep-lying centre forward, Don Revie.

It was almost kick-off time and it was only then that I remembered. I'd forgotten all about the wedding. Billy and Maggie would be going down the aisle. They'd be exchanging their vows any minute, everyone smiling and blissful. Susan would be cooing, Andy would be pulling the ring out of a waistcoat pocket, Mrs Edwards would be smiling proudly at her eldest son. And yet, for all that, it didn't begin to match what I was feeling as I stood on that expanse of terrace and gazed over at the Twin Towers.

The Queen was introduced to the players, followed by Harold Wilson and General Montgomery.

'I was one of Monty's army, you know,' said the dad standing next to me. 'I fought with him in the desert. Wonderful man.' Liverpool's captain, Ron Yeats, towered over his opposite number, the diminutive Bobby Collins. And then the whistle, and they were off.

The first half passed without incident, apart from an early injury to fullback Gerry Byrne. 'The Wembley curse,' muttered the man next to me. 'It happens every year: someone gets injured in the cup final, spoils the game. Maybe one of these days they'll allow substitutes.' But Byrne picked himself up and, after treatment from the Liverpool physio, Bob Paisley, carried on. We roared our hearts out. It was half-time before I knew it. The dad next to me offered me a piece of chocolate and promised me the game would get better. 'They're nervous. Don't want to lose,' he claimed. But it didn't get much better. Chances were few and far between in the second half as well. The pitch was clearly heavy and slippery. As the half wore on, I started to become increasingly anxious that Liverpool would do something inane: a flap by Tommy Lawrence, a miskick by Gerry Byrne, who was looking decidedly uncomfortable with his shoulder injury, or a misdirected header by Ron Yeats. It only needed one mistake and all could be lost.

Full-time and it was still goalless. Nobody could remember the last time they'd played extra time in an FA Cup final. Liverpool hadn't played poorly but Leeds had somehow managed to keep going on the rain-sodden pitch. You felt Leeds could only improve in extra time. Luck seemed to be in short supply for us with the Leeds goalkeeper making some impressive stops.

It's in games like this that you begin to fear the worst; Liverpool dominating but the other side sneaking off with the win. There was a numbness about the place. People sighed, drew breath, shook their heads, pushed their way towards the toilets. It didn't look good. I just knew what was going to happen. The scenario was stretching out in front of me. Leeds would sneak a goal with five minutes to go and that would be it.

'I don't think our luck's in today,' I told the dad next to me.

'Luck? There's no such thing as luck,' he snarled back. 'Luck is for weak men. It's an excuse. You make your own luck.'

I could see Bill Shankly out on the pitch talking to the players as they took a breather for a few minutes. What was he telling them? He was gesticulating, his arms waving one way and then the other, like a traffic cop in New York. Bob Paisley was rubbing seized-up muscles and talking to Gerry Byrne, whose shoulder seemed to be giving him trouble. And then they were off again, the crowd finding its voice. 'LIV-ER-POOL, LIV-ER-POOL, LIV-ER-POOL'. We might have been tired but we still had our role to play. And then, with just three minutes gone, Willie Stevenson set off on a run, slipped the ball to Gerry Byrne, who chipped it into the area, and the golden-haired Roger Hunt came diving in to head Liverpool into the lead. Pandemonium. The man next to me hurled his arms around me and began a dance. I felt smothered by his giant figure. My heart began to pound. Maybe I was wrong, maybe we would win. 'Why didn't they do that ten minutes ago?' I yelled.

But it was short lived. Eight minutes later little Billy Bremner, lurking on the edge of the area, latched on to a Charlton header and unleashed a shot that ripped into the back of the Liverpool net. Leeds were on equal terms. The deflation was intense. I knew it. I just bloody knew it. 'It's not going to be our day,' I told the giant next to me. 'Don't worry, son, we can beat this lot dead easy. If we can score once, we can score twice.' I didn't like to tell him that this argument worked both ways with Leeds just as capable of scoring another. I could hardly look. Down at the other end of Wembley there was ecstasy. The Leeds fans were jumping up and down. I wanted to pray. More than anything I could imagine at that moment, I wanted Liverpool to win. Oh please, please, don't let Leeds win.

Half-time in extra time came and we looked weary. The wet pitch was taking its toll. Some players were pulling up with cramp, others looked exhausted. From the sidelines, Shankly was urging them on. 'One last effort lads. We can still do it.' I could feel my entire body shaking. Thump, thump, thump, every sinew pounding as the blood heaved its way through my veins. My head was throbbing with the intensity.

And now Ian Callaghan had the ball. Cutting down the wing, he whipped in a cross that seemed to elude every Leeds defender. For a second or two time stood still. A snapshot that would be ingrained on my mind forever. The old black and white picture. And who should be there to swivel like a salmon in midair but Ian St John? Like a bullet, the ball smacked into the Leeds net: 2–1 to Liverpool. St John was lost beneath a carpet of red shirts. There was a momentary silence, a disbelief, as we all drew breath. And then Wembley erupted. The roar was deafening. We all leapt into the air. Never before had Wembley seen or heard anything like this. There was chaos. 'That's it! They'll not come back from that!' yelled the giant. 'It's our cup.' But that didn't stop me fretting for the next ten minutes. I hardly dared to look and with every Leeds attack I feared the worst. It was, I swear, the longest ten minutes ever. But then came the final whistle. The relief, the delirium, it was explosive. 'LIV-ER-POOL, LIV-ER-POOL, LIV-ER-POOL'. Shankly was on the pitch hugging each Liverpool player one by one.

'I told yer! I told yer we'd do it!' yelled the giant. 'We've won the bloody cup.' Shankly, who had discarded his white mac to reveal a smart suit and a flashy tie, was still congratulating his players. We were jumping up and down. The Leeds players had collapsed onto the pitch but we didn't care. And now Ron Yeats was leading his men wearily up the steps to receive the trophy from the Queen. The first time ever.

'Ee-aye-addio, we won der cup! We won der cup! We won der cup! Ee-aye-addio, we won der cup!' bellowed the Liverpool crowd. It was to become our new theme song, to be repeated many times over the years. I imagined Dad at home in front of the telly, tucking into a sandwich and a cup of tea; Mum pleased as anything; Peter and his brother sitting in their back room, begrudging; Dixie Dean remembering the moment he'd walked up those same steps to receive the same trophy; everyone at the wedding listening to Andy as he began his best man's speech.

In London that night the fans tossed red dye into the fountains of Trafalgar Square. They swarmed over Eros, hung red scarves over his arm, and then hit Soho. Liverpool supporters celebrated as they had never celebrated before. The stories reverberated around every office and pub over the following week. Football supporting would never be quite the same again. Fans might have seen the Kop on television and might even have heard that they sang songs but it wasn't until that Saturday when the Liverpool followers poured into London in droves that the reality hit home. Football supporting was about to become a participation event. 'Ee-aye-addio, we won der cup! We won der cup! We won der cup! Ee-aye-addio, we won der cup!' We'd sing it all the way down Wembley Way, and all the way home. We'd sing it forever.

thirteen

Nights to Remember

Dad had promised to meet me off the train and drop me off at the wedding reception. He'd just bought his first car, a yellow Triumph Herald, and was eager for any excuse to drive it. 'I'll see you at the ticket barrier,' he'd said. But spotting me was going to be the problem. As the train rolled into Lime Street station, round two of the partying began. Ever since the game had ended there had been one long celebration. The combination of victory and alcohol now induced a fresh cocktail of revelry as the victorious army returned to its barracks. It was not entirely to be recommended.

As I stepped down onto the platform someone grabbed hold of me by the hips, turned me around and pushed me. Suddenly I found myself leading a conga down the platform. There must have been three hundred people behind me. 'We've won the cup! We've won the cup! Eey-aye-addio, we've won the cup!' we sang as we conga'd, the noise echoing into the rafters and glass roof of the station. Down the platform I took them, swaying in one direction, then curving in a giant semi-circle towards the rear of the station before heading back towards the ticket barrier. Spotting the conga line, more joined in, some ahead of me so that I was no longer leading the charge, many more behind. At the ticket barrier, the collectors looked on in amusement and just waved us through. The waiting crowd applauded, cheered and even joined in as the conga continued its journey around the station. People threw themselves into the arms of those waiting for them on the concourse, danced a jig and then were on their way, mostly to the nearest pub on Lime Street. Liverpool had won the cup and the whole city was beginning its celebration. From somewhere in this vast drove a hand grabbed at me, rescuing me from another trip around the station. It was my father. He had a broad grin on his face. I leapt into his arms. 'We did it! Did you watch?' A silly question. 'What a noise, it was fantastic! We won the cup!' We walked off, he with his arm around me, and made our way to the car.

Susan, however, wasn't quite sure how to greet me. On the one hand, she knew that Liverpool had won and was pleased for me, if not especially for the team. On the other hand, she was still simmering that I had put Liverpool Football Club before her. But she was also pleased that I had at least arrived and that she now had someone to dance with, although, I have to confess, she looked to be dancing close enough to Dave as I walked though the door. Eventually she pulled herself away from him.

'How did the wedding go?' I asked.

'Okay.'

'How was the food?'

'Fine. I saved you some cake.'

'Who did you sit next to?'

'Dave.' I smiled bleakly. 'So you won then?' she added.

'Yeah. Great!' Billy caught sight of me and wandered over. 'Congratulations,' I said, shaking his hand warmly. 'How's married life?'

'Thanks,' he said, 'it's great. So far, so good,' but then just couldn't resist having a dig. 'Glad you could show up.' Andy was far more enthusiastic. He came bounding over, throwing his arms around me. 'Fantastic! Come and tell us about it. I didn't find out until I got to the reception. Who scored? What was it like?' I was weary but the adrenaline of the day was still pumping through me. I even went and gave the bride a kiss. Given the look on her face I was surprised I didn't turn into a frog. But I wasn't going to let it spoil either her day or mine. Maggie was never a stunner but

I have to confess that on this particular day she looked quite acceptable.

'How did it go Maggie?' I asked, exuding all the charm I could muster.

'Wonderful,' she replied with a forced smile. 'You should try it. It doesn't hurt.'

'Yeah, well maybe I will some day.' I managed to stop myself before I got too carried away. She looked at me quizzically like she'd just forced a major admission from me but I knew it was only the adrenaline talking. Thankfully, Susan wasn't within hearing distance. She was off, dancing to the Harry Dixon Trio with Dave again. Andy and I settled into a corner near the bar while I told him of the day's adventures: how Ian St John had dived to score the winner and how the noise of the Liverpool fans had reverberated around Wembley. 'It was unbelievable, Andy, the noise was fantastic. You should have heard it. Everyone was singing, "Ee-aye-addio, we won der cup!"'

Martin had settled into an alcove as well, along with Karen and the bride and groom. There's nothing like a wedding to bring out the romance in people and marriage was clearly item number one on their agendas. Its infection was catching and Martin and Karen were in danger of getting the bug. 'I'll give them a year,' I told Andy, 'before they're at it as well.' Just then Mrs Edwards appeared. She was looking radiant, her slim hips and full bosom amplified in an off-cream suit. 'Hello Stephen,' she said. 'Did you have a good day?' I smiled and daringly told her that she was looking very smart but deliberately didn't use the word attractive.

'Now which of you boys is going to dance with me?' she asked. We both looked blank.

'Come on, it can't be that bad.'

'I can't waltz,' explained Andy who, like me, was irked that Maggie's parents had insisted on the melodic tones of Harry Dixon and his Trio rather than the more pulsating beat of the Rhythmics.

'Well, seeing as you missed the wedding, Stephen, *you* can dance with me,' she said pulling me up and giving me little option. 'But I can't waltz either,' I burbled.

'Doesn't matter, I'll teach you,' she said, grinning. So here I was, my fantasies finally fulfilled, the Cup on its way to Anfield and me in the arms of Mrs Edwards. She held my hand and gently placed her other hand in the small of my back. 'Now, follow me, do what I do. One, two, three; one, two, three.' I tried but it didn't come naturally. We stumbled across the floor, most of the time staring down at our feet. At the end of the dance I was eager to escape but she insisted on one more try. 'You're doing very well but this time don't spend all your time looking down. Be natural.'

But how could I? Especially when Harry Dixon strode to the microphone and gave us his hands-on-bum, cheek-to-cheek rendition of Roy Orbison's 'Only The Lonely'. Mrs Edwards pulled me to her so tightly that it was impossible for me to look down. I could feel a thrusting in my loins. Oh God, no! I was in danger of embarrassing myself. But she just looked at me and smiled, her arms locked behind my back. I glanced over to the bar where the bucolic Mr Edwards was supping brown ale with his pals.

'Now, off we go. One, two, three, remember? No, don't look down.' I wasn't sure *where* to look but could feel her face close to mine, her hair gently brushing against my face. Her skin was as tanned and soft as suede. I could feel her firm bosom pressed against my chest and the inside of her thigh rubbing up against my leg each time we turned. Her eyes were dancing with the music. I'd never thought of waltzing as being sensuous but here on the floor with Mrs Edwards, to the sound of the Harry Dixon Trio, it got as seductive as it could be. I just wanted her to take me and teach me all that she knew, to smother me with kisses, to let me feel her hard breasts. But it was all fantasy. The dance ended and she slipped away from my dreams.

I felt that everybody must have been staring at me, wondering what we were up to, but when I returned to Andy it was never even mentioned. I thought he might have taken the piss, but not a word. Even Susan hadn't noticed. She came strolling over as the Harry Dixon Trio burst into their version of 'Let's Twist Again', and insisted on dragging me onto the floor for a dance. Yet, even though Susan's skirt finished halfway up her thighs, it didn't seem half as sensual as Mrs Edwards' firm breasts. I glanced in Mrs Edwards' direction as we danced and from the bar she flashed me a smile and a wink.

I hadn't told Susan about the following day. I left the subject until much later when I knew she'd be in a more responsive mood. It was almost 2 a.m. before I finally got around to telling her. By then she'd calmed down, had had a few drinks, a few dances and had begun to enjoy herself. We took a taxi home and as I kissed her outside her house I plucked up courage. 'Fancy coming to see Liverpool bringing the cup back tomorrow?' I asked, my hands slipping inside her blouse.

'Your hands are cold,' she sighed. 'When tomorrow?'

'Teatime, I think the train arrives about six-ish. It should be great. It's the first time they will ever have brought the cup home. An historic moment. They say that the day Liverpool bring the cup back to the city, the Liver Bird will up and fly off.' She laughed at that and wriggled closer to me. 'There should be a good few people there. It'll be fun. We could go and have a drink afterwards.' She thrust her pelvis hard against me. 'Liverpool! Is that all you think of?' she whispered, as she ran her tongue up and down my cheek. The cup final, a wedding and now this. It couldn't get any better.

'No,' I said. 'Most of the time I think of you.' She liked that, it encouraged her all the more. I'd obviously been forgiven, or maybe it was simply the drink.

But just as it was getting interesting a light flashed on in an upstairs room and a bedroom curtain flickered. I could just make out the silhouette of her mother. 'Damn!' said Susan. 'I was just beginning to enjoy that. I'd better go in soon or my mother'll be coming down.'

'So what about tomorrow?' I asked, anxiously. Much to my surprise, she wasn't wholly against the idea.

'Okay.' she said. 'The only problem is, I've promised to go and see my Auntie Jean in Tuebrook in the afternoon. Maybe I could meet you somewhere in Liverpool.' That was no problem, so we agreed to meet under the naked man above the entrance to Lewis's department store at 5.30 p.m. It was one of those favourite spots where people always meet up. I kissed her goodnight, quickly fumbled inside her blouse again, and danced my way home through the dimly lit streets, still bubbling on the adrenaline. It had been a long day: a cup final, a wedding and a bit of hanky-panky with Susan. What more could a man want?

The next day I took the train over to Liverpool and got off at Central Station. The train was fairly full but, if I thought that was bad, I was in for a shock when I saw the station. It was heaving. Lewis's was just outside the station but the exit was totally blocked by the crowd. It was impossible to get out. I went out by another exit and tried to head in the direction of Lewis's but again it was impossible. I was stranded and it was only 5.15 p.m. The team weren't scheduled to arrive at Lime Street until 6.25 p.m. The only ways I could go were either further into town or across the road. Getting any closer to Lewis's was simply out of the question. But what about Susan? I guessed she would have seen the crowd and turned tail. No way would she have managed to get anywhere near Lewis's.

I decided to dodge across the road and see if it was any easier on that side. It was, marginally, but by taking a few side roads I succeeded in finding a spot on the opposite side of the road from Lime Street station. The crowd around St George's Hall was as solid as could be imagined. It was a hundred deep. The entire St George's plateau bedecked in red. They were swarming all over the statue of Prince Albert on his horse: sitting alongside, on top of him, dangling from his shoulders. They were on the balcony of the Empire Theatre, clutching the hoarding that advertised their next production, *My Fair Lady*. To the left of the station Lime Street had been totally taken over by fans, filling almost every inch of the road, leaving just a narrow channel through which it was apparent the bus carrying the team would drive. Elsewhere it was one massive sea of humanity. Red scarves, red bobble hats, the occasional flag and banner. Trying to make my way any closer to the station was hopeless. I found myself pressed against the wall of the ABC Cinema but at least I could see something of the station. Fans had climbed lamp-posts, were hanging out of upstairs windows in the pubs of Lime Street and were perched on ledges high above the ground. Some twenty youths were even on the roof of the Crown Hotel. It seemed there was no room anywhere for anyone to move.

It was oppressive. A dullish May evening, the crowd expectant. Women were fainting left, right and centre. Over the road, on a high set of advertising hoardings, thirty or so lads were perched, acting as scouts. For almost an hour they kept up a chant of 'LIV-ER-POOL, bang, bang bang,' thumping their heels hard against the hoarding. Then as the sound suddenly rose to a crescendo you knew something was happening. Some lads had stood up and were now clapping while others banged even harder with their heels.

The crowd surged forward, pressing even more, and then out of the station came a procession of coaches, headed by a police car and lorry filled with photographers. Behind that, flanked by police motorbikes, came an open-topped coach bearing the placard 'Liverpool FC Cup Winners 1965'. And there on top of the first coach was the FA Cup, held aloft by captain Ron Yeats, dressed in a smart suit. And behind him waving to the crowds of delirious supporters was Bill Shankly himself. I gave him a special wave, hoping he might see me but in that vast crowd there was never a chance.

Suddenly people were chanting the name of Shankly to the same rhythmic clapping that they had used for Liverpool. It was bizarre, thousands were worshipping his name. It was as if he was some god or other. I'd heard the players' names chanted many times, particularly Ian St John, but never the manager. It was as if the crowd were acknowledging his role, the part he had played in transforming the club from a ramshackle second division outfit to league champions and cup-winners. He was their hero, the person who had masterminded the miracle. I jumped up and down, shouting, chanting along with everyone else. What would Uncle Horace and Auntie Gertie have thought to see this, their former next-door neighbour holding the cup up while his name was being chanted by thousands? It was bizarre, it was bedlam. I had never seen anything like it. And nor, for that matter, had football. Teams had brought the FA Cup home before but always to respectful, applauding crowds, never to a gathering like this and certainly never to this kind of adulation. It seemed the entire population of the city was on the streets and most of them were chanting Shankly's name.

The noise level rose to eardrum-bursting point as everyone, male, female, young, old, chanted 'SHANK-LEE, SHANK-LEE, SHANK-LEE.' And then, within a minute, they were gone, the three coaches steadily making their way down Lime Street and turning right at Lewis's before heading past Central Station, down Church Street and into Lord Street before making towards Castle Street and the Town Hall. And with that, everyone fell in behind the coaches and began racing after them, still cheering, still chanting his name.

It was only then that I realised just how many people were crammed into all the other streets. I had never seen such a crowd before. Bigger than VE Day, said the papers the next day. Bigger than the crowds that greeted Lord Kitchener's recruiting army. Bigger than the crowds that celebrated the ending of the Boer War. Bigger even than the crowd that welcomed home the British Expeditionary Force at the end of the First World War. It was the biggest crowd ever seen in the city centre. Never before had such a crowd greeted a football team. Not even Real Madrid, or the mighty Hungarians had received such adulation. It was more akin to a New York Yankees ticker tape welcome down Fifth Avenue. It was the beginning of something new, football fanaticism on a scale hitherto unknown in this country, or for that matter anywhere else.

It was almost impossible to move. Everyone was delirious with excitement. We climbed on people's backs, we hugged those standing next to us. 'Oh, when St John . . . oh, when St John . . . oh, when St John comes marching in,' we sang. Thousands spilled onto the roads, everyone pouring in one direction. Making any headway down Church Street was slow, the road becoming more and more densely packed as we neared the Town Hall. I decided to turn off Church Street and make my way through a side street that was not part of the route. The chances were that it would not be so busy. Unfortunately thousands of others had the same idea. But in the end I managed to squeeze onto the appropriately named St John Street. It was as tightly packed as imaginable. I was still a quarter of a mile from the Town Hall, which I could see in the distance, but getting any nearer was hopeless, so dense was the crowd.

I could just make out the figures of the players as they appeared one by one on the balcony of the Town Hall, the FA Cup glinting in the evening sunlight as it was lifted aloft, first by Ron Yeats and then by each member of the team in turn. Finally, Bill Shankly, dressed in red shirt and tie, kissed the cup and clutching it with both hands leaned over the balcony to the mightiest roar of the evening. And again the continual rhythmic clapping and chanting of 'LIV-ER-POOL, LIV-ER-POOL, LIV-ER-POOL', followed by 'SHANK-LEE, SHANK-LEE, SHANK-LEE'. In the side roads there were ambulances parked everywhere with St John officers treating the walking wounded and a hundred and one cases of heat exhaustion and fainting. It was chaotic. It was a city out of control, gone totally wild. On the television, later that evening, it was headline news. The cameras with the players on the balcony of the Town Hall scanned the streets and all that could be seen were ecstatic faces. A reporter described it as possibly the largest gathering of people ever seen in Britain. This was the beginning of football mania.

I took the ferry home, glad of the fresh air and the open space of the sea. On a choppy swell, we weaved in and out of the ships that were anchored in the river awaiting a berth. Behind us in the distance the Pier Head, the Liver Buildings and the Cunard offices. It was only then that I noticed. The Liver Bird: it was still there, gazing across the river from its high perch above the Liver Buildings. It hadn't flown away as folklore had foretold. I wondered how many other people had looked and smiled to themselves on seeing it still there. We'd won the cup and brought it home and still the Liver Bird remained. It seemed like a good omen. Then I remembered Susan.

As soon as I reached the top of our street I stopped off at the telephone box and rang her.

'And where were you?' she asked, tetchily.

'I couldn't get anywhere near Lewis's,' I explained. 'I came out of the station and there were thousands, the exists were crammed. It was impossible. Where were you?'

'I was at Lewis's, waiting for you.'

'Christ, how did you manage to get there?' I was completely taken aback. I had not for one moment imagined that she would have made it. I'm not quite sure what I did imagine but Susan waiting for me outside Lewis's was not it.

'I stood there for two hours waiting,' she said. 'I was terrified, I almost fainted. Everyone was pushing and shoving. It was awful. And now I'm tired and I want to go to bed.'

'I'm sorry,' I said, 'I didn't think you'd be there.'

'Well where did you think I'd be? I'm just sick of you and football. You think more of Liverpool than you do of me. I think it's about time you made your choice – me or Liverpool. I'm going to bed now. I'm tired. So think about it.' And with that she slammed down the phone.

I guessed she hadn't really meant it. Maybe she was right. Maybe I hadn't paid her enough attention lately. The FA Cup and the European Cup *had* been distracting. I decided to leave it a few days, let her cool down. Then I wouldn't have to confront her about going to Anfield on Tuesday evening to see Liverpool play Inter Milan in the semi-final of the European Cup. But it left me feeling despondent. I liked Susan. She was usually cheerful and bright. She was good fun. That's why she was so popular. What's more, she liked me and most of the time she showed it. I didn't want to lose her but I knew I'd have to work hard to talk her round.

'I'm knocking off at four,' announced Phil at lunchtime as he flicked a Subbuteo figure of Ian St John straight into the goal. The Polaris plans had been rolled up and the green beige Subbuteo pitch had been carefully laid down as we acted out that evening's European Cup semi-final against Inter Milan. Both Barry and Phil had been briefly assigned to the Polaris office. Phil was looking very smug with himself. 'There'll be bloody thousands going. You know what it was like on Sunday. They reckoned there were over half a million on the streets. The chances of getting in are zilch if you don't get there early.' We all looked at him, knowing that he was almost certainly right.

'How come you're getting away so early?' I asked.

'I've been in to see Ted and he says it's okay.'

'Right,' said Barry. 'That's it. I'm going in to see Ted as well.' He took careful aim and sent the ball spinning into the back of the net. 'Goal! 4–1 Liverpool.'

'You can't,' I replied. 'He'll say no.'

'I can but try. Phil's right, you know. We won't have a chance of getting in.' Immediately after lunch he was knocking on Ted's door. A couple of minutes later he emerged from his office, face beaming. 'No sweat,' he said. 'He says I can go at four.'

'Bloody hell!' I said, knowing that that left me in a spot. If I clocked off at five, as usual, the chances were that I wouldn't be at Anfield until six and by then the queues would be horrendous. 'I'm tellin' yer, everyone will be making for the ground straight from work. It's one of the biggest games in the club's history and everyone'll wanna see the cup as well.'

I needed to beat the rush hour. But the chances of me getting time off as well now looked decidedly slim as I would be the third to go begging to Ted.

'Go on,' said Barry encouragingly. 'He can only say no.'

So, off I went. Ted Nichols was a decent sort, creamy-faced and with a quiff of ginger hair, and although he was only in his late thirties he had recently been given an honour in the Queen's birthday list for services to the nation's defence. He was a man of few words but when he did speak it was usually gentle and thoughtful. He looked up and smiled as I walked in.

'Now, I wonder what you might want?' he asked, stretching back in his chair.

I returned his smile but before I could say anything he nodded. 'I suppose if I've agreed to one, I have to agree to you as well. Now bugger off. And don't send anyone else in. You're the last!'

'I'll give you a lift on the bike if you want,' suggested Barry, when he spotted me smiling as I came out of the office. 'We'll be there by five easily.'

'No, it's alright,' I said. 'I think me mate Andy down the yard wants to go as well. I'm off down the Engine Shop to check it out,' I added, donning white overalls and a tin hat. I told Alf my usual story, that I was going down to the slipway to check something out on the submarine. Ten minutes later I found Andy eating a sandwich and nattering to Martin.

'Fancy coming to the game tonight?' I asked.

'We won't get in, will we?' asked Andy, flinging a crust onto the floor.

'Well we will if we get there early. I've managed to get some time off. I'm leaving at four. Come on, you haven't been for ages. This is one night that you'll never forget.'

'Aye, okay. I suppose I could clock off early. I'll only lose half an hour's pay,' said Andy.

'Warra bout you Marty, fancy it?'

'Nah,' he replied, 'I'm seeing Karen tonight.'

'Bloody hell, Martin! You're getting worse than Billy. You're always seeing her these days. Are you in love or something?' He looked at us blankly.

'We're only goin' to the pictures,' he said, suddenly getting defensive. That was it, there was no persuading him. Anyhow, it would have been a miracle if he had said yes.

'How come you're not seeing Sue?'

'Christ! After Sunday? You're joking,' said Andy, sniggering.

'Why? What happened?' asked Martin.

'Oh, Christ, you haven't gone and told him, have you?'

Andy shook his head. 'No, honest, I haven't.'

But the cat was out of the bag, so I thought I might as well admit it.

'Oh, I lost her. I arranged to meet her in Liverpool on Sunday evening to see the cup coming back home and I couldn't find her.'

'Why not?'

'Why not? 'Cos there was fucking half a million people there. I'd said I'd meet her under Lewis's statue and I couldn't get anywhere near it. Never saw her all night. I rang her later and she went ape. Said she'd been there for hours and was scared stiff by the huge crowd. She told me to choose between her and Liverpool. Then she slammed the phone down on me.'

Martin burst out laughing. 'Not much choice there, then. I suppose it'll be Liverpool.'

'Bloody hell! You didn't tell me that bit,' interjected Andy. 'So what are you doing about her?'

'Oh, I'll just let her cool off, call her in a few days. She'll be alright then.'

'Aye, you wanna watch that Dave, you know,' said Martin. 'He was dancing a bit close to her the other night. Reckon she might have the hots for him. He fancies her, you know.' Andy laughed.

'He doesn't, does he?' I asked. And with that they both fell about laughing. I knew they were only joking but it made me think.

'I've got the car here,' said Andy.

'See you at the main gate, just after four,' I said, already relishing the prospect of a memorable evening.

Without the car it would have been well after five. The traffic was already heavy with thousands stringing along the Scotland Road and up Everton Valley. There was a palpable air of excitement. People were laughing and bounding along like kangaroos; red scarves were everywhere. The queues outside the Kop were building up and the turnstiles already open. We guessed there would be no problem getting in, it was just a matter of waiting and being patient. Half an hour later, though, and I would not have fancied our chances of making it.

By five thirty we were ensconced in the Kop – trapped might be a better description. Half an hour later, the gates were firmly closed, leaving us with a couple of hours of painful waiting. It was becoming the norm as Liverpool's increasing successes attracted bumper gates each game – twenty-five thousand on the Kop alone – and you were in the thick of it. It was like being in a sea, tossed gently backwards and forwards by a powerful swell over which you had no control. And when there was a corner or a goal incident down at the Kop end, the gentle sea became a mighty ocean in a storm, as the crowd, pushing themselves up on the shoulders of the man in front, spilled dangerously forward. From elsewhere in the ground you could see them tumble, chasms opening up, and then being swallowed again as the brief excitement ended. To say that it was dangerous is an understatement; to say that there was never an accident is a miracle. It was the stuff of young men, the thrill of the exuberance, the adrenaline of togetherness. Little wonder my father never enjoyed being on the Kop. One minute you were standing close to your pal, the next, the crowd had crashed forward, regrouped, and your friend was lost, carried away on a wave in this roaring sea of humanity. Another crashing wave and he'd suddenly reappear gasping for breath. You laughed and waited for the next storm. We'd invented crowd surfing long before the gig-goers of the 1990s. It was a chaos, a typically unrestrained Hieronymus Bosch painting. Wild faces, open mouths, a fog of steam and smoke, a sea of red and the continuous throb of noise.

To while away the time, we began to sing. Over the tannoy they always played the latest hits, usually those of one Liverpool group or other. By 1965 the charts had been invaded by a plethora of Liverpool groups. Not only the Beatles but also Gerry and the Pacemakers, Billy J Kramer, Cilla Black, the Searchers, the Swinging Blue Jeans. All of them had enjoyed number-one hits. The Mersey beat, as the papers dubbed it, had swept across the world. It was a new kind of music that found recognition among young people wherever it was heard. It seemed to epitomise the times. The Swinging Sixties had arrived.

They said that singing had first been heard on the Kop shortly after it was built in 1906. If it was, it was no more than the occasional chorus to accompany a parading band. In the 1940s they had community singing with the Kop regularly displaying its cynicism by changing the lyrics or even singing a totally different song from the one the band was playing. And then, as Liverpool climbed out of the second division, the Kop had invented chanting. Now it was taking things a step further. Singing wasn't unique at sporting events. The crowd at Cardiff Arms Park had sung Welsh hymns for years. But that was the Welsh, always singing – and always singing bloody hymns at that! But it had never been transferred to football. You didn't hear them singing at Ninian Park or Vetch Field. And nor had Welsh rugby union supporters ever sung the hits of the day, just bloody hymns.

And so we joined in the hits as they were played over the tannoy, in time adapting and changing the lyrics, to suit our team or opponents. It was those interminable hours of standing on the Kop, waiting for the game to start. Sometimes we'd be in the ground for hours before kick-off. It was too crammed to read, too uncomfortable to smoke, and the only sustenance that could be had was from a tea-bar perched up in the top corner. There was little to do but chat and sing.

Tonight the Kop was in full cry, as exuberant as it had ever been. To a small group of Italian fans squeezed into the Kop end of the Kemlyn Road stand we explained, in no certain terms, who had won the war. Well, it was only 20 years since hostilities had ceased. And, if they didn't already know, we informed them that Mussolini was dead. And to the tune of that Italian favourite 'Santa Lucia' we told them to 'Go back to Italy.' But most of all we repeatedly chanted for the FA Cup. We all wanted to see it again. Sunday had given us a flavour, the cup was back in the city, now we wanted to see it for the first time at Anfield.

I soon lost Andy in the crowd as wave upon wave of bodies cascaded past me. And then Inter Milan appeared, racing towards us for their pre-match kick-in. A wall of whistles greeted them. How dare they? Did they not understand that this was the Liverpool end? They quickly turned tail and ran in the opposite direction. A flag of surrender might just as well have been raised at that moment. But more was to come. The cry of 'ee-aye-addio, we wanna see der cup' grew louder as kick-off approached. And then Liverpool appeared to a cacophony of sound, a roar that could surely be heard across the Mersey. The eleven men ran down the pitch towards us. Then, out of the tunnel appeared the injured Gerry Byrne and Gordon Milne, holding aloft the FA Cup glittering in the lights of Anfield. It was a Shankly masterstroke. Neither before, nor since, has Anfield ever witnessed such a scene of delirium and noise. Slowly the pair walked around the pitch, down to the Anfield Road end and past the Kemlyn Road stand before reaching us in the Kop. The hairs on the back of the neck stood as rigid as the Inter Milan players, who watched in disbelief. Grown men cried. We hugged each other, pressed on each other's shoulders and spilled in torrents down the Kop. We had a taste of glory and we wanted more.

Within four minutes we were a goal ahead. At half-time we led 2–1. And then, with fifteen minutes remaining, St John made it 3–1. There had never been anything like it. We were surely on course to reach the final, the first English club to do so. As the teams left the pitch, Shankly turned and waved to the Kop. It was a calculated wave, an acknowledgement to the fans that they had played their role. This was it. This was what it was all about. An all-consuming commitment to your team. It didn't get any better. Following them to Wembley, bringing the cup back home, cheering from the Kop, humiliating the world's number-one side and on the verge of a place in the European Cup final. This was what belonging to Liverpool was all about: the Liverpool family. Loyalty, passion, belief – it was something you could almost touch. It had an enduring and authentic quality. We might have had our bad points but you couldn't doubt our loyalty. Life would never be quite the same again. It was a contract and I had signed up for life. In a way, Shankly was right, football was a religion and I had been converted. It was a bit like Catholicism; once a Catholic, always a Catholic. I had entered through the portals of the church and been blessed. I was here to stay. At that point it seemed I could never be separated from my city, from my team.

fourteen

A Bloody Nose

A year later, Liverpool were champions once more. Two titles and an FA Cup – all within a couple of seasons. It was heady stuff. And within days of the title being clinched we were off to Glasgow to see Liverpool face Borussia Dortmund in the final of the European Cup-winners Cup. Barry and I had watched all the European home games – Juventus, Standard Liege, Honved, Celtic – and no way were we going to pass up the opportunity of seeing them win a European trophy. We had already suffered a major disappointment. As the last four teams went into the semi-final draw, the hope was that Liverpool and Glasgow Celtic would be drawn apart. We were eagerly anticipating a final against Celtic at Hampden in front of 120,000. Sadly, it was not to be as we drew Celtic in the semi-final. That clash was, in itself, one of the most memorable nights in Anfield's history.

All day it rained, through murky Preston, through the soaking Borders and into the grey mists of industrial Strathclyde. You could barely see Glasgow. A damp smog hung over the city, the pallid buildings merging into the greyness of the rain. We were turfed off the train. Briefly raising a rousing chorus or two, we marched off, dispersing into the drizzle and haze of no-man's land.

For a short while we sheltered in the shops, finally growing weary, then ate fish and chips in a shop doorway until the soggy newspaper finally dribbled into pieces. After that we hung around until the pubs opened before marching towards Hampden.

'The rain has to stop sometime,' promised Barry, as he wiped his steamed-up glasses and peered into his pint. But it didn't. It poured the entire evening, sending streams of water gushing down the empty terraces. Pools gathered near the pitch, around the dugout and on the track.

We were a sorry bunch. The Celtic supporters stayed at home. The terraces, where near on 150,000 had once gathered to cheer on Scotland against the old enemy, stood bare and sad. Only 41,000 spectators showed up, a fraction of what we had expected. They were virtually all Liverpool fans. It couldn't get worse. But of course it did. Borussia won 2–1 in extra time with a fierce shot from Libuda that was disastrously deflected into the net by Ron Yeats. There was little he could do about it. We tramped back to the station. It was still raining and we were drenched to the bone. On the train Barry peeled off his trousers and tried to dry them on the heater until the ticket inspector made him put them back on. We had no food, no money, we were dripping wet, hungry, thirsty, and defeated. It was enough to make you want to start going shopping on a Saturday afternoon. Never let it be said that supporting a football team is easy. On the contrary, it can be an ordeal. And we were suffering.

It's tempting to say that World Cup fever gripped Merseyside that summer but sadly it isn't true. The fact is that the nation didn't really get excited until we had actually won the cup, and, anyhow, on Merseyside we enjoyed something of a detached enthusiasm for the England team. We were always for the underdog and England did not represent the underdog. The underdog was North Korea.

Goodison Park and Old Trafford had been chosen as the northwest venues for the Group Three matches. That meant we welcomed the holders Brazil, along with Bulgaria, Hungary and Portugal. Peter and I were ecstatic at the prospect of seeing the likes of the Brazilians Pele, Gilmar, Gerson, Garrincha, and Jairzinho, while Portugal boasted Europe's finest player – Eusebio

– plus a few others. As for Hungary, it wasn't that long since the Mighty Magyars had humiliated England one misty afternoon at Wembley.

It all began well enough for the Brazilians as they beat Bulgaria 2–0 in the opening game at Goodison. Pele and Garrincha scored. Meanwhile, predictably, Portugal beat Hungary 3–1 at Manchester. Then came a classic at Goodison as Hungary, reminiscent of their forebears, defeated the ageing Brazilians 3–1 in pouring rain. The star of the show was a young Hungarian, Albert, who ran the Brazilians ragged with his mercurial sprints and passes. The Portuguese then beat the Bulgarians at Old Trafford and suddenly Brazil were in danger of being eliminated. The crunch came at Everton as the two-time winners met the new-found arrogance of Portugal. In a desperate effort to stay in the competition, Brazil had made nine changes, giving World Cup debuts to no fewer than seven newcomers. A barely fit Pele returned to the action but after being hacked down a couple of times by the disrespectful Portuguese, he limped off draped in a grey blanket, his World Cup over for another four years. Peter and I watched disgusted, ashamed that the Portuguese should have resorted to such tactics when they boasted such talent themselves. Portugal and Hungary were through to the quarter-finals and we sat back to welcome the return of Portugal to Goodison, this time to face the surprise package of the competition, North Korea, who had humiliated the might of Italy at Ayresome Park. It was the biggest shock since the USA had humbled England in Belo Horizonte sixteen years earlier. Portugal, of course, would be a different matter.

Peter and I crammed into the Gwladys Street end of Goodison Park, along with his brother and another sixty thousand, in anticipation of watching Pele's heir apparent. '6–0,' said Peter. His brother nodded in agreement. 'And Eusebio'll get a hat-trick.'

It only took 40-odd seconds for that prediction to be overturned as North Korea shot into a sensational lead. We shrugged our shoulders and then watched in growing admiration as the plucky Koreans continued to take the game to the Portuguese. But none of us dared imagine what was about to happen. It took another 20 minutes for Korea to score a second goal. And then, two minutes later, we could barely believe what we were seeing as the North Koreans snatched a third to make it 3–0. There was stunned silence all around Goodison. This was the signal for a dramatic U-turn by the crowd. Until then we had expected an emphatic victory by the tournament's new favourites, Portugal, but now we delighted in seeing the form book turned upside down. The chant went up for North Korea. In a way, that was their undoing. The North Koreans, intoxicated by the adrenaline of the crowd, carried on attacking, regardless. They should have sat back and protected their lead. Instead they went in search of more goals. Eusebio, now playing the game of his life, began almost single-handedly to demolish a dream. By half-time it was 3–2 with both goals coming from the Benfica star. You could see what was coming. Nevertheless, we carried on cheering for the naïve little men from the other side of the world. But it was not to be. In the second half Eusebio added two more goals to his tally and even had a hand in his team's fifth goal as Portugal eventually ran out 5–3 winners. We had seen a game that would live on in the memory and we had played our part in the carnival as well, roaring our support for the underdog. Sod England, we wanted the North Koreans to win the World Cup.

By 1967 Bill Shankly was well on his way to becoming a footballing legend. He had become the most successful Liverpool manager in history. Two league titles, the FA Cup and European Cup-winners Cup finalists were enough to endear him to any Liverpool fan. But more than that, he had also endeared himself to the wider community. Even Evertonians grudgingly acknowledged that he was something special. Shankly's one-liners, his anecdotes, his enthusiasm were turning him into a footballing favourite. He was a gift to the media. And yet he could so easily have become a comic character. What made him so endearing was that much that he said had a ring of truth about it. 'Our grass is greener than theirs.' Well, it might or might not have been, but you understood what he was getting at. 'Football is more important than life.' Of course it wasn't, but football fans understood precisely what he was implying. He was a showman and an impresario. But he was also a preacher. He had a strong moral code, a respect for old-fashioned values, a decency and a faith in the working man. He believed the fans were far more important than anyone else in the game, more important than the players, directors, managers. It was the fans who put money in the players' pockets every week and the fans to whom they should be thankful. It was the latter sentiment that perhaps endeared him most to Liverpudlians and football fans everywhere. Shankly had come as a stranger to the city of Liverpool. Within five years the city had opened its heart to him. Had he stood for Mayor he would have been elected unopposed. Nobody had a bad word to say of him. Admiration for Shankly had scaled new heights.

And yet there was humiliation for us that season. We were in the European Cup again and so had a chance to eradicate the nightmares of Hampden and our devastating 3–0 defeat against Inter Milan at the San Siro the season before that. But it did not go according to plan. In the preliminary round we came unstuck against the unknown Romanian outfit Petrolul Ploietsi. We won comfortably enough at Anfield but then lost 3–1 in the wilds of Romania. We needed the replay in Brussels to assure us of a place in the next round where we found ourselves facing the little-known team Ajax of Amsterdam. It was the last time they would ever be referred to as the 'little-known'. And once more the weather dealt us a cruel blow. The mist drifted in off the North Sea and shrouded Amsterdam in a blanket of fog. It was impossible to see one side of the pitch from the other. Shankly even claimed to have walked on the pitch and to have chatted to some of the players, all unnoticed by the referee or the other officials. Liverpool lost 5–1 and, although we blamed the fog, the fact was that we had especially failed to cope with a young lad called Johan Cruyff. Still, we'd do them at Anfield.

Shankly was defiant. That late away goal by Chris Lawler would save us, he claimed. We only needed to win 4–0. For days he ranted to anyone willing to listen about how the game should never have been allowed to continue and what we'd do to Ajax once we had them on Merseyside. When a misguided journalist pointed out that the fog affected both sides, Shankly simply told him that Ajax knew the pitch better than we did. No problem, of course we'd cuff them. I was taken in just as much as the rest of the 53,000 who turned up convinced that we could do it. Oh dear! After a goalless first half and a peerless display of passing, Rinus Michel's side went ahead shortly after the interval. Liverpool soon equalised but it was obvious to everyone, and probably Shankly as well, that there was no coming back. It ended 2–2.

As we tumbled out of the Kop, I wondered aloud if Liverpool weren't looking a little weary. Roger Hunt had been a star of England's exhausting World Cup victory during the summer, Ian Callaghan had also been involved, and the efforts of the previous season looked to have taken their toll on the others. In hindsight, it was indeed the beginning of the end of that glorious Liverpool side.

''Ave any of you lot done anything for dis thesis for general studies?' asked Gobbo, as he shovelled another load of chips into his mouth. It was little wonder he looked sickly and overweight. Around the table, heads shook. We were sitting in the canteen at the local technical college having our lunch. I was obliged to come here one day a week to study for a diploma in naval architecture. It sounded grand but was possibly the dullest course ever devised by academia. Equally I was probably the most obtuse student to have ever undertaken such a course.

The college was one of those precise, early-sixties constructions, overloaded with glass, characterless and with possibly the most inhospitable canteen ever known to mankind. The food was simply appalling. At lunchtime and in the evening we were forced to eat chips with either beans, fish or cheese pie. Even the pigs would have turned up their snouts at this grub. It was inedible. But there was little alternative.

Frank was the only one prepared to own up to having done any work. 'I've been doing something about mountaineering,' he admitted, raising his voice to overcome the noise of rattling cutlery. We all knew Frank was a fanatical climber, off to Snowdonia every weekend. 'It's about the Alps, and climbing the north face of the Eiger. I'm going to go there one day and climb it,' he said. Gobbo stared at him. 'Seriously,' added Frank.

'Warra bout you?' asked Gobbo, turning towards me.

'I'm not going to climb the fucking Eiger.'

'No, the essay, dickhead.' Everyone laughed.

'Well, I've got a few ideas.'

'Such as?'

'I'm not going to tell you.'

'Fuckin' teacher's pet, you are? Wants to keep it for Mr Latham. Fuckin' bum boy, that Latham is, with his dicky bow and poncy walk. Old queer. And look at your hair. You look like a fuckin' girl with hair that long. Fuckin' Linda, that's what we should call you.'

'Well, I was thinking about doing something about T E Lawrence.'

'Tommy Lawrence? What do you mean, Tommy Lawrence!'

There are times when you know you should never have opened your mouth. This was one such occasion and I was about to compound it.

'No! I mean Lawrence of Arabia. I've been reading a book about him.'

'Warra yer readin' a book about 'im for Linda?' he asked, queue for much sniggering.

'It's quite interesting. I saw the film and then spotted this book in the library, so I borrowed it.' Gobbo rolled his eyes.

''Ee was a queer as well, wasn't he?'

'I dunno.'

'Ballocks, of course he was. He used to shag little boys. I've seen the movie as well. There's those two little Arab boys following him around everywhere, doing everything they can for him. Him and bloody Latham.'

'Well, it didn't say that in the film, did it?'

'Everyone knows he was a queer. What's it say in that book of yours.'

'Haven't got to that bit yet.'

'You're well suspect you are Linda,' laughed Gobbo from across the canteen table. 'We all know you went to that Magic Clock pub the other week.'

'That was just for a look.'

'Just for a look, my arse. You don't go to a queer pub just to look.'

'Well, we did.'

'And now yer reading about Lawrence of Arabia.'

I tried to explain that, no, I wasn't gay. And I wasn't so sure that T E Lawrence was either, but my argument seemed to be falling on deaf ears. I decided to let the subject drop and returned to my attempts at eating a plate of dried chips and beans.

'Christ, this food is shite,' muttered Peter, pushing his plate aside. Most of us nodded in approval, apart from Gobbo, who picked up his plate and wandered off to get some more. He was the only one of us who could stomach it, but at least it allowed us a brief respite from his prejudices.

Peter had only lasted a couple of years at Ford's. The money was good but he soon found the pace of the production line at the new factory too stressful. That, coupled with the hour-long journey to Halewood, had left him debilitated and sick one winter. He took to his bed and didn't budge for a month. 'Couldn't you get yourself a different job?' I suggested. He agreed. 'That's what my dad says as well.' So, instead of trekking to Ford's, he was now cycling just a few miles to a new factory within spitting distance of the seagulls and windy sea front at Moreton, where they made chocolate. The result of all this was that Peter now found himself sitting next to me in the canteen at the same technical college. And due to my declining academic progress we had even wound up in the same mechanical-engineering class. All those years knowing him and this was the first time we had ever sat in the same classroom; at last, a sectarian-free education.

'Take no notice of him,' he urged, as he spotted Gobbo ambling back in our direction with another plateful of chips that resembled the wood clippings gardeners throw onto flower borders. 'He's just an ignorant git.' Gobbo sat down and chomped in silence but I could tell his mind was churning. He wasn't going to let up.

I was studying a cocktail of subjects including mechanical engineering, naval architecture, engineering drawing, maths and general studies. After successfully completing three years I would be awarded an Ordinary National Diploma in naval architecture. After that, a further two years would bring a Higher National Diploma. Well, that had been the plan. Such a dream might have been part of my initial ambition but within months any such thoughts had quickly been eradicated.

I failed one subject in my first year and, although I was allowed to progress to the second year, I was forced to repeat the subject I'd failed. I failed it again the following year, but this time I was not allowed to progress to the third year. Instead I found myself repeating what I had done the previous year. And so it went on until eventually they decided that I should drop the Ordinary National Diploma altogether and instead sit for a much simpler, craft-based qualification in mechanical engineering – the one most apprentices down the yard were tackling. It was a disastrous decision. The work might have been less demanding but I still managed to fail. The reason was fairly obvious. It was mindlessly boring and I loathed every minute of it. I was now going backwards. At this rate I was likely to be repeating the O-levels I had already passed. And no doubt I would fail those as well. Gobbo had also failed his exams, though in his case it was a lack of ability rather than effort.

The remainder of the lunchtime passed in unpleasant silence and the approach of two o' clock came as a relief. I picked up my bag and umbrella and marched off down the corridor towards the classroom with Peter in tow and my stomach churning with dried chips and mashed baked beans. Gobbo followed, not too far behind. I could hear him and some of the others snorting.

'Hey Linda! Yer look a right fuckin' ponce with dat umbrella,' he was saying for the benefit of anyone within listening distance, and deliberately loud enough for me to hear. I decided to ignore him. 'Look at him, marching along with his tight little arse. You're a freak Linda, a fuckin' hipless freak.' Inside the classroom little was happening. It seemed our teacher was off ill and we were awaiting a replacement. Gobbo sat behind Peter and me.

'Hey, Linda,' he started up again. 'Suppose you're looking forward to seeing your friend Mr Latham later, aren't you? Nice little teacher's friend. Yes, Mr Latham, no, Mr Latham, three bags fuckin' full, Mr Latham.'

With that I'd had enough. I turned and snapped at him. 'Fuckin' shurrup, will yer? Yer just an ignorant twat.'

Unfortunately, it was just what he wanted to hear. It gave him an excuse. With one grand gesture he simply butted me in the face, his forehead meeting the bridge of my nose with the kind of vengeance that Ron Yeats might head a ball out of defence. Blood began to dribble out of my nose and down my face. Tears welled up in my eyes. He reached forward, ready to repeat the action, but was pulled back. There was a commotion. Peter was now threatening him. I'd been humiliated. 'Want to make something of it?' he was asking Peter, as the two squared up. At that point the cavalry arrived in the barrel shape of George Moston, our stand-in mechanical-drawing teacher. He could see something had happened but didn't want to get too involved. 'Go clean yourself up,' he suggested as I hugged a handkerchief to my face pathetically. I declined his offer, aware that to leave the classroom would only add further to the humiliation I had already suffered. He shrugged his shoulders and the class settled down to producing yet another reduced-scale drawing of a ship's double bottom.

Over tea, Peter was suitably sympathetic. 'He'll only try and wind you up again,' he urged, as we sat down to another plateful of chips, this time with cheese pie, in the sombre half-lit canteen. Nobody was saying much, especially to me. Gobbo and the others sat at the other end of the table. I was the leper of the group, stuck down the far end with Peter. 'It could be worse,' said Peter. 'Just think, you could be a Tranmere supporter. Then you'd really have something to be miserable about.'

General studies for most was as tedious a subject as could be imagined, a pot-pourri of politics, media, art, music and anything else under the sun that Harold Latham, our teacher, fancied exploring. For me, it was the one bit of light relief in the day, just about the only subject I found in any way stimulating.

Harold Latham was indeed a dapper character with his silvery hair and bow tie, but this evening his usual good humour had given way to an unusual anger. Not surprising, really, when you had to spend your evening in this burial chamber teaching the likes of us. Apart from Frank nobody had much idea what they were going to write about for their dissertations. That made Latham even more unhappy. Gobbo snarled behind cupped hands. The rest sniggered. Given the events of earlier in the day, I decided to keep my head down and remain silent.

'Could I do something about Coronation Street?' asked one of the second-year apprentices. Everyone burst out laughing. Mr Latham tried to be accommodating. 'Well, what, exactly?'

'I dunno.'

Harold looked at him, exasperated. 'Well, you could look at the programme's importance. I mean, why do people watch it?' The lad shrugged.

'Well, do *you* watch it?' asked Harold.

'No, well, sometimes. Me mum watches it, though.' There was more laughter. Harold was banging his head against a brick wall and was finally losing patience. 'What about you?' he asked, suddenly putting me on the spot. 'You're usually full of ideas.' This was the question I was dreading.

'Well, I thought possibly of doing something about apartheid, but I really wondered if I could write something about Bill Shankly.' There were hoots of laughter. Harold told everyone to shut up.

'Bill Shankly? The Liverpool manager?' he asked quizzically. I nodded.

'Why do you want to do something about him?'

'Well, I'm a Liverpool supporter, you see, and I've met him.'

'Like 'ell you have,' muttered Gobbo.

'Yes, he has,' shouted Peter jumping to my aid. 'I've seen a photograph of him and Shankly.' The class was in danger of getting out of hand.

'Go on. Tell me why you want to write about him?'

'Well, I think he's a very interesting man. He's very political, a socialist. He worked down the mines.'

'So what would you write about?'

'I'd write something about his career and about the fact that he's a socialist. I read an interview he'd done in a newspaper and he talked about working down the mines and why he believes in socialism and trade unions, so I'd base some of it on that. And he's something of a hero now in Liverpool, people look up to him.'

'Well, I think that's quite interesting.'

'Go 'way sir,' yelled Gobbo.

'If he can write about Shankly, can I write about the Golden Vision, sir?' asked someone else.

'Who's the Golden Vision?' asked Harold.

'Christ, don't you know sir? It's Alex Young of Everton.'

Harold still looked blank. 'Well, I don't mind who you write about as long as you can manage two thousand words.'

'Two thousand words, sir? Bloody hell, that's a lot! That's a book, that is.'

'If nobody else has got any sensible ideas, why don't you all go off to the library for an hour and look at some books. See if you can get some ideas. Be back here for eight o'clock.' He told me to remain behind.

'That's quite an interesting idea you've got there,' he said, turning to me, once everyone had left the room. 'Do you think you can write two thousand words?'

'Yeah,' I said. 'I don't see why not. I like writing, I've written a few articles for the union journal.'

'What about?'

'Well, I did one about apartheid and I did another about the shipbuilding industry.'

'I'd like to see them.'

'I did have another idea but I didn't want to mention it with everyone else around 'cos they'd only take the piss. I had thought of doing something about T E Lawrence.' Harold looked at me puzzled.

'You mean Lawrence of Arabia? I take it you've seen the film.'

'Yes, I think he's really interesting. I think his role in the Middle East in the First World War was crucial. There's a lot we still don't know about. And then after the war he felt that he was let down when they carved up the Middle East in the Treaty of Versailles. He'd made promises to people but the governments of Europe didn't keep those promises. He was never the same after that.'

'You really are interested in politics, aren't you?'

'Well, I'm quite involved with the union. I'm on a few committees and I've done the articles.'

'Writing something about Lawrence would be very difficult. Have you read any books about him?'

'I'm halfway through *The Seven Pillars of Wisdom*. My girlfriend works in the library, so she's ordered some books for me.'

'Good. Well, it's up to you, Bill Shankly, T E Lawrence, I don't mind which. I've noticed you've always got something to say in class. Always got an opinion. You seem to be interested in what's going on around you. What do you want to do with your life?'

'I don't know. I don't particularly like working at Laird's but I'm not sure what I really want to do.'

'Have you ever thought about studying something like politics or sociology?'

'Socio what?'

'Sociology, it's the way society works, about how we live our lives, things like social problems, families, communities, political systems and so on.'

'No.'

'Why not?'

'Well, I'm not that bright. I've only got a few GCEs. I can't even pass the exams here. Anyhow, I didn't know you could study politics.'

'Of course you can, it's just like any other subject.'

'That sounds good. And where would I study it?'

'Well, you could do an A-level or you could go to an evening class. Studying politics is something that needs a more mature approach, knowing a little bit about life. Your trade union activities would help you enormously.'

'Do you think so?'

'It's not just about being bright, you know. There's much more to learning than being intelligent. It's about motivation and application, having the determination to succeed. You can have all the qualifications in the world but if you haven't got the focus and determination to do something with them, then you'll not be as successful as maybe you could be. In fact, it's still possible to go to university at your age, even older. There are colleges for mature students. I went to college when I was thirty. I used to work as a clerk in a bank, hated it. I was a bit like you. I got interested in the union and decided to get myself an education. But I'm not really interested in football, I'm afraid. I don't know anything about Bill Shankly. And I certainly didn't know what you've just been telling me about him. But it's obviously of interest to a lot of people.'

Someone burst into the room. 'Hey, sir! There's a fight! Gobbo and your mate are 'avin' a go at each other.' We all rushed out to see the two of them scrapping all over the floor farther down the corridor. Other classroom doors were being flung open to find out what the commotion was. Harold ran towards them but was beaten to it by at least two other teachers who pulled the pair apart. Gobbo had blood trickling from his nose and was breathing heavily; Peter was even paler than usual, his hands trembling and his hair ruffled The two pulled themselves up and were promptly frogmarched in the direction of the office of Bill Webster, the notorious College Kommandant whose reputation stretched from one side of the Mersey to the other, and no doubt to Germany and back as well. It didn't look good.

'What was all that about?' asked Harold, as we strolled back towards the classroom.

'I think it was something to do with me. They'd been taking the mickey out of me earlier. It was partly to do with that Lawrence of Arabia idea. That's why I didn't want to mention it in class. Gobbo had a go at me. He head-butted me and Peter nearly had a fight with him then. But Mr Moston came into the classroom before anything happened.'

'Christ! When will you lads learn?' The fracas had disrupted any hope of concentrated thought. Once Harold had everyone back in class he told us to come up with an idea by the following week and then dismissed us all half an hour early. I wandered down the stairs, deliberately sauntering past Webster's office, half expecting to hear screams as someone's nails were ripped from their fingers. As I turned the corner, I spotted Harold coming down the stairs from the opposite direction and heading towards Webster's office. He knocked on the door and went in. I decided to sit on the steps by the college entrance and wait for Peter. It was the least I could do, even though it might mean a further confrontation with Gobbo.

I didn't have to wait too long. Ten minutes later Peter appeared, swinging his rucksack over his shoulder.

'What happened?'

'He's giving Gobbo a right ballocking.'

'Warra bout you.'

'Nuthin'. Harold came into Webster's office and we were sent outside for a few minutes. Then I was called back in, told to grow up and not try settling scores with my fists, and then told to go home. Gobbo's still in there with Webster laying into him. It's a bit odd, really, 'cos Webster was giving us all hell until Harold appeared. Do you think Harold said something to Webster?'

'Well, he asked me what had happened, so I told him about this afternoon and how Gobbo had hit me and had then threatened you. Maybe he went and told Webster.'

'Bloody hell! Good old Harold!'

'I think I owe him one,' I said.

'I think maybe we both do,' replied Peter as we jumped on the bus.

'So? What happened between you and Gobbo?' I asked, as we settled down. 'Nuthin'. Doesn't matter. But I gave him one. Got my punch in first. Stuck one right on his nose, I did.' He started chuckling. 'Hey, are you really going to write something about Bill Shankly?'

'I don't know. I told Harold about the Lawrence of Arabia idea as well, and he quite liked that. What do y' reckon?'

'I reckon you should do Shankly. Much more interesting. Maybe I should do Matt Busby.'

I didn't take much persuading. Shankly it was, although Susan was a bit annoyed after she'd ordered all those books on T E Lawrence. 'I'd still like to read them, though,' I told her.

But writing something about Bill Shankly proved far more difficult than I had envisaged. At least with T E Lawrence there were books I could refer to. With Shankly there was nothing. I looked through some old programmes and found one or two articles about his career but I was struggling and beginning to wish I'd opted for Lawrence. I decided to seek Harold's advice.

'Well, it's a challenge,' he said, 'and the real task is for you to overcome that challenge. Lawrence would certainly be easier but with Shankly you'd be doing something original. Have you thought of writing to him, asking him if he'll do an interview? Then you could ask him all the questions you need to know, about his career and about his beliefs.'

'I think he'd be too busy to talk to me, although I did write to him once before, when I was after a cup final ticket.'

'And did he reply?'

'Yes, and I went to the ground and saw him and he gave me a ticket. He used to live next door to my uncle and aunt in Huddersfield and I met him when I was quite small and had my photograph taken with him.'

'Well, you could remind him all about that in your letter and tell him that you're doing the project for college. He might agree to meet you.' And so, out came the typewriter again and I composed yet another letter to the great man.

Dear Mr Shankly,

You may remember that we have met in the past. You were the next door neighbour to my uncle and aunt when you lived in Huddersfield. One day I had my photograph taken with you. I also wrote to you before the FA Cup final and came to see you at Anfield. You very kindly found a ticket for me. I wondered if you might be able to help me again. I have to write a 2,000 word project for my course work at technical college and I have chosen to write something about you. I don't know whether you

have any information about your career which you could send
me or anything which you have written. I'd really like to come
and interview you but I realise that you are a very busy man. If
it is possible, could I come and interview you one evening as I
work during the day, or at a weekend. I look forward to hearing
from you.

Yours sincerely,

Stephen Kelly

Writing to Shankly had once more jogged my memory about the
old photograph of the two of us at Uncle Horace's house. So I
began yet another search through all the old albums and bundles
of photographs, this time more determined than ever to unearth
it. I pulled out the red-backed album containing all my mother's
family pictures, but I drew a blank. There were plenty of pictures
of Horace and Gertie, even one or two of them with me, but none
with Bill Shankly. Next, I went through the box containing mostly
my father's family. But again I failed to find what I was looking
for. I spent two hours assiduously searching, but still nothing. It
had been lost. It was depressing. I hated losing things. It was
illogical. How could it possibly be lost? Things were only ever
mislaid. It was a prize, something that I ought to have been able
to keep for the whole of my life. I even began to wonder if such a
picture actually existed. It was so long ago. The memory could be
playing tricks.

'If you do go to see him, maybe you could take a camera with you
and have another picture taken,' suggested my mother. Well, it
was a good idea. A couple of days later a letter arrived.

Liverpool Football Club Ltd., Anfield Road, Liverpool 4.
Telegraphic Address: Goalkeeper.

Dear Stephen,

Thank you for your letter. Unfortunately I do not have any
written information about my career as a professional
footballer and manager. However I would be delighted to let
you come and interview me. If you could come to my house one
Sunday afternoon I am sure that I would be able to spare you

*half an hour or so to talk about my career. I hope that this will
be okay.*

Yours sincerely,

W. Shankly
Manager

Although the letter was on official Liverpool-Football-Club-
headed notepaper, he had handwritten his own address at the top
of the page.

'I think I have an idea where that is,' said Dad. 'I'll check with
some of the lads at work, they'll know. I'll drive you over if you like.'
And so, after lunch one Sunday, we sped through the Mersey
Tunnel and made our way to West Derby. The house was situated
down a neat cul-de-sac, ironically, at the back of Everton's training
ground. 'He probably decided to buy this house so that he could
spy on Everton from his bedroom window while they were
training,' joked Dad. He probably wasn't far off the mark. They
were pleasant houses, not dissimilar from Uncle Horace's old
house in Huddersfield: neat, semi-detached, thirties-built,
suburban with three bedrooms and a pinch of a garden at the front.
I was shaking. What if he wasn't in? Would he still remember the
letter? Would he be busy? Maybe he'd still be down at the training
ground or doing something important with his family. 'Go on,' said
Dad, 'he won't bite. Now, have you got everything you need?' I had.
I'd even persuaded Andy to let me borrow his small tape recorder
so that I could record the interview.

'I'll wait here,' said Dad. Give me a call when you've finished and
I'll come and take a photograph of the two of you.'

I knocked nervously on the door. No answer. I knocked again,
still no answer. I looked towards Dad sitting in the car. I began to
walk away, but just as I reached the garden gate the front door shot
open.

A pretty girl, roughly the same age as me, was standing in the
doorway. She was wearing a short, dark skirt and a white blouse.
'Is it the paper boy?' asked an unmistakable voice from behind her.
'I don't think so,' she said, moving aside to allow the familiar figure
of Bill Shankly through the porch. As I approached the door, I
noticed the girl had soft blue eyes.

'Oh, hello Mr Shankly,' I said explaining the reason for my calling.

'Aye, I do remember. You wanted to do an interview. Aye, well, yes, you best come in,' he said.

'Are you sure you're not too busy?'

'No, no problem. Go sit yourself in the room there. Would you like a cup of tea?' And off he went to make the tea. From upstairs I could hear a record player, the sound of the Beach Boys. I guessed the girl must be in her bedroom. I looked around the room, searching for signs of a footballing career, but there were none. It was a tidy room with a few newspapers scattered around. A television sat in the corner. There was a glass-fronted bookcase containing a couple of dozen books, some encyclopaedias and an orderly stack of *Reader's Digest*s. I sat on the settee, took out my tape recorder, and a pencil and paper. I'd made a list of questions. A minute later, he popped his head round the door. 'Milk and sugar?' I nodded. He spotted my tape recorder. 'Are you wanting to record this? Well, I'll just go and tell the girls to turn the music down a bit.' And with that he bounded up the stairs.

'So, this is for your college work is it?' he asked, as he returned to the room. 'I don't think I've ever been interviewed for a college project before, usually just newspapermen. Wonderful thing, education. Very important. I didn't have much, you know.'

I pulled out an old photograph of Uncle Horace and Auntie Gertie that I'd decided to bring along to show him. He leaned forward, with his elbows on his knees. 'Oh yes, I remember Horace and his wife. Always had such a nice garden. My wife was very fond of your aunt. Aye. And are your uncle and aunt still alive?'

'No, they both died a few years ago.'

'Oh, I am sorry. We used to get a Christmas card off them. Right then, what is it you want to know?' I pressed the on-button on the tape recorder and for more than an hour we chatted about his career with Carlisle and Preston, and then his managerial days with Carlisle, Grimsby, Workington and Huddersfield, and, of course, his war days. And in between, our conversation was peppered with his home-spun philosophy. As he spoke, you could see the energy in his eyes as they gripped you in his gaze. He reminded me of McGill: authoritative, yet equally persuasive. He could not have been kinder. On a Sunday afternoon, when there were surely more fruitful ways of spending his time, he was devoting an hour or more to chatting to a fan.

'I get people coming here all the time,' he joked. 'They just knock on the door wanting an autograph, wanting to talk about football, wanting to tell me all sorts about the team. Sometimes they want to tell me off, tell me I'm not picking the right side. You're a fan, aren't you?'

I nodded. 'Yes, I go to every game. I go on the Kop.'

'What do you think of the team at the moment?'

'Well.' I was suddenly struck dumb, being asked my opinion of the side by the manager himself. 'Oh, great, great, yes, playing great.'

'Might need some more new players soon, though. We've got some difficult games coming up but we're doing alright so far. Well, if you'll excuse me, I suppose I'd better go and see what those two girls are up to. Finish my chores. Have y' far to go home?'

'No, not really, just Birkenhead.'

'You've come all the way from Birkenhead, just to talk to me?'

'Well, my dad brought me in the car. He's sitting in it, waiting.'

'Oh, you should have said. He could have come in and waited here in the warm, had a cup of tea. It's cold out there today.'

And with that I shook his hand, thanked him and waved goodbye as I closed the garden gate. As I glanced back at the house a curtain in an upstairs bedroom twitched. Two girls peered out, then flicked the curtain shut when they spotted me looking at them.

I jumped back in the car.

'What about the photograph?' asked Dad. 'I thought you were going to call me to come and take a picture.' In all the excitement I had totally forgotten.

'Go and knock on the door again,' suggested Dad.

'No,' I said. 'I've troubled him enough. Let's leave it.'

'He won't mind.'

'No,' I insisted. 'It's my fault. It doesn't matter.'

'Is there someone else you could interview who might be able to give you a different perspective?' suggested Harold.

'I could interview some fans.'

'Yes, that would be good. What about a journalist, a reporter on one of the local papers? I know someone who works for the *Liverpool Echo*. If you like, I could have a word with him and see if he could have a word with one of their sports writers.' And so a further line of investigation was set up.

I stayed in, night after night, forgoing evenings out with the lads and Susan, while painstakingly I bashed away on the typewriter with just two fingers. I wrote a long section about Shankly's footballing career, then another about his managerial career before Liverpool, then a long chapter on Liverpool itself. I put in quotes from my interview with him and also inserted quotes from the man from the *Echo*. Finally, I wrote a chapter about his influence on the city of Liverpool and talked to fans about how important he had become. The whole thesis ran to five thousand words, far more than had been necessary. But it had been fun and challenging. Harold was impressed when I handed it to him, each page numbered and carefully typed and bound. He took it away to read, promising an opinion the following week.

A couple of days later, I was surprised to receive a telephone call in the office. It was Harold. 'I hope you don't mind me calling you at work,' he said, 'but I just wanted to say that I've read your thesis and that I think it's really good. It's very readable and makes some good points. Just wanted to let you know. We'll talk some more about it when you're next in college. We'll have to see about getting you a proper education. Maybe you should start by reading a decent newspaper every day.'

fifteen

Green, Red or Orange

It has been argued that, apart from London, no city in Britain arouses more diverse opinion than Liverpool. It is viewed by the media and the chattering classes as a hotbed of thievery, urban dereliction, work-shies and drug addicts, and as a community with a chip on its shoulder. At times it has equally been described as a centre of extraordinary creativity, the music capital of the world, the foremost footballing city in Europe, a city of writers, a city of wits. All of which was encouraged by a band of professional Scousers who liked to indulge either in image-making or regurgitating a few legends of their own. I'll not name names.

The politics of Liverpool has been equally diverse, illogical and non-conformist, much of it determined by passion, religion, bitterness or jealousy. At times those old-fashioned determinants of class and poverty seem to have played only a minor role. At the turn of the nineteenth century, and indeed up until the 1930s, religion was the main factor in the makeup of the city. Parliamentary and council candidates were 'orange' or 'green'. It wasn't until mass unemployment struck the city in the thirties that any semblance of class politics began to emerge.

The Communist Party in Liverpool enjoyed a brief flirtation

with the electorate under the dutiful leadership of Jack and Bessie Braddock. Then, in an astonishing about-turn, the Braddocks quit their beloved party and began a dramatic shift from left to right. They joined the Labour Party and by the 1940s had turned the Liverpool Labour Party into a bastion of reaction and a bitter enemy of the Communist Party, employing not dissimilar centralist tactics to those they had learned in the Communist Party itself. At times, they seemed more concerned with outdoing the Cold War antics of Senator McCarthy than with opposing the Tories. But in truth Liverpool was always too anarchic a city for the discipline and organisation required by communism.

By the 1960s, Liberalism was on the rise in the city as the left, yet again, tore its own heart out. But it was to be a momentary and bewildering period – and then Militant added to the confusion in the 1980s. I had been wary of joining the Labour Party, although its victories in the 1964 and 1966 general elections had been more than welcome. After the patrician era of Macmillan and the aristocratic years of Alec Douglas-Home, Harold Wilson was a breath of fresh air in British politics. He was young, intellectual, working class; a new breed of politician who epitomised the sixties. He spun a good line, talking up his white-hot technological revolution, even though we were still bogged down in boardroom inertia and class division.

I felt a certain affinity, given that he had been born in Huddersfield and had then migrated to the Wirral, even going to a school we regularly played at rugby. He had also found himself a Merseyside constituency, although you could never claim that he was ever a part of Merseyside's baffling politics. Yet for all his effusiveness, Wilson would prove to be just as much trapped in the armlock of orthodoxy as any of his Labour predecessors. But in 1964 he was undoubtedly different from the breed who had immediately preceded him.

The politics of my union were such that there was little encouragement to join the Labour Party. We opposed the Vietnam War, then in its infancy, any notion of a prices-and-incomes policy, apartheid in South Africa, and Labour's failure to introduce sweeping nationalisation. For all our illusory support of the Labour government, we regularly seemed to be at odds with it. And of course, it was true, as George continued to remind us, that many of the union's most active participants were members of the Communist Party. And an impressive bunch they were. The more I mingled with them the more their colour rubbed off on me. Their organisation and discipline were admirable. They could get things done. Hardly a week passed without me attending a meeting of one kind or another. I was gradually being granted access to their inner circle, even being invited to their caucus meetings, held on the Friday evening before the Saturday Divisional meeting. I was regarded as 'safe', a 'sympathiser' who would, with time, see sense and join up. But I never did.

Since the weekend in Blackpool I had been active as the youth representative on the Merseyside Divisional Committee. A political education was under way. The Kitson meeting had been a notable success and had earned me considerable trust even though it had not led to his release, which, I guess, was the main aim. Not that anyone ever imagined it would but at least it brought his plight to the attention of more people. After half a dozen meetings I was told that the union was starting up a national youth committee. Would I like to be the Merseyside representative? asked Alf, the division's executive member, pulling me aside one Saturday morning after our meeting. 'Only once a month and a free night in a London hotel,' he added, by way of inducement. That was enough for me, even though meetings occasionally clashed with a Liverpool home game. The appointment was soon confirmed.

I was now in the big time, swanning down to London on a Friday evening, relishing a meal on the train, overnighting in a hotel close to Euston before an all-day meeting on the Saturday. After one such meeting in April 1967, I returned to Liverpool to be met by Susan at the station. She had a broad grin on her face.

'I've won,' she said.

'Won what?'

'The National. I've won ten pounds.' I'd forgotten it was the Grand National that day.

'I backed Foinavon and it won at 100–1. I had a shilling on each way. It was astonishing. All the horses fell at Beechers.' She handed me a copy of the *Football Echo*. There it was: 'Foinavon Wins Most Sensational National in years. 100–1 Long shot.' It seemed there had been a massive pile-up first time around at Beechers. Foinavon, having refused the fence at its first attempt, then squeezed through the chaos to jump it at the second, and had raced into an unbeatable lead.

'Come on. I'll buy you a drink with my winnings,' she said, steering me along Lime Street and babbling on about what an amazing race it had been. As I placed a drink on her table, I told her my news.

'Someone at the meeting asked me if I would be interested in going to university, to some college in Oxford.'

'In Oxford?'

'Yeah, it's a trade union college, for mature students.'

'But how could you go there?'

'Well, the union has a scholarship. It sends one student there each year.'

'How long's it for?'

'Two years. You have to enter an exam and have an interview.'

'What about your job?'

'I'm out of my apprenticeship now. I'm free to do what I want.'

'You're on good money, though.'

'Yeah, but I can't stand that place any longer.'

'But you'd have to leave home.'

'I suppose so, although I could come back most weekends.'

'Do you fancy it?'

'Don't know really. I've hardly thought about it. I really enjoyed doing that thesis on Bill Shankly. The teacher really liked it, said it was good. I got a good mark for it.' She took out a cigarette and handed one to me.

'Oxford, wow. What do you study at this college?'

'I don't know that much about it really, but I think politics, history, English . . .' Suddenly there was a thunderous crash. For a brief moment I was not sure what had happened. It was as if a brick had been hurled through the window. In the far corner of the room a table full of glasses had been sent flying. We all turned, just in time to see a fist shoot out and a man in his mid-twenties keel over. The man who had punched him brushed past another table, sending drinks tumbling over an elderly woman. A voice was raised and her husband, a short, smartly dressed man with spiky grey hair, was on his feet attempting to protect his wife. He told the man to calm down. He was promptly punched in the face and crashed headlong into his table. Mayhem ensued. Glasses flew everywhere, bottles bounced, the bar staff ducked, everyone was on their feet. Within seconds it resembled something out of an old Western as a bar-room brawl broke out. Bottles sailed across the room, smashing against the mirror at the back of the bar. Bodies and blood spilled everywhere. The man who had been felled initially was up on his feet, brandishing a smashed bottle in his hand. I grabbed hold of a screaming Susan and dragged her away and out of the pub before we found ourselves involved. She was shaking. She wasn't the only one. 'Just another Saturday night in Liverpool,' I told her, 'or maybe one too many people winning on the National.' Talk of Oxford was forgotten, superseded by the bar-room brawl.

It wasn't until the next day that the subject was raised again. Susan seemed tearful.

'I've been thinking about you going to Oxford,' she told me, as I walked her home.

'Hang on, I haven't decided anything yet.'

'I know, but are you sure you really want to go?'

'I don't know. I haven't thought any more about it. Anyhow, I probably wouldn't pass the exam.'

'You've got a good job and what would you do when you finished, would you go back to Laird's? Two years is a long time, you know.' I had to confess that I hadn't thought about what I'd do afterwards but certainly Cammell Laird was not on the agenda.

'And what about us?' Ah, now I could see her line of reasoning.

'Well? What difference would it make to us? I'd still come home most weekends to see you.'

'But I'd miss you.'

'I'd miss you too. Don't worry about it. As I say, I probably wouldn't get in, anyhow. And please don't say anything to anyone else.' She didn't look convinced. But the more I thought about it, the more appealing it became. Oxford! That would be one up on everybody, all those people who thought I was dumb. Imagine Lennie's face when he found out, Gobbo as well – and George. They'd be gobsmacked. I had nothing to lose. I was single and if I was ever going to jump it had to be done before I got much older. It could be a new start. It would get me away from Laird's although what I would do afterwards was, with the recklessness of youth, a dilemma that I wasn't going to confront at this point. I dismissed Susan's misgivings without a thought.

Susan continued to be her usual self, especially as the Oxford question was barely mentioned over the next six months. Then an advert appeared in the union journal inviting applications for the scholarship. I had no choice; it was decision time, time to go public. First port of call – parents. Much to my surprise, Mother was enthusiastic. She recognised that I was unhappy at Laird's and was never going to get anywhere. Dad was the opposite. I'd expected him to be supportive, but no. 'You've got to think about security,' he told me. 'You've got a good job and you're on good money. Jobs don't come easy, you know, especially around here. I lived through the thirties, remember. I saw poverty. I saw men begging for work. I saw people being means-tested.'

'There you go, over the top again. This is not the thirties, Dad.'

'Well, seeing things like that leaves an indelible memory. I know it might sound like a good opportunity but if you become a student you won't have any money for two years. What will you live on?' I explained that the scholarship came with a grant and that it would probably be enough to survive on. 'And I could always get a job during the vacations as well,' I added. But he remained sceptical.

'And what will you do when you've finished?' I still didn't know the answer to that one. 'You wanted to go to acting school a couple of years ago.' That idea had never really taken off. I knew I'd never be more than a decent rep actor. 'Then you thought about youth work.' True, but I'd seen it at close range at the YMCA and knew it was a thankless job. 'Now you want to go to Oxford.' I'd tried to be reasonable but it wasn't working. Now I was getting angry.

'He should try writing, that's what he's good at and he's had those articles published in the union magazine,' interrupted Mother from the kitchen. Nice idea, Mum, but you don't become a writer overnight and I certainly didn't want to be a journalist. They represented the lowest of the low. 'I thought I might try union work,' I said. 'There's always full-time jobs being advertised in the our union.' I could see that appealed a bit more. A union job was a serious possibility, especially if I was to pick up a scholarship. They'd probably expect something in return, like a few years devoted to union work. But the discussion was going nowhere and the conversation petered out, unresolved and disputed.

The following evening, Dad asked if he could see the advert. 'Not much point,' I muttered throwing the magazine to him. But something was brewing within. He asked a few questions but made no comments. I remained silent and cussed.

I returned from Anfield at the weekend full of high spirits. Liverpool had just given Leeds United something of a footballing lesson, but more memorably the Leeds goalkeeper, Gary Sprake, had committed one of the greatest howlers the game has ever seen. He'd taken a back pass in his own area, picked up the ball, bounced it a few times and with no one anywhere near him had gone to throw the ball out to a defender. As he pulled his arm back the ball spun out of his hand and flew into the back of the net. We had watched in amazement. I had never seen anything like it. Barry didn't even think it was a goal. 'He'll disallow it,' Barry reckoned, gazing in astonishment. But the referee pointed decisively to the centre spot. The Liverpool players didn't know what to do. Who do you congratulate? They simply stood there, raised their arms and looked towards Sprake with a degree of sympathy, which was more than he received from his own team-mates, who scowled at him. The Kop howled with laughter and then – quick as a flash – began to bellow out a hit of the time, 'Careless Hands'. It was instantaneous – a forlorn Sprake hadn't even retrieved the ball from the back of the net. The entire stadium roared with laughter. Even the referee couldn't resist a smile. The Leeds players were less than amused.

I related this tale in graphic detail to my father, showing him precisely how Sprake had swept his arm back and the acute angle from which the ball had shot out of his hand.

'Fancy a pint at the club?' he asked, after tea. Mum nodded. 'Go on, that'll be nice for you both.' I wasn't seeing Susan that night, so I agreed. Gary Sprake might have been cold-shouldered by his own team-mates that evening but at least he had inadvertently melted the week-long iciness that had engulfed my father and me.

We sat in the corner beneath a garish painting of Our Lady. It was still early evening. A few regulars were in the other bar playing billiards but in the lounge all was calm and peaceful.

'It's a bit quieter than the pub I was in the other week,' I told him. 'There was a dreadful fight, fists flying everywhere. This old man, about your age, stood up to protect his wife and was punched in the face. It was unbelievable. It was just like something in the movies. I had to get Susan out quick, it was really nasty. Bottles were flying everywhere.'

'Liverpool can be a hard place. There were times when you couldn't take women into pubs at all. There's even some pubs today where you still wouldn't take a woman, especially down by the docks. Spit and sawdust.'

Dad had joined a club belonging to the local Catholic church. It happened to be where Peter's dad drank, as well as a few of his other pals. It seemed an anomaly that Our Lady's Church of the Bleeding Heart, Ambassadors of God, were also Ambassadors for the other kind of 'Holy Water'.

'So, when's the application have to be in?' he asked.

'A couple of weeks.'

'I've been talking to your mother.' He twitched his shoulders. I'd guessed she might have had a word. 'And you know we'll back you if that's what you really want.' I told him I'd been thinking more seriously about it and it really was.

'Well, as long as you're sure.'

'I can't stand the office, there's no future there for me. I know it's not a bad job, but it's not what I want.'

'It'll be like starting all over again and you're already in your twenties. Once you go you'll probably not come back here, you know.'

'Oh, I don't know. There might be a job for me somewhere on Merseyside.' But I was lying. He knew it and I knew it. As he said those words it began to dawn upon me that this really was a watershed. He was right, I might never come back, but that didn't bother me. Where I'd end up was in the lap of the gods but it almost certainly wouldn't be on Merseyside. Would I miss it? I wasn't sure. I'd miss the football. There was no doubt about that. But what else would I miss? I wouldn't miss the narrow-mindedness of some of my colleagues, nor the insularity. I'd miss the humour, Saturday nights. And friends? Well, they were moving on in one way or another. Billy was married, Martin was engaged, Peter was halfway down the aisle, and Barry wasn't that far behind. We were just growing older, shifting directions, leaving our youth behind, taking on new responsibilities. I didn't want to get left behind.

From somewhere to the back of me came a voice. 'Hello, Tommy!' It was Bill Dean, his cherubic face beaming. Dad shook his hand and went off to the bar to buy him a drink. The great centre forward eased himself into a chair alongside me. 'Getting old,' he said, puffing slightly, his voice hinting at too many close encounters with smoky tap rooms. 'Almost as bad as Everton.' He was wearing a smart worsted suit. 'Not good today, shouldn't lose like that at Stoke. I hear you had great fun at Anfield this afternoon.' I nodded, and told him all about it. 'Did you ever see anything like that?' I asked.

'No, can't say as I ever did. You see funny things on the pitch, though, things the referee misses. I scored for England once, playing abroad, somewhere in the Bahamas, I think.' He smiled. 'Hit the ball so hard it burst the net and finished up in the crowd. The referee gave a goal kick, wouldn't believe it had gone into the net.' He laughed. 'That'll haunt Sprake for the rest of his days.'

Dad returned with a trayful of drinks. 'Lad's thinking of going to Oxford,' he told him as he sat down.

'Hang on Dad, I might not pass the exam.'

'Of course you will,' he said smiling.

I'd figured that persuading Susan would not be difficult but, judging from her initial reaction, it was clear that I had underestimated her. The subject had barely been raised since we had been so rudely interrupted by the flying fists on Grand National night and the longer it went on the more anxious I was becoming. Sooner or later I would have to broach the issue once more. I could sense that she didn't want to talk about it but time was pressing. As we strolled through the park the next day, I eventually plucked up courage.

'I've been thinking some more about that chance to go to Ruskin College.' She half stopped and looked at me.

'And?'

'Well, I've decided to give it a go. I've got nothing to lose.'

'When do you have to apply?'

'By the end of February, so I've still got plenty of time to decide. What do you think?'

'What does it matter what I think?'

We'd been seeing each for some time now but you can never fully understand someone. She was about to shock me.

'There's something I want you to know. I've been meaning to tell you for a while but the right moment never seemed to come.' She coughed nervously. 'You won't go mad, will you?' We sat down on a damp bench overlooking the park pond. A couple of ducks, chased by a posse of small children, skidded off across the water to the safety of a small island.

'I've always been worried that someone might have said something to you.'

'About what?'

'Well . . .' She hesitated. 'I had a baby two years ago. That's why I had to leave school and disappear for a year or so.' I suddenly remembered the rumours, but there was never any evidence and she had returned claiming that her father had had to go north to work for a short period and that all the family had joined him in Sunderland. It seemed a perfectly reasonable explanation and the whispers had long since died down. I said nothing, not because I was shocked but because I wasn't quite sure how to react.

'I went for a weekend up to the Lake District with this man. He was older than me and married and I got pregnant. God, I wasn't even sixteen. It was so stupid. He just took advantage of me. I had to leave school, so I went up to my nanna's in Sunderland. My mum came as well.' She looked at me, her azure eyes welling with tears. 'And now you'll hate me.'

'No I won't. Come on, we've all done things we regret.'

'Yes, but not carrying a stigma and a memory that lasts forever. How do you think I feel? Somebody else has my baby. I had to give it away. I don't even know who has it or where it is?' There still seemed little I could say.

'I hate him! I hate him! He ruined my life!' she cried. I put my arm round her.

'No he didn't, because you've got me now.'

'He did, because it'll always be with me. I wanted to go to university as well and because of him I had to leave school. And I've had to find a job and I'll never go to college now.' There were floods of tears. 'And you'll go off to college, and probably won't come back home, and I'll be stuck here forever, and when anybody finds out about my having a baby they won't want to know me.'

'But it's not made me change my mind about you. Everything will work out for the best.'

'If that's what you really want, you should apply.'

I didn't feel like going home. I just wanted to walk, sort out the muddle in my head. Everything was coming at me too quickly. I sauntered quietly around the park a couple of times mulling it all over, until the park keeper spotted me and waved his bunch of keys. It was time for him to lock up. Even then, I took the long way home. There was no doubt I was shocked by what Susan had told me, although I was not entirely surprised. It all added up and I wondered how I'd come to forget the tittle-tattle. Maybe I'd forgotten deliberately, just pushed it to the back of my mind. I didn't feel any different towards Susan. In fact, I felt all the more drawn to her. And yet. As I approached the top of our road, a thought suddenly occurred to me. Such is the irresponsibility and carelessness of youth that I had forgotten to ask if it was a boy or a girl. Too late now to ever ask.

sixteen

Fellow Travellers

I'd seen little of Jim McGill since the dispute at Laird's. Not long after that he had been promoted to become the union's national organiser and was now based at head office in London. Walking into one of our Saturday morning divisional meetings a few weeks later, I couldn't help but hear his infectious laughter and soft Scottish tones ringing around the room. He was talking to Vince and Alf. I felt a sudden lift to my spirits. At the end of the meeting McGill tugged at my arm as I was about to leave. He said he wanted a word and suggested a stroll up Parliament Hill. It suited me, it was wintry sunshine and I had time to while away before making for Anfield. We sat on the steps in front of the cocoa-bricked brute of an Anglican cathedral.

'Wonderful view from up here,' he said. 'You can see the whole span of the Mersey; from Runcorn in the east there to as far as the Mersey Bar in the west. In fact, if you stand up you'll probably be able to see Ireland, maybe even America.

'I used to know this old shipwright. He worked over there at Laird's,' he said, laughing and pointing across the river. 'Bit before your time. He was a member of the Communist Party, been in the party for donkey's years. Fought in Spain with the International

Brigade and was a leading member of the National Unemployed Workers' Movement in the early thirties. Got imprisoned for organising demonstrations against the means test in Liverpool and Birkenhead. I remember coming up here with him once and he said to me, "When I die I want a Viking burial. I want to be put on a boat and I want it set on fire and pushed down the slipway at Laird's towards the Pier Head. That'll do me," he said. "Floating across the Mersey, that's how I want to go. I want people to understand that Birkenhead and Liverpool are one and the same place. They've got the same problems, the same humour, the same culture." He then added that he wanted to be remembered as an old Viking warrior because he'd spent all his life fighting for the two cities.' McGill laughed. 'Wonderful old man he was.'

'So what happened to him?'

'Well, when he did die we were in a bit of a quandary. Some of the lads were all for making some kind of raft and setting it alight one night and trying to float it across the Mersey. But that was a bit of a crazy idea. So we did the next best thing. We took a ferry boat from Woodside to the Pier Head with his ashes in a churn and we tossed his remains into the Mersey halfway between Birkenhead and Liverpool.' McGill burst into one of his uproarious laughs.

'You know, captains and merchants used to have their homes up here. They were crafty old buggers. They came here so that they could see the sprawl of these docks below and know the business of the day before anyone else and before the incoming tide brought in the flotillas of ships from Africa, the Indies and the Americas. They used to have telescopes up in their lofts and at first light every morning they'd be up there spying out on the Mersey to see what ships were waiting to come in. And if it was one of their own they'd be straight down to the dock and start making plans for a speedy berthing and unloading. That way they were always one ahead of the game.'

I guessed that it was similar with the wives and children of the sailors. They'd be up here as well, scouring the Mersey in hope of spotting a three-masted schooner making for the port, perhaps carrying a husband, a son or a lover. It was the same in the whaling port of Nantucket – three thousand miles directly east of here. There, wives would climb the 92 steps to the lookout post on the tower of the Congregationalist church for a first sighting of a whaling vessel returning from a voyage that might have been two, three or even four years in duration. And, as in Liverpool, the more wealthy wives had their own conning towers atop their smart wooden-built captains' homes in Orange Street.

Wives on either side of that vast expanse of ocean must have experienced the same confused apprehension at the prospect of their menfolk disembarking. A mixture of joy, relief and – surely – trepidation; a fear and unease about who or what they might be greeting. People may not change but, all too often, their feelings do. It was claimed that the Quaker women of Nantucket secreted sexual aids about their homes, ready to be produced in the privacy of dark wistful nights long after their husbands had departed. And no doubt when their ships were spotted the aids would be secreted again; the chimney was a popular hiding place. Such was the plight of the whaling widow. Maybe the women of Liverpool felt much, or even did much, the same, although their loved ones were rarely away for such long periods.

'Are you away to Anfield this afternoon?' asked McGill, offering me a cigarette.

I nodded. 'Are *you* a football fan?'

'Oh aye.' I must have looked slightly surprised. 'I come from Glasgow, remember.'

'Who's your team?'

'Celtic of course, always has been since I was a wee bairn. Oh aye, I was at the Liverpool–Celtic game at Anfield a few years back. Bloody robbed we were. That should have been a penalty in the last few minutes.' He smirked. 'I met your man Shankly recently. He was on a radio programme with me. We had a long chat afterwards. I hadn't realised he worked down the mines.' The ash from his cigarette blew in a swirl of wind. I told him how I'd done an interview with Shankly for my college work.

'It's a small city, this,' he said looking up. 'It looks big from up here but it isn't. Sometimes I think it's more like an overgrown village. A bit like Glasgow. You don't need to know that many people to know what's going on. Not like London. There's a lot in common between Liverpool and Glasgow, you know. The people have got the same character, faced the same hardships in life. They live hard and play hard. Liverpool can be a bit narrow, though, whereas we Scots go out, we explore, we're adventurers, we like to change the world.' He was being mischievous. 'Sometimes you Liverpudlians have limited horizons. You think the world ticks around Liverpool but it doesn't. There's a big, big world out there. Don't get me wrong, like. I love the city, wonderful people, always make you welcome. But you can be a bit introspective. Look at Alf, he'll never leave. He wants to stay here, work at Plessey's and remain a lay official. We've offered him full-time union jobs all over the country. We need him, but we can't persuade him to leave. He's a good lad, very astute, but he needs to get away. And what about you? Have you thought any more about Ruskin College?'

'I didn't know you knew.'

He smiled. 'Well, there you are, see? Liverpool is a small city, everybody knows everybody's business. Anyhow, I'm chairing the selection committee. So, have you thought about it?'

'Oh, I don't know. It's a big decision. I might not even pass the exam. It might be too difficult.'

'I wouldn't worry too much about that. The main thing is the interview. We have to know that you're committed to the union, the right kind of person. Your name's been mentioned by quite a few at head office. There won't be that many applying. So, what other worries do you have?'

'I suppose I'm a bit like Len. I just wish the college was in Liverpool. On the one hand I don't want to leave 'cos all my pals are here.'

'Girlfriend?'

'Yeah.'

'Serious?'

'Not sure really.'

'Then you're not serious.' There was a pause, then he added, 'But you were saying, on the other hand . . .?'

'Well, I don't much enjoy being a draughtsman. I'm interested in politics. I seem to spend all my time either doing union work or going to football matches. I feel mixed up about it all.'

'Tell me,' he said, 'what would your man Shankly say?'

'I dunno, never thought about that.'

'I'll tell you what he'd say. He'd say if you've got the skill and the talent, you've got to move on, you've got to go where your ability takes you. He moved on. He didn't stay down the mines, did he?'

Across the river, Birkenhead and the Cammell Laird shipyard glimmered in the midday sunshine. You could spot the engine shop where I was wasting so many furtive hours gossiping with Andy and the lads. On the slipways a new sixty-thousand-ton oil tanker was taking shape, alongside it the bare bones of the shed hiding the Polaris submarines from prying eyes. Hot metal rising into the sky. Cranes were swinging round with gigantic girders dangling like plywood. You could even see the occasional flash of a welding arc or a spray of sparks.

'Look, how many ships do you see over there?' he asked.

'Two.'

'Exactly. When I first became organiser here, there were half a dozen and before that there'd have been eight or nine. The slipways were chock-full of activity. Times aren't good. And do you think they'll get any better? Course they won't. It's finished. Mark my words, in ten years' time there'll be nothing over there. They won't be building ships in this country by then. I was brought up on the Clyde, my father worked all his life in the yards. When I was serving my time at John Brown's there were eight or nine yards on the river. And today? There's Fairfields and Stephens on the south bank, Connel's and Yarrow's on the north bank and John Brown's. And that's it. The government doesn't care and, anyhow, it probably wouldn't make any difference. Japan, Brazil, that's where they'll be making ships, not here. It makes me angry to think that the great tradition of shipbuilding is going to end. How long have they been building ships here?'

'A hundred years?'

'More, almost a hundred and fifty.' He paused for a moment, then added, 'And what else do they do in Birkenhead?'

'There's the docks.'

'Yes, the docks. It's just the same. I used to take the kids on the ferry boat across the river when they were young and the boat used to weave in and out of the traffic in the river. There were dozens of ships. You must remember it. And where are they now? How many ships will you find in Birkenhead docks today? I'll tell you: a handful. I fear for Birkenhead and Liverpool.'

'But they'll always need ships.'

'True. But they won't always need Cammell Laird to build them and the Liverpool dockers to load them. It's finished. But don't tell anybody I told you.' He smiled and pulled himself up, stretching to his impressive height. 'I'm off. Think about it. Remember your man Shankly.' He waved goodbye, leaving me to gaze across the grey rooftops of Toxteth.

Maybe he was right. Although I had never settled into the life of a shipbuilder, I still remained fond of ships. No two ships are ever the same. Even if they build a sister ship, and that in itself is a rarity, they still vary. There will always be minor distinctions, a modification here, a refinement there. For years afterwards I would be able to recall the number and the name of all the ships I had worked on, from oil tankers to cable layers, from ferry boats to cargo ships, from guided-missile destroyers to nuclear-powered submarines, every one of them was special.

Ships are not unlike houses. Ask any sailor and he'll tell you that they have their own personalities. Some ships you never really engage with, others you feel perfectly at ease with. The nightly groans of steel pressing against steel in the twist of the sea can unleash terrible emotions while equally the throb of the engine room can be like the comforting sound of a purring cat.

I enjoyed watching the superstructure, day by day spiralling upwards on the slipway, until some dignitary arrived to launch the new child into the real world. We'd cheer as the steel hulk slid down the slipway and into the Mersey. And then it would lie in the basin for months to be fitted out until it was spick and span, ready to accommodate its crew. A lick of paint, a spit of polish, successful sea trials, and only then would it finally and officially be handed over to its owners. *Mercury, Sepia, Devonshire, Resolution, Overchurch, Ajax*; ships that would sail a million miles and more. It would be churlish not to feel proud of them. And yet here I was, thinking of turning my back on them, leaving them all behind.

The builders of ships have much the same association with their ship as any seaman. Ships begin with a number, the next in line on the order book, and on launch assume their legitimate name. Shipbuilding, like any craft, is part devotion. And all those trades: shipwrights, riveters, welders, millwrights, blacksmiths, draughtsmen, tracers, fitters, joiners, electricians, plumbers, boilermakers, caulkers, even the famous rivet catcher.

*

I was nervous about talking to Susan again. If her brave confession had been meant to undermine or colour any decision I was about to make, she had certainly been successful. I thought I'd come to some kind of resolution but her announcement had knocked me for six. I suddenly felt a deeper empathy with her and didn't want to leave her. After all, she was good-hearted, attractive, bright and yet vulnerable and in need of support. And here I was planning to disappear to the other end of the country.

'You'd be daft to leave her,' Billy told me. I don't know why I had ever thought of confiding in him but after a couple of pints one evening my tongue got the better of me. 'Once you've gone that'll be it. She won't hang around and, anyhow, you'll lose interest. You can't keep a relationship going from two hundred miles. Can't think why you want to be going off, anyhow. You've finished your apprenticeship, you should be on good money now. At your age, you should be thinking about settling down. What does she think about it?' I shrugged my shoulders.

'Well, if you ask me, you should get yourself married while you've got the chance. It's alright you know. Martin's getting married next year and Andy won't be far behind.' It was true; Martin was set to marry Janet's friend in the spring and, while Andy and my cousin had not lasted much more than a month, he'd subsequently met someone else. He'd even mothballed his guitar.

'She's a nice girl, Susan. What more do you want? She likes you, you like her. She's fun, good looking. What's her mum like?'

'She's alright.'

'Well, there you go.'

'What do you mean?'

'They always turn out like their mums. If the mum's alright, the daughter'll be alright.' I didn't like to ask him if he'd had a good look at Maggie's mum lately. 'You can't have everything in life, you know.'

'Why not?'

''Cos life ain't like that. Oxford! Honestly! You'd probably fail the exam, anyhow.' He paused. 'We're thinking of buying a dog, you know.'

I wondered if Barry might have an angle on this, so I confided in him one Saturday as we stood on the Kop watching Liverpool play Southampton.

'Oxford? You're joking. How are you goin' to get into Oxford? You keep failing your exams at the tech,' he joked. I tried to explain that I was interested in politics whereas I wasn't that much interested in designing ships.

'How long will it be?'

'Only two years.'

'And then you'll come back to Laird's?'

'Er, no.'

'You mean you'll leave Laird's.'

'Yeah.'

'Not come back?'

'What's wrong with that?'

'But it's a good job, good prospects. Where'll you find a better job.'

'I don't know.'

'Well, what'll you do afterwards?'

'I don't know?'

'Bloody hell, Steve. You don't know much. You're taking a bit of a risk, aren't you? Anyhow, they're all snobs down there. You won't fit in. Don't they all swan about in gowns and go to balls?'

It was the wrong place to have entered into any such discussion. But by half-time Barry had thought some more. 'You'd be waving goodbye to all this. Bloody hell, when would you see them?'

'Well, I'd be back in the vacations.'

'In the what?'

'In the vacations, the holidays.'

'Vacations, hey? You're sounding poncy already. Anyrate, that's if they're at home. You'd only see a couple of games a season. They haven't even got a football team in Oxford.'

'Yes they have, they're in the third division.'

'Exactly, they haven't got a football team.'

'But they're top; they might be in the second division next season.'

'Yeah, well, if you want to watch second-division football, you're welcome to it. You must have a screw loose. It's totally different, you know. You'll be telling me next you're going to start supporting Tranmere.'

By full time Liverpool had won 2–0.

'Look what you'd be missing,' said Barry, as we were surfed

down the Kop steps and into the Walton Breck Road. 'We'll win the league again next season.' I had to agree with him. A good win, fifty thousand inside Anfield, close to the top of the first division. It was giving up a lot.

It felt like a tug of war was going on with me in the middle. Susan was feeling threatened.

'You might meet someone else,' she said. 'When you get down there and see all those rich, beautiful girls, you won't be interested in me.' I told her not to be so silly.

'But they will, they'll all be better looking than me and more intelligent. You'll forget all about me and you'll be off having a good time.

'There's a philosopher I read about somewhere who says that life is about instinct,' I told her. 'He says that the thing to do in life is to follow your instinct all the time. Don't sit down and start analysing it too much. He reckons that the more you think about something, the more you debate it, the more confusing it becomes. He says it's like walking through a maze. You follow your nose. But if you sit down and think about where you've been or where you're going you just get lost and the chances are you never escape. But if you keep going, follow your instinct, eventually you'll get it right and get out. Sure, you'll make mistakes, but with time you get there.'

'So does everybody get there with time?'

'Maybe. It's just about learning from your experiences.'

'But we get lots of instincts. We want to do lots of things. How do you know yours is the one to follow? If we followed all our instincts we'd be in all sorts of trouble and have no money either. Look what happened to me when I followed my instinct. I got pregnant.' I was about to counter that but thought better of it. There was an uneasy silence.

'You can work it out mathematically as well, you know,' I continued. 'There's a formula that you can apply to any dilemma; it's supposed to give you the answer.'

'Sounds to me like you're already at Oxford,' replied Susan, sardonically. There was a silence.

'McGill spoke to me the other day. He wanted to know if I was going to apply.'

'What did you say?'

'I said I didn't know, I hadn't decided. I asked him about the exam though. He said not to worry. He's in charge of the selection, he's chairing the committee. He says the interview's just as important and he'll be doing the interview – not by himself, I suppose, but he'd be there. He seemed to think I should apply.'

'I think you have decided, haven't you?'

I nodded. 'I guess so.'

'Well it's up to you. You know I don't want you to go but if it's what you want, you should, as that man says, follow your instinct. As long as you're sure that's what you want. We'll just have to manage. I suppose I'll see you every month or so.'

I could understand Susan's hesitancy. I'd be off doing something exciting. She'd still be slaving away in the library. She'd have nothing to do at weekends and no doubt she'd spend all her time looking forward to our monthly meetings and then the vacation. Plus I'd have no money to take her anywhere, no meals, no dances, no holidays together. And at the end of it all there was still a huge question mark. Would I find a job and, if so, where would it be? If it wasn't in Liverpool would she want to follow me? Would we get married? I didn't know the answer to these questions any more than she did. I was asking a lot of her. While for me there seemed certainty, for her there was nothing but uncertainty.

seventeen

A Surprising Promotion

There comes a time when you wonder if you should quit while you're winning and move on. I was just about reaching that point. It's much the same with supporting a football club as anything else. I'd had a good run for my money. Half a dozen years of success: the second division title, two league championships, the FA Cup, European Cup-winners Cup finalists and European Cup semi-finalists. It was more than most fans dare dream of. I'd sung from the Kop, shaken Bill Shankly's hand, thrown snowballs on the pitch, queued overnight, conga-ed down Wembley Way, even shed tears on a sodden raw night at Hampden. I'd pursued Liverpool loyally to most parts of the country clutching my red scarf and sandwiches. But now, the team was undoubtedly growing old; to the trained eye it showed signs of weariness. Even Shankly had admitted that.

Jack London once argued that boxers needed to be hungry to win titles and that once they had achieved their ambition the hunger dissipated. Football was no different. After winning so much there had to be a lack of motivation and direction. The players had captured more medals than most professional players can hope for. Roger Hunt had even led the line in the World Cup final. Shankly, of course, would never knowingly allow the team to grow fat and complacent but even he, with his boundless enthusiasm, couldn't keep them hungry forever.

They were still at the top, or thereabouts. They'd been together for the best part of six or seven years but it clearly couldn't go on forever. The autumn leaves may have been turning but they were hardly dropping off the branches. Yet the future alarmed me. Memories of second-division football were still fresh in the mind and nobody was confident enough to predict that Liverpool would have a long-term future in the top flight. It was the old pessimism creeping up on me again, the fear that one day we would slip through the trapdoor yet again and into second-division oblivion. Leyton Orient, Barnsley and Stockport County held little or no appeal. Once the likes of Hunt, St John and the almighty Yeats had gone the side would surely surrender. They needed new blood. Tony Hateley had arrived, the most expensive player in the country, and although he opened promisingly with an early hat-trick in the 6–0 rout of Newcastle, he had faded once the pitches had become heavy and cumbersome. The only other striking new face was Emlyn Hughes. Now here was a player. From the moment I first saw him I knew precisely what Shankly had meant when he said that one day Hughes would captain England. He was powerful, and for a big man he possessed unusual pace, he could win the ball, distribute it and drive the team forward. I liked Hughes but they needed more like him.

I couldn't bear to support them if they were struggling and me having to face the likes of Bluenose every day with his carping remarks and the twins with their echoing comments. It was bad enough with Peter. United were even going well in the European Cup. Maybe this was as good a time as any to call it a day. Forget about football altogether.

But, of course, football isn't like that; you can't suddenly drop your commitment. Well, *I* couldn't. 'Why don't you just support another side,' suggested Susan kindly. I didn't like to tell her that you couldn't suddenly start following a different team. That was tantamount to treachery. She didn't understand. I was hooked, even though it might have been comforting to imagine that I could draw a line under it all. It was never really a debate, just one of those unnecessary ideas you toss around in your head in the small hours of the night. Happily, by morning sanity had returned. I was addicted and that was it.

It wasn't like Ted to call me into his office. That meant he wanted to talk to me about something important. But what would he want to talk to *me* about. Normally he never needed to say more than a few words; he'd just poke his head round his door, shout something or stroll over to my desk. But this was the nearest to a written invitation. 'Can I have a word with you after lunch,' he asked, 'say 2 p.m.' I spent the rest of the morning worrying, trying to figure out if there was something I had done wrong. I couldn't think of anything. I might not have been wholly committed to the job but I did as much as I needed to do, and did it efficiently.

Later that morning the reason began to filter through. A re-organisation and restructuring of the office was taking place. Ted was seeing just about everybody to tell them their future. Harry wandered out with a smile on his face but his lips were sealed. Vic came out as well, looking extremely pleased and promptly announced that he and Harry had been promoted. The office was being spilt into two new divisions and *they* would be heading them, with Ted Nichols as the supremo. A few others went in to see Ted and returned to tell us which division they had been assigned to. Then it was my turn.

'As you may have gathered,' began Ted, painstakingly unpicking a paper clip, 'the office is being re-structured to bring us in line with Barrow. We need to have similar organisations, especially now as we're approaching the fitting-out stages. We're going to create a new production co-ordinating department and I'd like you to help run it as an assistant section leader.' I was staggered. Not in a hundred years would I have guessed that Ted would think of promoting me.

'The department will co-ordinate some aspects of production with the yard. It's fairly similar to what you've already been doing, so shouldn't be too different. It won't be a big department, of course. You'll co-ordinate ordering and delivery, and ensure that it is in line with Barrow.' He smiled and tossed the paperclip into a bin. His eyes searched thoughtfully around his office. He had a lean, drawn-out face with smooth, delicate skin. 'You didn't expect that, did you?' I shook my head. 'Well, I've spoken to Harry and he says you're doing a good job, so we'll give it a try. I'm going to give you a couple of apprentices to work with you, plus someone to do the clerking. You'll be stationed up the far end of the office and you'll be part of Harry's new empire. You'll be okay and, of course, there'll be a pay rise.'

Six months earlier, there had been a major pay settlement. I hadn't long been out of my apprenticeship and had expected only a small rise but had been pleasantly surprised when I discovered that I had been awarded a substantial increase, taking my salary to just over one thousand pounds a year. Now more money was on the way. 'You're pay will go up to twelve hundred pounds,' announced Ted, rising from his swivel chair. 'It's a good opportunity for you, so grab it. You won't let me down, will you? And get your bloody hair cut as well.' I walked out of his office feeling ten feet tall.

The office was abuzz with the new changes and my mini-promotion was hot news. At lunchtime I strolled over to the Ships Drawing Office to see Barry. He'd already heard. 'Christ, you'll be able to afford to go in the stands at Anfield now.'

'I might even be able to afford a season ticket,' I added.

'You wouldn't, would you?'

'No, don't worry, I'll always be a Kopite. They'll have to pull it down before I go elsewhere.'

'It's because you're thick with the union,' sneered George from a nearby desk. 'Buying you off. It's always the fucking same, union officials getting the jobs, joining management.'

'It's hardly fucking management,' I told him. 'It's only a bit of a promotion and, anyhow, you all scoffed when I went over there, you told me it was a dead end and boring. You could have gone if you'd wanted.'

'What you going do about Oxford?' asked Barry, when George had disappeared.

'Christ, I'd not thought about that.' And I hadn't. All thoughts of Oxford had been obliterated. I was wallowing in my success

After work I dashed into town. It was lashing down with rain, a slate-grey, heavy afternoon of swirling wind and long faces. Susan was at work in the library and I wanted to surprise her and tell her my news. She was delighted but puzzled. 'I thought you didn't get on too well in the office,' she said. 'Obviously somebody thinks you're doing a good job.' She didn't mention Oxford. We agreed to meet up after she had finished work and have a celebratory meal. I decided not to say anything to my parents. I knew they'd be thrilled and that any question of my going to Oxford would certainly be off their agenda. They'd only be trying to persuade me otherwise and I wasn't sure of my own feelings yet. Instead I dropped in on Andy.

'Go on up, he's in his bedroom,' said Andy's mum, answering the door. She was a slight, forceful woman with smouldering eyes and round red-veined cheeks. Andy was sitting on the bed strumming his guitar. His room was an Aladdin's cave full of knick-knacks: karabiners, fossils, pewter mugs, records, boxes of guitar music and reels of tapes. You could amuse yourself for hours just rummaging around; Andy usually did. He looked up as I walked in and began singing, his red hair shaking in rhythm.

'*Some other guy now, taken my love away from me. Oh now, some of other guy now.*'

'I thought you'd put that in mothballs,' I said, pointing to the guitar. He put it down, picked up a yellow duster and began to polish the instrument.

'I have, just cleaning it up. I'm going to sell it. Someone at work's offered me twenty-five pounds.'

'Seems a shame that.'

'Well, you know how it is. The group thing never worked out. And I haven't got any time, anyhow. Thought I might buy a camera. I could take some pictures of Susan for you if you like.'

'Yeah, she'd like that. Hey, guess what? I've been promoted.'

'Bloody hell, really? But you're never in the office.'

'I know, seems a bit daft really. I've been made an assistant section leader and production co-ordinator for Polaris. Sounds fancy, doesn't it? More money, a couple of apprentices to shout at.'

'Wow that's fantastic. Congratulations. Don't suppose you'll be dropping in on the Engine Shop every five minutes any more.' For a moment there was a silence as Andy tried to re-tune the guitar.

'Do you really like living here, Andy?'

'You mean this house?'

'No, Birkenhead, Liverpool?'

'Yeah, of course I do. Why?'

'Do you think you'll stay here forever?'

'I don't know but I suppose so, can't see any reason why I should leave. Anyhow, where else am I going to go. The job's alright. I'll probably get married, buy a house, you know. What about you?'

'I don't want to still be here in fifty years' time, working at Laird's from nine to five and then sneaking off down the pub for last orders.'

'Could be worse off, you know. You should be loyal to where you were born and bred.'

'Why?'

''Cos.' He paused, placing his guitar lovingly in its solid top case. ''Cos that's where your family and friends are. You belong here.'

'But you can make friends in other places. Isn't there more to life than Birkenhead and Liverpool? There's a big world out there.'

'Don't you think you're getting a bit above yourself? You're never happy these days. What's wrong with working at Laird's? You could do a lot worse. Some of us are going to be stuck there forever. Maybe we like it. But you're going around slagging it off.'

'No I'm not.'

'Yes you are. You want to get away. You're saying it's not good enough for you. It's sod the poor buggers like me, Billy and Martin who have to carry on there. It's not good enough for you but it's good enough for us.' I looked at him despondently. I had to admit I hadn't thought of it that way.

'Anyhow, I thought you liked all the football and the music,' he continued.

'I do, but the music's finished now, they've all gone. It's not the same as it was.'

'And why has it finished?'

'What d'ye mean, why has it finished? It's finished 'cos everyone was successful.'

'Well exactly, what you really mean is that they've all buggered off, gone down to the bright lights of London, the Beatles, Gerry, the Big Three, Billy J Kramer, they've all gone. Where are they now? They're not up here in bloody Liverpool. They're off somewhere else, London, New York, wherever.'

'They might come back.'

'Ballocks! No way will they come back. They've gone, made their money, and they're off to the bright lights. Not good enough for them up here. You won't see them in Liverpool again. And that's why there's no music scene here any more. A sniff of success and they all desert Liverpool.' He paused, then remembered his previous question. 'And warra bout the football?'

'Yeah, that's still great but there has to be more to life than going to Anfield every week, even if they do win. Can't remember the last time I saw them lose up here.'

'People aren't the same down south, you know. They're stuck up, snobby. Is that what you really want? People up here are genuine, friendly, loyal. They look after you. You shouldn't turn your back on your friends and family.'

'But I'm not.'

'You might think you're not but I can tell you others think different. Some of the lads in the YM were going on about it the other night. Some of them reckon you're getting too big for your boots. Don't get me wrong, not that I think that way, but there's talk.' It was a tad depressing hearing that. Andy refused to name names but I wondered and had my suspicions. I couldn't get it out of my head all evening.

'Am I really getting too big for my boots?' I asked Susan, as we sat waiting for our food in a Chinese restaurant in town. She didn't answer. 'I know I've been promoted and I'm very grateful to get an opportunity but I'm still not convinced that Laird's is the place for me. Is it really disloyal to think that? I know some of the lads are going to stay at Laird's and that's great, if they like it. I have no problem with that. But I just don't like it that much.'

'What about Oxford?' I'd been waiting for her to ask that all evening and I still hadn't worked out an answer. I pulled a face. Fortunately the waiter brought our food and momentarily broke up a difficult train of conversation. But, of course, it had to come back.

'I'd still like to go,' I said. 'But it's more difficult now. I haven't even told my parents yet.'

'Why not?' she snapped. I didn't want to tell her the truth, that I knew they'd be excited and destroy any thoughts of going to Oxford, so I muttered something about them not being around and that I'd tell them later. The fates seemed to be conspiring, trying to tell me that I shouldn't leave, shouldn't be thinking of going to somewhere like Oxford. I'd always criticised Laird's because I was never given an opportunity but here was my big chance and I was threatening to kick it into touch. No, that wasn't altogether true. It wasn't just the opportunity. I never enjoyed the work. I never even liked most of the people I worked with. Maybe I was becoming a snob. Susan didn't really want me to go, my parents certainly wouldn't want me to go now that I'd been promoted and the lads reckoned I was getting above myself. What chance did I have?

'Have you got a pay rise with the new job?' asked Susan.

'Yeah, another two hundred pounds a year.' I could see her line of questioning; cash tills ringing, wedding bells clanging. I might just as well give in now, accept my station in life and get on with it. I don't suppose it would be all that bad: decent job, nice girlfriend/wife, money to buy a house, plenty of friends, union activities, going to Anfield every other Saturday. You could want for a lot more, Steve.

I arrived home late – but not too late to catch my parents. I couldn't leave it any longer.

'Well, that's a turn-up for the book. Congratulations,' was Dad's predictable response. 'I always knew you had it in you. You must be pleased?'

'Yes, I suppose so.'

'And have they given you a pay rise as well?'

'Yes, another two hundred pounds.'

Mother was impressed too. 'When do you start?' she asked.

'Next week.'

'So where does this leave Oxford?' Ah yes, that question.

'I'm not sure,' I confessed.

'Why didn't you tell us at tea time?' said Dad.

'I don't know. I just needed to think. I'm confused.' Dad gave Mum one of those looks.

'But I thought you wanted to go to Oxford.'

'I do.'

'So, what's the problem?'

'What do you mean, what's the problem? The problem is that I've been promoted, got a good opportunity and now I'm not so sure about anything. I did want to go to Oxford but I'd be throwing this chance away. Susan doesn't want me to go, my pals think I'm getting ideas above myself. Maybe I should just stay and get on with it like everybody else.'

'But is that what you really want?'

'No, I don't suppose it is.'

'Well there you are, there's your answer. Look, you've got to do what you want to do in life. Don't be like me. If you've set your heart on something and you believe it's right, then go for it. Don't worry about what other people think. You've got to take risks. Remember, you don't win competitions if you don't enter.' Now this was something I hadn't expected.

'I never took risks,' he continued. 'I could have left the Gas Board and gone to work at Belmont's but I didn't. I should have done. I'd have been much better off. But my generation never took chances. Go for it, to hell with Cammell Laird's. You've served your apprenticeship, you've been promoted. You can always fall back on that if it doesn't work out.'

'He's right, you know,' continued my mother as he left the room. 'We could have moved house as well but he wouldn't take the risk. He doesn't want you to be like he was.'

I have to confess to being somewhat surprised by their response. I had guessed that my promotion would only have consolidated their hope that I would remain at Laird's. But no, on the contrary, they were now encouraging me to leave and take up any offer to go to Oxford. I was as confused as ever.

eighteen

The Long Goodbye

Some nights I had a terror of sleeping. I would lie paralysed, afraid of slipping into an unconsciousness over which I had no control. I not only feared that I might never wake up, but also that if I did fall asleep a whole night would have slipped by without my knowing anything about it. Eight dark hours totally comatose. Absolute nothingness. The world could change in that time and I would know nothing. Assassinations, political upheavals, earthquakes, midnight transfer deals. Sleep was akin to death. I would lie there fending off sleep for what seemed an eternity until inevitably tiredness would overcome me and I would crash into the black hole of the night. It was while I lay there on the edge of sleep that I would encounter other equally terrifying thoughts. Chief among these was not only Liverpool's future but my own and the reckless gamble I seemed intent on executing. At times Liverpool's prospects and my own seemed to be inevitably intertwined. Large question marks hung over both. Not for the present but for the future.

For the moment, however, the truth was that everything appeared comfortable. How could I be so despairing? Liverpool were soaring high, challenging in a four-way battle for the league title with Leeds and the two Manchester clubs. Including Everton, the four north-west clubs had dominated English football throughout the 1960s. Leeds, for all their ability and zeal, were in danger of forever being bridesmaids and never brides. Manchester United, meanwhile, were intent on realising Matt Busby's dream of becoming the first English club to win the European Cup. I say English because Celtic had pipped them to it the previous year.

It could have been Liverpool's title, and probably should have been, but two defeats in their final six games left them trailing Manchester City by three points. United finished second and the balance of power shifted from Merseyside to Manchester.

As for my own future, while events seemed to be conspiring to detain me in Birkenhead, I was blindly pursuing my Oxford application. I sat the examination, one of three people in a bare office close to the Mersey Tunnel, and was asked to discuss the issue of the closed shop. A couple of weeks later I was invited to attend an interview in Oxford.

Jim McGill, flanked by the college principal and his deputy, and another union official, sat with a jumble of papers on the floor. It was a neat, airy room with half a dozen comfortable chairs and overlooked a well-stocked garden of flowering laburnums and sycamores. The college principal, a round, ruddy-faced man with a hearty laugh, welcomed me in, poured a coffee and wondered how I saw the future of the shipbuilding industry. I waxed lyrical about its failure to invest, its inability to seize new opportunities, its poor management, and its appalling industrial relations. It was a favourite theme and my six years at Laird's had provided an insight into how not to run a company.

'Maybe we should just give up building ships and move on to building something else,' suggested the deputy principal. I stole a glance at McGill. He sat nonplussed.

'Yes, why not?' I began. He looked surprised. 'There's plenty of other things we could be doing, provided there's the investment.'

'Such as?' interrupted the deputy abruptly.

'Well, we could be building oil platforms, for one thing. In some parts of the world they're already beginning to drill in the sea for oil. If it's successful then that could one day become a much bigger market. If other countries can build ships so cheaply that we can't possibly compete with them, then we have to maybe specialise in the more high-tech end of the market. But it will mean investment in training people and being prepared to take risks.' And so the interview went on, spanning the worldwide economy, nationalisation and equal pay, until the principal asked me what I understood by the term Marxism. I didn't want to admit that it was not much, so I waffled something about equality. I didn't sound convincing.

I came out, my head buzzing, my confidence punctured but with McGill promising to let me know within the fortnight. Had I perceived any hint from McGill? No, I decided. He'd said nothing, given no clues. I knew I'd done okay when I talked about shipbuilding, even nationalisation, but Marxism! They might just as well have been talking in a different language. I'd been flummoxed. I ambled back to the station through the streets of Oxford in the June sunshine. I'd never been to Oxford before. It was a different world: students larking on bicycles, students rushing about in gowns, students laughing in the spring sunshine. It was bookish, sedate, ordered – a far cry from the chaos of Liverpool. Maybe this was what everybody meant about the difference between north and south. And yet I didn't feel overawed. On the contrary, I felt excited by it all. I wanted to be a part of it.

As soon as the letter thudded through the door, I knew I was in. It was almost a package and was franked 'Ruskin College, Oxford'. I guessed that if I hadn't been offered a place, all that I would get would be a simple brown envelope. But this was a bulky foolscap envelope. My heart leapt. This was it. I wanted to cherish the moment. I slowly opened the envelope. I had guessed right. I started in October.

As I sauntered towards Ted's office to tell him of my impending departure, I couldn't help but feel that leaving them all behind would be a wrench. You couldn't avoid the sea and all that it meant in either Liverpool or Birkenhead, and to have been a part of it was to have been on the path of history, slippery and downward though that path was proving to be. Within a few years, Cammell Laird would be bankrupt. The slips would become overwhelmed by weed and the dry docks would seize up, while the mighty wharves of the Pier Head would, after years of ghostly silence, become expensive shopping arcades and homes for rich foreign footballers. Maybe McGill was right, I was the last of a breed of shipbuilders and sailors.

I left my letter in Ted's office and wandered back to my own desk, unrolled a plan and waited. This was going to be my moment, the moment I had been anticipating for years. From where I was sitting I would be able to watch him enter his office, spot the letter, open it and then indulge myself in his reaction.

Ted looked up in astonishment and waved me to come in. 'Well! You do surprise me,' he said. Ted was as kindly as ever. I never bore any grudge against him. He genuinely wanted to know how it had all come about. 'It's a big step, you're throwing up a lot,' he warned, brushing his hair aside. 'What will you do afterwards? Will you want to come back here?' I told him that was unlikely. 'But I've just promoted you. I thought that would be a huge opportunity for you.' He looked disappointed.

'I know, and I am grateful for what you did, but I've been thinking about this for a while. When you promoted me I didn't want to say anything in case it never happened.'

'Well, I'll be sorry to see you go. Is there anything I can do to make you change your mind?' I shook my head.

'I envy you, in some ways. I never went to university, you know. But I did have the chance. I did really well in my Higher National Diploma and the college asked if I'd like to go to Newcastle University. But I ummed and aahed. I was courting and I'd just been made deputy head of Admiralty. It seemed a lot to give up, so I said no. I regret that now. My lad went off to university last year. I really envied him. He's grown up such a lot. I've been up to see him a couple of times. He's having a great time. He's in various clubs and doing all these sports I never got the chance to try. It made me realise what I'd missed.'

He wished me luck and promised he'd find some work for me during the holidays if ever I wanted it. I'd not said anything to anyone else apart from Barry. This was my secret, my ambition, and I was about to have my moment by imparting the news to the world.

Gobbo was speechless – well, for a moment. 'Oxford, fuckin' Oxford! How could you get into Oxford? You can't even pass your second-year OND.' They were all looking at me as I

marched through the Ships Drawing Office. Stan was flabber-
gasted as well. His son was at Cambridge studying archaeology.
'My lad spent all those years struggling to get A-levels to get into
Oxbridge.' He shook his head in disbelief. I marched on. George
couldn't even bring himself to say 'well done'. Eric thought it
was one up on 'the buggers who run this office'. Phil agreed and
said 'good on yer' but warned that I'd be missing a few league
titles at Anfield.

My parents had been overjoyed and were backing me all the
way. Birkenhead's a one-eyed city,' said my father. 'Always was and
always will be.' Susan was more restrained. She was happy for me
but she wasn't happy for herself. It would be another few months
before I went but I guessed they would be troublesome times. And
indeed they were.

'Do you want to take any photographs?' asked Mum. I was sitting
in the bedroom packing, throwing clothes, books and a few other
things into a large trunk.

'What for?'

'It might remind you of us all.'

'I'm not going forever,' I snapped.

'Well, I'll leave the album and the box here in case you change
your mind.' When she'd gone I picked it up, lay on the bed and
flicked through them. Photographs of holidays past, weddings,
school, aunts, uncles and grandparents, soldiers in uniform, newly
born babies. The usual. Mum came back into the room and
spotted me rummaging through the pictures.

'Oh, I remember that,' she said, looking over my shoulder. 'That
was taken in the Isle of Man. On our honeymoon, we were. It was
such a beautiful summer. The war was just over and it was the first
holiday either of us had had for years. I must sort all those pictures
out one day.' She retreated once more.

I found a recent photo of Susan, looking sultry and thoughtful,
taken by Andy with his new camera. 'I've found some more
photographs,' shouted Mum, from her bedroom. 'They were stuck
at the back of the drawer.'

She brought them in. Some were in an old envelope. I opened
it and flicked through the half-dozen photos inside. And then,
suddenly, there it was. Me and Bill Shankly. Shanks was

standing on the other side of a garden fence, me in front of him. We were both smiling. I'd almost convinced myself that the photo did not exist except in my imagination. It was at least twelve years old and I hadn't seen it since that day Dad brought it back from the chemist's. 'I was looking for this a few months ago, remember, to take with me when I went to do the interview with Bill Shankly. I couldn't find it anywhere. I thought it'd been lost.'

'That was at Auntie Gertie's,' said Mum, taking the picture from me. 'Oh she had such lovely roses. You were about ten at the time. You should take that with you. You could pin that over your desk,' she suggested.

I changed my mind. Yes, I would take some photos with me. And yes, I would pin it over my desk. I'd take that picture of Susan. I also pulled out a photograph of Peter and me, two kids on the beach at New Brighton performing cartwheels. I'd been in a convalescent home that summer and had spent a glorious few months running around in only a pair of shorts. I returned home a deep brown. Me so sun-tanned, Peter as white as creamy milk, both of us in woollen swimming trunks. And there was a picture of Barry and me with the twin towers of Wembley stadium in the background, just before the 1965 FA Cup final. We were holding our scarves above our heads. Barry had just stolen a ticket off a tout and was looking more than a little pleased with himself. I took the photos out, along with the one of Bill Shankly, and put them in a clean envelope for safe keeping. I told Susan I had her photograph and that I would pin it up in my room. She liked that. I thought it best not to tell her that it would be sharing a space with Bill Shankly.

That afternoon, I paid my final respects at Anfield. We were facing Leicester City. It wasn't the ideal valedictory match: we won 4–0. It might have been better if we had lost, then at least I could claim not to be missing too much. They introduced a new lad that day, eighteen-year-old Alun Evans, just signed from Wolverhampton Wanderers for one hundred thousand pounds. It was a record fee paid out for a teenager but he scored on his debut, as Liverpool ran riot, to show just why Shankly had reached for his cheque book. Suddenly, the pessimism and doubts of the previous months gave way to a burst of optimism. If Shankly could lash out so much money on a youngster like this, then there was hope. Evans, rakish and athletic, cut a fleeting figure, like a gazelle on the chase, sprinting, turning, bursting with effort and grace. With his long blond Beatle haircut, you knew it wouldn't be long before he was a favourite of the Kop. He was one for the future. Or so it seemed that mild October afternoon.

As we poured into the Walton Breck Road after the game, I noticed that something was missing.

'Hey, my scarf, it's gone! Where is it?' I fumbled around inside my jacket but couldn't find it. Nor was it in any of my pockets. I must have dropped it somewhere.

'You'll never find it now,' said Barry, as we stood outside the Kop gates watching the vast hoard of supporters flood past us and melt into the Liverpool streets.

'We'll have to go back and find it.'

'But it could be anywhere. You could have lost it during the game.'

'No, I'm sure I had it. I must have had it at the start 'cos I had it above my head when we were singing "You'll Never Walk Alone".'

'What about later?'

'No, I don't remember. I don't think I had it when we sang towards the end of the game.'

In that case, it's probably somewhere on the Kop. You'll never find it now.' I was all for going back in but they were already closing the gates of the Kop. 'You'll have to write in,' said the gateman, 'or come next week. They always find dozens of scarves and shoes. You wouldn't believe some of the things they find here.'

'Best to come back Monday,' said the other gateman, 'that's when they sweep the Kop.'

'But I can't. I won't be here.' The gateman shrugged.

'Come on,' said Barry, 'it's only a scarf.'

'It might be "only a scarf" to you mate but it's my *lucky* scarf. And my mum knitted it for me. I've had it years. It went to the cup final with me. It's been everywhere, that scarf, seen almost every home game Liverpool's played in the past seven years. It was lucky, that scarf. That's it now. They'll not have any more luck. They're finished.'

'Anyrate, you won't be needing it now. You won't be coming any more.'

'I will. I'll need it for the Christmas games and for next Easter. If they get bloody relegated it'll be your fault. You'll be the one to blame.'

'Come on,' he said, 'I'm going home.' And with that we both drifted off into the evening. The roads were still trapped with cars and the queues for the buses stretched for miles.

'I'm going to start walking,' I said. 'We'll be here for ages, waiting for a bus.'

'Okay,' said Barry, 'well, I guess that's it. I'll have to come by myself next week.'

'Well, give them a cheer from me. And see if you can find my scarf.'

'Will do. Get in touch when you're back next and we'll come see a game together.' He shook my hand, then turned and began to wander off in the opposite direction. Then he called out, 'Hey!' I turned around. He was holding a red and white scarf above his head. My scarf! 'Don't worry,' he shouted, 'I noticed you dropped it coming off the Kop. I'll look after it. It's gone to a good home.'

'Hey! You bugger!' I yelled. But he only laughed and ran off into the distance waving my scarf around his head.

'What would you like to do for your final night?' asked Susan.

'Well, I suppose say goodbye to everyone at the YM, see Andy, the lads, maybe have a drink. How about you, anything you'd like to do?'

'No, just be with you,' she replied. And so we spent our final evening: me saying goodbye to all the lads and ending up in the pub. It hadn't hit me until then. I'd had my interview in June, been offered a place in July and then had a couple of months to forget about it. It was only a few days since I'd finished at Laird's. It had all been so slow. I had been overwhelmed with excitement, yet life had continued largely as if nothing had happened. But now, as I sat in the pub, it slowly began to dawn on me. This was it. Tomorrow I'd be gone. It was goodbye, Laird's, goodbye Susan, goodbye lads, goodbye parents, goodbye Liverpool. All those dreams about to be realised. It was frightening. Susan tried hard not to cry but in the end there were floods of tears. It didn't help. By the time I got home I was a wreck. I ended up talking to Dad until the early hours. 'Do you fancy a whisky?' he asked. He must have known it would never be quite the same again, losing a son after all those years. Of course it wouldn't be the end but it would be different. I was an only child and at that moment I began to see in the pained eyes of my parents the dilemma of saying goodbye to a child. The house would be quieter, they would be left to find comfort and conversation in each other. Just the two of them. It hadn't been like that for them in twenty odd years.

'Make sure you enjoy it. I believe in you,' said Dad. 'If it doesn't work out, you know there'll always be room for you here.'

'Thanks, but it will work out.'

'Yes, I know it will.'

I barely slept. It might have been the whisky, the excitement or just the jumble in my head. Whatever it was, I couldn't escape the fact that life was about to change more dramatically than it had in the previous twenty years. The truth of what I had done had finally and irrevocably hit me. I was taciturn all morning as Dad drove Mum, Susan and me to the station.

We wandered silently up the platform, nobody quite sure what to say. Doors were slamming. This was it. Dad shook my hand. 'Good luck. Oh, and don't forget the newspaper,' he said, suddenly remembering that he still had it. Mum gave me a hug. Susan wept buckets. I jumped onto the train and pulled the window down. A whistle blew. The train suddenly shuddered and then barged forward uncomfortably for a few feet before bumping its way along the platform. Susan gave me a final kiss through the half-open window. 'Write to me, won't you?' She raced up the platform, following the train, tears streaming from her eyes. In the growing distance behind her, my parents waved. We had run out of platform. And then they were almost gone.

The train painfully eased out of the station and began to make its fretful way through the inky cutting that takes you out of Lime Street. There was darkness. A final look but they were gone. No Susan, no Mum, no Dad. I was on my own. The train edged its way through the gorge carved by railway navvies a century earlier, now overgrown with a variety of mosses, foliage and bushes, before descending into blackness and then emerging into the cutting once more. There was a smell of damp. I pulled up the window and returned to my seat as the train hit the suburbs of Liverpool.

I was exhausted from my sleepless night. My eyes were sticky and tearful, my nose was running. I felt spaced out. I pulled out a handkerchief and blew my nose, surreptitiously drying the tears on my face. I felt a mess. I wanted to go and throw my head under a tap of cold water.

I was alone. For the first time in my life I was genuinely on my own. I might have been embarking on a thrilling adventure but the reality was only just beginning to hit me. I wouldn't see any of them for months. What the hell had I done? I desperately needed some distraction.

I reached into my new briefcase and spotted the large envelope that Peter had left for me. I'd forgotten all about it last night. I had assumed it was a good-luck card and had not got around to opening it. I pulled it out and tore it open. Inside was a large card. Out of it fell a football programme. Arsenal v. Liverpool, 1950 FA Cup final. On the card Peter had written:

Good luck Steve. Thought you might like this!
Peter.
PS. Just in case you might have forgotten, Manchester United 4 Benfica 1

I flicked through the programme but none of it went in. Too many doubts were racing through my head. Why? Why? Why, was I doing this? I was off on an adventure, leaving everyone behind. Was there any sense to it? And what about Susan? Oh God, I wouldn't see her for weeks, maybe even months. What would she be like when I got back? Would she still want to know me? And my mum, trying to be so brave on the platform. She'd be in floods of tears by now. She'd be inconsolable all day. And there was me telling her not to worry, that I'd be fine. How could she not worry? I imagined I might be a parent one day, waving goodbye to a child. How would I feel? I knew I'd never really be back. It was the end of a chapter. I'd never live at home again. I was off to college and that was it. Although I had no inkling as to what might happen after that, I sensed that I'd never live on Merseyside again. It was goodbye Liverpool.

I was shaking. In 1916 lads four years younger than me were going to their deaths on the Somme. And here was I, in my early twenties, and venturing into the real world alone for the first time. What right had I got to feel afraid. It was pathetic.

The train was rattling through jumbled suburbs, past gardens where washing dangled in the breeze, past busy factories, and schools where kids hurried towards the gates. They'd be just about clocking on at Laird's now. Barry would be nattering to anyone and everyone about Saturday's game, Lennie would be storm-trooping into the Ships Drawing Office, carefully placing his bowler on the hat stand, Ted and Harry would be brewing themselves a cup of tea. And no doubt Gobbo would be biting at someone's ankles.

An elderly man across the aisle lowered his newspaper and threw me a glance. I half smiled back, wondering if he could see my tear-stained face. I picked up my own newspaper. 'No Injuries for Derby Clash', read the headline in the *Daily Post*. I could barely get beyond the headline. Liverpool were playing Everton at Anfield that evening. And I wouldn't be there. That's all they'd be talking about in the office. Bluenose'd be ribbing Phil and Eric and Barry would be telling the twins what Liverpool were going to do to them. Yes, I'd even miss the pathetic banter of Bluenose.

Ten minutes down the line and panic was setting in. Liverpool was barely behind me but it was beginning to feel a million miles away. The train rumbled on past sidings, freight trains, through deserted commuter stations. My throat had gone dry, my head was pounding. I was thinking of Susan. I was terrified. I didn't know anybody, I was on my own, no one to turn to, no friends. I'd have to go out there and make new friends. I was leaving Liverpool behind. Liverpool might not have been ideal but at least I knew it and understood it. I began to understand Peter's dad, going down to join Tottenham and then running scared when he got to Euston Station. I wondered if he'd regretted it all his life. I didn't want to be like that. I didn't want to go through life regretting things. I didn't want to find myself saying, 'if only, if only I'd had the chance'. Here was the chance. I was bottling it.

I couldn't go through with it. When it came to it, I didn't have
the nerve. I was all talk, big ambitions, 'going to do this, going to
do that. Sort the world's problems out'. I had all the solutions:
socialism, peace, equality, negotiation. That was all very well but
you had to be prepared to sacrifice, to go to lengths to achieve it.
And I wasn't so sure that I could sacrifice.

And what about Anfield? No more regular Saturday afternoons
trekking across Stanley Park or up Everton Valley. No more
scouring the local paper for the latest gossip from Melwood. No
more hanging on Shankly's every word. True, I could still go
occasionally but would it be the same? Would I still have that
edge, that commitment? Maybe something else would have come
into my life. Who knew where I'd be in another five years' time. A
pint before the game, the chat in the pub on a Saturday evening,
the banter in the office on a Monday morning. There'd certainly be
none of that, wherever I was.

But if I did go back, what was I going to say? Was I suddenly
going to appear in front of the lads that night and confess, 'No I
couldn't face the prospect of leaving.' They'd all said goodbye
last night, shook my hand, wished me luck. I guessed Susan
would be glad to see me land on her doorstep, and my mum as
well. But maybe they'd also feel a little disappointed that I
hadn't done it.

Late afternoon and the tension in the office would be
mounting as kick-off time approached. This was the biggest
game of the season, Liverpool v. Everton. The game we most
wanted to see, the first fixture you looked for when the new list
appeared in the summer. Bluenose would be warming up for the
evening, the barbs in the office becoming more caustic. Barry
would soon be packing his things ready for a quick getaway, a
bite to eat in the pub, racing up Everton valley, then on to the
Kop. He'd be going through all the usual rituals; through the
same turnstile, going to the same toilet, buying the programme
from the same seller. Then edging his way towards his usual
spec, down the same aisle, skipping under the same barrier. I
wondered whether he'd be wearing my scarf.

The train arched its way across the Mersey estuary. Lakes of
water on the mud sands glistened in the morning sun. A mile or
two ahead was Runcorn, first stop. This was it. If I was going to get

off, just as well to get off now and catch the next train back to Lime Street. There'd be one along within the half-hour. I could be back at home by eleven. But then what would I do? I didn't have a job to go to, although I guessed Ted and George would have me back. But then there was the humiliation. Gobbo standing there, hands on hips: 'Look at him, he went off to the other side of the world and came back after managing twenty miles.' Not that Gobbo would have the guts to go any further.

Yeah, I'd show him. I couldn't face the humiliation, the thought of having to explain to everyone that 'no, I couldn't do it'. I'd be a laughing stock. I could hardly go spouting on about socialism and solving the world's problems if I couldn't even manage to get beyond Runcorn.

Phil would be settling into his stand seat now. The atmosphere would be electric. The songs, the chants, the Kop becoming more packed, the crowd beginning to sway. And down in the dressing room, a still young Emlyn Hughes would be nervously tying his laces, still unused to the tension that surrounds derby games. And Alun Evans, about to play in his first ever derby, must have been wondering what had hit him. Tommy Smith might be saying a few words to calm him down. Big Ron Yeats would be sharing a joke with Ian St John. Roger Hunt would be polishing up his boots, getting that extra shine so that the ball would skim off his toe at an ever faster pace. Tommy Lawrence would be sharpening up his reflexes, hurling a ball against the wall.

And then I remembered the question Jim McGill had posed: what would Shankly think about my leaving? Would he accuse me of deserting him, the team, the city? What would he have done? No, he'd moved around. He'd left home when he was eighteen, deserted the coalfields of Ayrshire and gone to Carlisle. It might not have been a million miles from home but he could so easily have stayed back in Glenbuck, played in the local side, the famed Cherry Pickers, and earned a living down the pit. It mightn't have been so bad a life. But no, he'd taken a chance. He'd left his family behind and gone off to join Carlisle United. It couldn't have been easy, not knowing anyone, taking a chance as a footballer. It wasn't all glamour in the 1930s. It was a hard slog in the third division north with not much glory. And a year later he joined Preston North End. Preston had brought him fame, a cup-winners' medal, Scottish international caps. And he hadn't stopped there. He'd moved on again to become a manager, returning briefly to Carlisle, then to Grimsby, Workington, Huddersfield. It hardly read like the idyllic pages of a travel brochure. He wasn't an immediate success as a manager but he kept at it until it all gelled with Liverpool. I could hear him saying, 'When the door opens you either walk through it or stand still.' And there he was, in front of me, adorning the back page of the *Daily Post*, talking about the team's chances against Everton, confident as ever. That was Shankly, a man of the people, a man who had once welcomed me, a stranger, into his home. He wasn't just a populist. He didn't just follow, he led as well. I rummaged in my bag and took out the envelope containing the photographs. I went straight to the picture of me and Bill Shankly.

Down in the tunnel, Bill Shankly would now be having a final word with each of his players telling them just how good they were and how they would destroy Everton. He'd be slapping them on the back, a friendly dig in the ribs. 'Good luck lads.' And from the tunnel they'd be able to hear the thunderous noise of the crowd beyond as it begins to wind up the decibels.

The train was slowing down as we clattered over the criss-cross iron girders of the Runcorn Bridge heading towards the station. Further up the Mersey you could spot Liverpool in the distance; to the south a battered old cargo ship stood poised to make its way up the Manchester Ship Canal. I looked at my bags. They were ready to be picked up. My newspaper, Peter's card, that photograph and a few other odds and ends lay on the table. Peter's card and the programme. How could I give him back the programme. Anyhow, I wanted it. I wasn't going to give that back to him. And what would I tell him if I did give it him back? What would I say: 'thanks, but no thanks'? No, he wasn't having that back, even if it meant . . .

The train bumped to a halt, brakes squealing, doors opening, windows rattling. Noise. Runcorn was bathed in autumn foliage. But inside my head a quiet stillness. Calm and peace. You're on your own now. Only you can make the decision. This is it: make or break.

Ron Yeats gets the nod from the referee. And here, at last, come Liverpool racing on to the pitch. The Kop is singing 'You'll Never

Walk Alone', scarves held aloft, gently swaying from one side to the other. The ground – red one end, blue the other. And now it's Everton's turn. A wall of whistles greets the enemy. The nerve ends tingle. This is it, when the blood pumps through the body, the anticipation, the excitement. And I wouldn't be there.